Paul Hattaway, a native New ⬚⬚⬚⬚⬚⬚⬚⬚ for most of his life. He is an ⬚⬚⬚⬚⬚ ⬚⬚ ⬚⬚ ⬚⬚⬚⬚⬚ ⬚⬚⬚⬚⬚⬚ ⬚⬚⬚ ⬚⬚ author of *The Heavenly Man*; *An Asian Harvest*; *Operation China*; and in The China Chronicles series: *Shandong, Guizhou, Zhejiang, Tibet,* and *Henan*; and many other books. He and his wife Joy are the founders of Asia Harvest (www.asiaharvest.org), which supports thousands of indigenous missionaries and has provided millions of Bibles to spiritually hungry Christians throughout Asia.

Also by Paul Hattaway:

The Heavenly Man

An Asian Harvest

Operation China

China's Book of Martyrs

The China Chronicles 1: Shandong

The China Chronicles 2: Guizhou

The China Chronicles 3: Zhejiang

The China Chronicles 4: Tibet

The China Chronicles 5: Henan

XINJIANG

China's Gateway to the World

Paul Hattaway

First published in 2022 by Piquant Editions in the UK
Also published in 2022 by Asia Harvest, **www.asiaharvest.org**

Piquant Editions
www.piquanteditions.com

ISBNs
978-1-80329-005-8 Print
978-1-80329-006-5 Mobi

British Library Cataloguing-in-Publication Data
A catalogue record of this book is available in the UK from the British Library.

ISBN 978-1-80329-005-8
Cover and Book Design: projectluz.com

Xinjiang

———◆———

新疆

شنجاڭ

"New Frontier"

Map of China showing Xinjiang

Pronounced:	Shin-jeung		
Old Spelling:	Sinkiang, Eastern Turkestan		
Population:	18,459,511 (2000)		
	21,725,815 (2010)		
	24,992,119 (2020)		
Area:	642,820 sq. miles (1,664,897 sq. km)		
Population Density:	30 people per sq. mile (13 per sq. km)		
Highest Elevation:	28,251 feet (8,611 meters)		
Capital City:	Urumqi	2,853,398	
Largest Cities (2010):	Korla	425,182	
	Yining	368,813	
	Karamay	353,299	
	Shihezi	313,768	
	Hami	310,500	
	Kashgar	310,448	
	Changji	303,938	
Administrative	Prefectures:	14	
Divisions:	Counties:	99	
	Towns:	1,005	
			Percent
Major Ethnic Groups	Uyghur	8,345,622	45.2
(2000):	Han Chinese	7,489,919	40.6
	Kazak	1,245,023	6.7
	Hui	839,837	4.5
	Kirgiz	158,775	0.9
	Mongol	149,857	0.8
	Dongxiang	55,841	0.3
	Tajik	39,493	0.2
	Xibe	34,566	0.2
	Manchu	19,493	0.1
	Uzbek	12,096	0.1
	Russian	8,935	0.1

Contents

Foreword   ix

Reactions to China Chronicles Books from
  Christians in China   x

The China Chronicles Overview   xiii

Introduction   1

Secrets from Beneath the Sand   15

Nestorians in Xinjiang   31

Catholics in Xinjiang   43

1890s   55

1900s and 1910s   66

George Hunter   78

Percy Mather   92

1920s   101

The Trio   117

1930s   124

Slaughter in the Desert   136

1940s   153

The Back to Jerusalem Evangelistic Band   162

The Northwest Spiritual Band   177

Simon Zhao   187

Contents

1950s and 1960s	196
1970s and 1980s	204
1990s	217
2000s	231
The Modern Back to Jerusalem Movement	254
2010s	273
2017—The Year Everything Changed in Xinjiang	282
Genocide	292
A Christian Lament for the Uyghurs	300
The Future of the Church in Xinjiang	306

Appendix

Table 1. Evangelical Christians in Xinjiang	311
Map of All Christians in Xinjiang	313
Table 2. All Christians in Xinjiang	314
Table 3. Ethnic Minority Groups in Xinjiang	318
Researching Christians in China	319
Map of China's Christians	322

Notes	323
Selected Bibliography	343
Contact Details	346

Foreword

Over many years and generations, the followers of Jesus in China have set their hearts to be the witnesses of Christ to the nation. Many have paid a great price for their ministry, and the brutal persecutions they have endured for the faith have often been unimaginable.

The Bible commands all believers to "Go into all the world and preach the gospel to all creation" (Mark 16:15). Many foreign missionaries responded to this command in the past, traveling to China to proclaim the Word of God. They blessed the land with their message of new life in Christ, and suffered greatly when the darkness clashed with God's light. Their faithful service despite great hardship was a beautiful example for Chinese believers to emulate as they served God.

China today still urgently needs more servants and laborers to take the gospel throughout the land. God is looking for people who will stand up and declare, "Lord, here am I. Please send me!"

The Day of our Lord is near. May your hearts be encouraged by the testimonies of what the Lord Jesus Christ has done in China, to the praise of His glorious Name!

May the Lord raise up more testimonies that will glorify His Name in our generation, the next generation, and forever more!

Lord, You are the victorious King. Blessed are those who follow you to the end!

A humble servant of Christ,
*Moses Xie (1918–2011)**

---

* The late Moses Xie wrote this Foreword for The China Chronicles prior to his death in 2011. He was a highly respected Chinese house church leader who spent 23 years of his life in prison for the Name of Jesus Christ.

ix

Reactions to China Chronicles Books from Christians in China

The book you have in your hands is part of The China Chronicles, which the author is primarily writing to bless and encourage the persecuted Church in China. Each book in the series is being translated into Chinese, and thousands of copies are being distributed free of charge throughout China's house church networks.

The Communist authorities in China have blocked the publication of most Christian books, especially those that deal with revival and persecution. Consequently, these China Chronicles books have been like living water to the thirsty Chinese believers who eagerly desire to read about the mighty acts God has performed in their nation. Here are just a few reactions from house church Christians:

> We never had a good understanding of how the Lord established His kingdom in our midst, but thanks to these precious books, now we know how God has achieved great and amazing works through His servants in each province. We continue to pray that more life-giving books will flow to us!
>
> (Brother Yang, Chongqing)

> We believe the revival fires of the Holy Spirit will again be lit in our generation, and the mighty power of the Lord will sweep millions of our countrymen and women into the family of God. These are really amazing books. Please send more!
>
> (Brother Jiang, Hubei Province)

It is very important for the children of God to understand the history of the Church in different parts of China. After all, history is His Story. These are precious books, offering us in-depth accounts of the history of the body of Christ. We eagerly await each book in the series, as they will give us a more comprehensive understanding of God's glorious work in China.

(Brother Zhai, Beijing)

My husband and I read your book together, and we shared many thoughts and tears as we discovered testimonies we have never heard before. Our spiritual lives have been deeply enriched and encouraged. We hope to receive new books in the series as soon as they are available.

(Sister Xu, Shanghai)

We live in Wuhan and read your book while our city was going through its unprecedented trial. As we read how the Lord established and empowered His Church, we realized that He has been in control in the past, He is in control in the present, and He will continue to be in control in the future. Thank you for sharing these priceless nuggets of gold with us!

(Brother Cai, Hubei Province)

I shared your book with my fellow brothers and sisters in our Bible study group. We all loved it. Such living and relevant Christian history is nowhere to be found in our country, and we treasure it. We beg you to send more of these books.

(Brother Zhou, Zhejiang Province)

I gave your book to my son, who is a college student. He studies history, but said that none of the textbooks in his school teach anything like this. It is eye-opening and refreshing to our souls.

(Sister Ping, Jiangxi Province)

As the sovereignty of our Lord Jesus Christ was revealed to us through all the incidents in history, we grew acutely aware that He is in complete control, and we have nothing to fear. As a result, we now have more confidence and faith in Him, knowing that He cares for us and that the Spirit of God is at work behind the scenes, weaving together a beautiful narrative as His salvation spreads throughout our nation.

(Brother Gong, Sichuan Province)

The China Chronicles Overview

Many people are aware of the extraordinary explosion of Christianity throughout China in recent decades, with the Church now numbering in excess of 100 million members. Few, however, know how this miracle has occurred. The China Chronicles are an ambitious project to document the advance of Christianity in each province of China, from the time the gospel was first introduced to the present day.

The genesis for this project came at a meeting I attended in the year 2000, where leaders of the Chinese house church movements expressed the need for their members to understand how God established His kingdom throughout China. As a result, it is planned that these books would be translated into Chinese and distributed widely among both the Church in China and overseas. Millions of Chinese Christians know little of their spiritual legacy, and my prayer is that multitudes will be strengthened, edified and challenged by these books to carry the torch of the Holy Spirit to their generation.

My intention is not to present readers with a dry list of names and dates, but to bring alive the marvelous stories of how God has caused His kingdom to take root and flourish in the world's most populated country. I consider it a great honor to write these books, especially as I have been entrusted, through hundreds of hours of interviews conducted throughout China, with many precious testimonies that have never previously been shared in public.

Another reason for compiling The China Chronicles is to have a record of God's mighty acts in China. As a new believer in the 1980s, I recall reading many reports from the Soviet Union of how Christian men and women were being brutally persecuted, yet the kingdom of God was growing rapidly, with many people meeting Jesus Christ. By the time the Soviet empire collapsed in the early 1990s, no one had systematically recorded the glorious deeds of the Holy Spirit during the Communist era. Tragically, the body of Christ has largely forgotten the miracles God performed in those decades behind the Iron Curtain, and we are much the poorer for it. Consequently, I am determined to preserve a record of God's work in China so that future generations of believers can learn about the wonderful events that have transformed tens of millions of lives there.

At the back of each volume will appear a detailed statistical analysis estimating the number of Christians living within each province of China. This is the first comprehensive survey of the number of believers in China—in every one of its more than 2,800 cities, districts, and counties—in nearly a century. Such a huge undertaking would be impossible without the cooperation and assistance of numerous organizations and individuals.

I appreciate mission organizations such as the International Mission Board, Overseas Missionary Fellowship, Revival Chinese Ministries International, and many others that graciously allowed me to access their archives, libraries, photographs, collections, and personal records. I am indebted to the many believers whose generosity exemplified Jesus' command: "Freely you have received; freely give" (Matthew 10:8).

Many Chinese believers, too numerous to list, have lovingly assisted in this endeavor. For example, I fondly recall the aged house church evangelist Elder Fu, who required two young men to assist him up the stairs to my hotel room because he was eager to be interviewed for this series. Although he had spent many years in prison for the gospel, this saint desperately wanted to testify of God's great works so that believers around the world could be inspired and encouraged to live a more consecrated life.

Finally, it would be remiss not to thank the Lord Jesus Christ. As you read these books, my prayer is that He will emerge from the pages not merely as a historical figure, but as Someone ever present Who is longing to seek and to save the lost by displaying His power and transformative grace.

Today, the Church in China is one of the strongest in the world, both spiritually and numerically. Yet little more than a century ago, China was considered one of the most difficult mission fields. The great Welsh missionary Griffith John once wrote,

> The good news is moving but very slowly. The people are as hard as steel. They are eaten up both soul and body by the world, and do not seem to feel that there can be reality in anything beyond sense. To them our doctrine is foolishness, our talk jargon. We discuss and beat them in argument. We reason them into silence and shame; but the whole effort falls upon them like showers upon a sandy desert.[1]

How things have changed! When it is all said and done, no person in China will be able to take credit for the amazing revival that has occurred. It will be clear that this great accomplishment is the handiwork of none other than the Lord Jesus Christ. We will stand in awe and declare:

> The LORD has done this,
>   and it is marvelous in our eyes.
> The LORD has done it this very day;
>   let us rejoice and be glad. (Ps 118:23–24)

Paul Hattaway

Publisher's Note: In The China Chronicles, we have avoided specific information such as individuals' names or details that could directly lead to the identification of house church workers. The exception to this rule is when a leader has already become so well known around the world that there is little point in concealing his or her identity in these books. This same principle applies to the use of photographs.

Several different systems for writing the sounds of Chinese characters in English have been used over the years, the main ones being the Wade-Giles system (introduced in 1912) and Pinyin (literally "spelling sounds"), which has been the accepted form in China since 1979. In The China Chronicles, all names of people and places are given in their Pinyin form. For example this means that the places formerly spelled Chung-king, Shantung, and Tien-tsin are now respectively Chongqing, Shandong, and Tianjin, and Mao Tse-tung becomes Mao Zedong, and so on. The only times we have retained the old spelling of names is when they are part of the title of a published book or article listed in the notes or bibliography.

Introduction

The spectacular Heavenly Lake in the Tianshan Range
Bei Baoke

A land of contrasts

Xinjiang is a vast region of northwest China that has been
shrouded in mystery and blocked off from the rest of China for
much of its long history. It sits at a strategic crossroad of Asia and
is a key gateway between China and the rest of the world. The
Xinjiang region contains extreme geographic features ranging
from K2—the second highest mountain in the world at 28,251
feet (8,611 meters) above sea level—to the Tarim Basin, which is
the second lowest point on earth at 505 feet (154 meters) below
sea level.

The landscape also ranges from stunningly beautiful to hide-
ously barren. Massive snow-capped mountains encircling the

region create sharp barriers between Xinjiang and the eight countries that border it: India, Pakistan, Afghanistan, Tajikistan, Kazakhstan, Kyrgyzstan, Russia, and Mongolia. A visitor wrote the following description of Xinjiang's unique topography in 1931:

> Xinjiang: a place of mystery and fascinating physical peculiarities! A land where rivers run into the ground, and then break forth again in oases and springs tens of miles from the places where they disappeared; where the winds blow from the northeast a steady gale for months on end, without a drop of rainfall; where ancient writings on wooden tablets, silk scrolls, and parchment, buried 2,000 years ago in the ruins of once-populous cities, can be unearthed today in a state of perfect preservation; where all transport is carried on camel back, and where camels get tipsy from eating a peculiar desert growth![1]

The center of Xinjiang is dominated by the huge Taklamakan Desert, which is significantly larger than the entire area of the United Kingdom and nearly as large as California. "Taklamakan" is a Turkic name that can be translated, "Many go in, but few come out." Freezing winters give way to blistering summers. Andir, in the western part of the desert, once registered a temperature of 67.2° Celsius (153° F).[2]

The largest of China's 31 provinces and regions, Xinjiang covers an area of about 643,000 square miles. Its size may be better understood when compared to other places around the world. Xinjiang is approximately two and a half times the size of Texas and is the same size as the combined area of the five large US states of Texas, Oklahoma, Kansas, Colorado, and New Mexico.

By another measure, Xinjiang is roughly the equivalent of the combined area of Germany, France, Italy, and Sweden. Whereas the population of these four European countries totals 207 million people, Xinjiang is home to just 25 million inhabitants and has a sparse distribution of just 30 people per square mile.

The traumatic events that have shaped Xinjiang throughout its history have resulted in sharp rises and falls in its population. After being decimated by various Muslim rebellions throughout the nineteenth century, the population had recovered to just 2.5 million by the time of the 1928 census before jumping by more than 70 percent within nine years to 4.3 million in 1937.

Also large-scale migration from other provinces has continued unabated since the 1950s, causing the population of Xinjiang to bloom to over 13 million by 1982 and 21 million at the time of the 2010 census. Future census figures for Xinjiang will be watched with interest as critics claim that hundreds of thousands of Uyghurs have been systematically killed in concentration camps since 2017, while forced sterilization programs have rendered large numbers of women unable to bear children.

POPULATION OF XINJIANG (1912 – 2010)		
Year	Population	Percent change
1912	2,098,000	—
1928	2,552,000	+21.6
1937	4,360,000	+70.8
1947	4,047,000	−7.2
1954	4,873,608	+20.4
1964	7,270,067	+49.2
1982	13,081,681	+79.9
1990	15,155,778	+15.9
2000	18,459,511	+21.8
2010	21,813,334	+18.2

Xinjiang's three regions

Xinjiang is divided by the Tianshan Mountains, which run from east to west. To the south of the range sits the Tarim Basin, while to the north is the Junggar Basin. The Tarim River flows into the massive salt marshes of Lopnur, where China conducted 46 nuclear tests between 1964 and 1996. The blast of one above ground test was estimated to have been 300 times more powerful than the one that flattened Hiroshima. The Chinese government has strenuously denied that these tests have had any adverse effects on the health of people in the area while also denying access to all independent research. Tellingly, however, cancer rates in Xinjiang are said to be 35 percent higher than in the rest of China.

The name "Xinjiang," which means "New Frontier," was only coined by the rulers of the Qing Dynasty in 1759. Historically, Xinjiang has been divided into three main geographic and cultural regions and contains every kind of terrain, from vast, sandy deserts without vegetation to glacial lakes and stunning fir forests.

Northern Xinjiang (sometimes called Dzungaria or Zungharia) refers to the area north of the majestic Tianshan Mountains near China's borders with Russia, Kazakhstan, Kyrgyzstan, and Mongolia. It is a relatively wealthy and developed region and includes the capital city Urumqi (pronounced Urum-chee)—a Mongol name meaning "a beautiful ranch."

Southern Xinjiang is comprised of the area south of the Tianshan Range and includes the Tarim Basin, which extends south to the edge of the Tibetan Plateau. The Karakoram Pass divides China from Pakistan, and the Pamir Mountains separate China from Tajikistan and Afghanistan.[3] Despite this region's abundant reserves of oil and natural gas, the people in southern Xinjiang are generally poorer than their northern counterparts.

Eastern Xinjiang includes the area around the eastern edge of the Tianshan Range which borders the Chinese provinces of Gansu and Qinghai. Eastern Xinjiang is markedly different from the other two regions, with some towns renowned for their abundance of delicious fruit including grapes, melons, figs, apricots, peaches, and pears. Cotton is also grown in abundance throughout Xinjiang, with approximately one-fourth of the world's cotton production coming from the province.

Marco Polo in Xinjiang

The Silk Road was constructed by nomadic Indo-European tribes as early as 1800 BC. The route, which connected with other routes and centuries later extended to the Roman Empire, was

Little has changed in some parts of Xinjiang since Marco Polo's visit. A street butcher in southern Xinjiang
RCMI

5

primarily used for trade, but also brought armies, philosophies, and religions into northwest China.

One of the first foreigners to visit Xinjiang was the famous Marco Polo, who traveled down the Silk Road in 1273 with his father and uncle. They entered China via the Pamir Mountains in west Xinjiang before continuing their journey across the vast region. After crossing the present border of China near today's Tashkurgan, Polo remarked,

> There are numbers of wild beasts of all sorts in this region. And when you leave this little country, and ride three days north-east, always among mountains, you get to such a height that 'tis said to be the highest place in the world! . . . The region is so lofty and cold that you do not even see any birds flying. And I must also notice that because of this great cold, fire does not burn so brightly, nor give out so much heat as usual, nor does it cook food so effectually. . . . The people dwell high up in the mountains, and are savage idolaters, living only by the chase, and clothing themselves in the skins of beasts. They are in truth an evil race.[4]

Polo reached today's city of Kashgar where he was among people who "worship Mohammed." He described the people of the city in terms not far removed from how they still are today:

> The inhabitants live by trade and handicrafts; they have beautiful gardens and vineyards, and fine estates, and grow a great deal of cotton. From this country many merchants go forth about the world on trading journeys. The natives are a wretched, niggardly set of people; they eat and drink in miserable fashion. There are in the country many Nestorian Christians, who have churches of their own. The people of the country have a peculiar language, and the territory extends for five days' journey.[5]

Next, Polo and his companions took the southern route around the massive Taklamakan Desert, first reaching the city of Yarkant (Shache), where he briefly noted,

The people follow the law of Mohammed, but there are also Nestorian and Jacobite Christians. They are subject to the Great Khan's nephew. They have plenty of everything, particularly cotton. They are also great craftsmen, but a large proportion of them have swollen legs, and great crops at the throat, which arises from some quality in their drinking water.[6]

Next came Hotan and a visit to the Lopnur area on the southern rim of the desert, where Polo found: "If a husband of any woman goes away on a journey and remains away for more than 20 days, as soon as that term is past the woman may marry another man, and the husband also may then marry whom he pleases."[7]

While crossing the remote desert in the Lopnur region, Polo remarked,

The whole of the province is sandy, and so is the road all the way from Lopnur, and much of the water you find is bitter and bad. . . . When an army passes through the land, the people escape with their wives, children, and cattle a distance of two- or three-days' journey into the sandy waste; and knowing the spots where the water is to be had, they are able to live there, and to keep their cattle alive, whilst it is impossible to discover them; for the wind immediately blows the sand over their tracks. . . .

There is a marvelous thing related of this desert, which is that when travelers are on the move by night, and one of them chances to lag behind or to fall asleep or the like, when he tries to gain his company again, he will hear spirits talking, and will suppose them to be his comrades. Sometimes the spirits will call him by name; and thus, many a traveler has been led astray so that he never finds his party. And in this way, many have perished.[8]

Finally after many weeks of toil, Polo reached Kumul (Hami) in northeast Xinjiang, which is the first major town travelers coming from China proper reach after passing through the Gansu corridor. The oasis town was the seat of a Nestorian bishop at the time of Polo's visit, although he made no mention of it. Instead, the intrepid explorer focused on some of the customs of the area:

> They live by the fruits of the earth, which they have in plenty, and dispose of to travelers. They are a people who take things very easily, for they mind nothing but playing and singing, and dancing and enjoying themselves.
>
> And it is the truth that if a foreigner comes to the house of one of these people to lodge, the host is delighted, and desires his wife to put herself entirely at the guest's disposal, while he himself gets out of the way, and comes back no more until the stranger has taken his departure. The guest may stay and enjoy the wife's society for as long as he likes, while the husband has no shame in the matter, but indeed considers it an honor. And all the men of this province are made wittols of by their wives in this way. The women themselves are fair and wanton.[9]

Marco Polo then left Xinjiang and entered areas in today's Gansu, Ningxia, and Inner Mongolia, where he reported the presence of more Nestorian Christians. Although he was not the first foreigner to cross the length of Xinjiang, Polo was the first to record his experiences in detail, which delighted and amazed astonished Europeans when his book was published many years later.

The arrival of Islam

Islam is generally believed to have arrived in Xinjiang in AD 708, when a Muslim delegation from Persia and Arabia, carrying many valuable gifts, entered Kashgar just 76 years after the death of Mohammed. Islam grew quickly in China so that by 742, one study found, there were already 5,358 mosques scattered throughout the country.[10]

According to one account, the introduction of Islam in the Kashgar area came about after Prince Nasr asked the local ruler to allow him to build a mosque on a space the size of an ox-hide so he could worship Allah. The ruler saw no threat in the request and granted permission, but the cunning prince "cut the ox-hide into narrow strips, connecting them to fences in a large plot of land and built the first mosque in Xinjiang."[11]

Uyghur control of the region reached its zenith by AD 842, and by 960, Sunni Islam had become the official religion after 200,000 families converted. The new Muslim rulers of Xinjiang regarded Nestorian Christians and Buddhists as heathens, and violent hostility emerged. In 1006, the Uyghurs thoroughly demolished the last Buddhist kingdom in the Tarim Basin. One source describes the early days of Islam in Xinjiang:

> The knowledge of Islam came to north China through the Uyghurs, that is, the Turks of Chinese Turkestan, and through them the trade in Persian drugs and rose water. Pearls, from the Indian Ocean, were carried in, while the Arabs traded in these articles. . . . Persians were mixed with them, and both together have given origin to the Chinese Muslims. As the Persians took the chief place in trade, the colloquial medium for the commerce carried on through the Uyghur country became Persian. . . . Mosques in China and in the Uyghur country were supplied with Persian teachers, because the Turks were not intellectually competent to teach the Qur'an.[12]

Uyghurs praying outside the Kashgar mosque in the late 1980s

The languages of Xinjiang

Xinjiang is a melting pot of several diverse linguistic threads. While the Chinese government has worked hard to implement Mandarin as the standard language of all education and media, Uyghur remains the dominant vernacular among the Muslim population. Uyghur is a member of the Turkic language family and is closely related to other Central Asian languages such as Uzbek, Kazak, and Kirgiz.[13] It is said that Uyghurs who travel to Turkey are able to be understood, with difficulty, if they first learn some of the many modern loanwords that have influenced Turkish vocabulary.

The written script used by the Uyghurs has an interesting background. At the end of the tenth century, a modified Arabic script like that used by Persian (Farsi) and Urdu people was introduced. In 1956, the Chinese government introduced a Cyrillic-based script in Xinjiang, similar to what the Soviet Union used, in a bid to control the Muslim ethnic groups in their republics. Just four years later the relationship between China and the Soviet Union soured, and the project was abandoned. In 1984 the authorities in Xinjiang adopted a new, modified Arabic-based script with Uyghur vowels added. This script is widely used today, although in recent years a trend has emerged among educated Uyghurs who want to replace Chinese influence with Western values. New "Romanized Uyghur" writing has proved popular with young people, as it enables them to use standard computer keyboards to compose emails and text messages.

The dialect of Chinese spoken in Xinjiang was traditionally labeled Northwestern Mandarin. But the influx of millions of Han from all parts of China over the past 60 years has blurred the distinctiveness of the dialect, and today the sharp tones of Beijing Mandarin are just as likely to be heard on the streets of Urumqi as the traditional Northwest Mandarin accent.

Xinjiang's lesser known ethnic groups

Apart from the dominant Uyghurs, smaller Muslim groups in Xinjiang—including Kazak, Kirgiz, and Uzbek—also use the Uyghur script, while the 60,000 Tajik people on the far western edge of China speak two different Indo-European languages that are related to Persian (Farsi) rather than to any of the Turkic varieties. The Tajik are followers of the Ismaili sect of Islam, which other Muslims in Xinjiang consider heretical.

Approximately 22,000 Uzbek people live in and around the city of Yining in northern Xinjiang, where they represent just a tiny sliver of the nearly 30 million Uzbek people throughout Central Asia. After the gospel made progress in Uzbekistan in the 1990s, a group of 40 Uzbek believers volunteered to plant

An Uzbek man from northern Xinjiang
Paul Hattaway

churches in other parts of Central Asia. Some crossed the border into Xinjiang, where today about 100 Uzbek people are followers of Jesus Christ.

Other officially recognized minority groups in Xinjiang include approximately one million Chinese-speaking Hui Muslims; 150,000 Mongols, and 60,000 Xibe and Manchu people, whose forefathers were soldiers left behind during the expansion of the Qing Dynasty from 1644 to 1912. Additionally, a cluster of small ethnic groups that are not recognized by the Chinese authorities are scattered throughout Xinjiang, some of whom are the remnants of centuries of conquest and migration along the Silk Road. These fascinating, little known groups include the 7,000 Ainu people of southern Xinjiang whose language is a mixture of Turkic and Persian; the 3,000 Akto Turkmen who say they came from Samarkand in Uzbekistan; and 800 Keriya people who claim to be the descendants of the Gug tribe who fled into the Taklamakan Desert centuries ago to escape the Ladakhi army that crossed the border from north India. Today 700 Nubra people in southwest Xinjiang speak Ladakhi and may be the descendants of those soldiers who chased the Keriya deep into the desert.

Ili in the northern tip of Xinjiang is home to several tiny people groups that may be on the verge of extinction. These include 300 Tuerke who are losing their language and customs due to intermarriage with Uzbek and Kazak people.

In eastern Xinjiang, 44,000 Lopnur Uyghurs speak a distinct language that may be related to Mongol, while 70,000 Yutian Uyghurs live in the very south of Xinjiang. Yutian was the capital of the Jumi Kingdom, which flourished until 1370. Today, the Yutian Uyghurs retain customs and clothing that differentiate them from all other Uyghur groups.

Finally in 1990, a Chinese oil exploration team came across an extraordinary community of just 300 Taklamakan Uyghurs who were living around an oasis in the heart of the remote, sandy wastes of the desert. They were described as having

> a gentle culture, living primitive lives in extreme isolation. Experts discovered this tribe had been out of touch with the world for 350 years. As a result, they knew nothing of the historical fact of the Qing (China's last dynasty) or about anything else up to the present time. . . . At the time of their discovery, the Taklamakan Uyghurs told the time by the sun, had no form of government or authority structure, and no schools or writing system.[14]

History of Christianity

The history of Christianity in Xinjiang is unique and can be split into two main eras. The first period details the astonishing influence of Nestorian Christianity from the seventh to thirteenth centuries, while a second main period covers the progress of the gospel in Xinjiang during the past 150 years.

Other books in The China Chronicles series may be more pleasant to read than this one. Xinjiang is a place where much barbaric cruelty has taken place over the centuries, and parts of this book may be difficult for some people to read. It is our hope to neither shock nor underplay events in Xinjiang, but to present the facts and hopefully help readers better understand the background behind the present tensions in this troubled region.

Researching material for this book has presented challenges unique among all the provinces of China. For example, few accounts of early missionary work in Xinjiang were produced in English. Instead, an extensive array of books were published in Swedish, only a few of which have ever been translated into English. For decades, Xinjiang was like a blank region on world maps, and the Swedish Mission was content to toil away in relative obscurity. As a result, many people reading this book will be learning about the tremendous work of the Swedish Christians for the first time almost a century after they were expelled from Xinjiang.

A special mention and word of thanks are owed to Sigfrid Moen and Margareta Höök of Sweden for kindly allowing the use of many of the best photographs in this book, which were taken by their families in the 1920s and 1930s. These invaluable images vividly portray the marvelous work of God Who delivered hundreds of Muslims throughout Xinjiang out of darkness and into the glorious light of Jesus Christ.

Secrets from Beneath the Sand

History tends to be the least favorite subject of many students at school. But it is crucial for readers of this book to have at least a basic understanding of the rise and fall of Xinjiang's kingdoms because recent events that have shocked the world cannot be properly understood apart from the historical context that has shaped life in the region over the past four millennia.

The ancient Silk Roads that connected China to the Middle East and beyond enabled waves of merchants, armies, and missionaries to enter the region. Buddhism, Christianity, and Islam all entered China through Xinjiang, as did other lesser known faiths including Zoroastrianism which came from Persia and flourished in Xinjiang for 1,000 years. Even today, some of the

The Kumtag Desert in eastern Xinjiang
Lu Jinrong

festivals celebrated by the Uyghur, Tajik, and other peoples in Xinjiang retain elements of the Zoroastrian fire worship religion.

Thousands of years of warfare and migration have seen the rise and fall of many dynasties and kingdoms in Xinjiang, and a long arm wrestling for power continues to the present day. More than twenty civilizations have claimed at least part of the region at one time or another, many of which have vanished beneath the desert sands.

Xinjiang is a land of closely guarded secrets, but occasionally outsiders are given a glimpse into its surprising and varied past. One such glimpse occurred in 2007 when the Chinese government allowed a team of *National Geographic* experts to examine a collection of mummies that had been excavated from an ancient cemetery near Hami, on the edge of the Taklamakan Desert. Due to the extremely dry climate in the area, the mummies were remarkably well preserved, and Chinese scholars waited with bated breath to see what conclusions the Western experts would reach.

After extensive DNA testing on the mummies, which they dated to as far back as 1,800 BC, *National Geographic* found that the mummies were Caucasian people, some of whom had blonde or red hair. Spencer Wells, who led the DNA testing, concluded that rather than having a single origin, the people came from Europe, Mesopotamia, and the Indus Valley in today's Pakistan and northwest India. Scientist Victor Mair wrote that he was "awed by the sight of the bodies . . . preserved for over three millennia. They are clearly of Caucasoid-Europoid extraction (long noses, deep-set eyes, blondish, light-brown or red hair, and so forth)."[1] Elsewhere Mair further notes, "The new finds are also forcing a re-examination of old Chinese books that describe historical or legendary figures of great height, with deep-set blue or green eyes, long noses, full beards, and red or blond hair. Scholars have traditionally scoffed at these accounts, but it now seems that they may be accurate."[2]

While many international scholars were not surprised by the findings, the report was rejected by the Chinese Communist Party because it contradicted their narrative that Xinjiang has always belonged to Han people and has been an indispensable part of the Chinese realm. In response, Chinese historian Ji Xianlin said that while China "supported and admired" the research by foreign experts, "Within China a small group of ethnic separatists have taken advantage of this opportunity to stir up trouble and are acting like buffoons. Some of them have even styled themselves the descendants of these ancient 'white people' with the aim of dividing the Motherland. But these perverse acts will not succeed."[3]

Despite protests from Beijing, it is clear that the earliest people in Xinjiang were fair-skinned Caucasians. Turkic and Mongol people arrived much later, and the Han are among the most recent arrivals in the area. Thus it is worth making a quick summary of some of the more prominent people groups that have shaped the long history of Xinjiang.

The Scythians

Although a centuries-long struggle is currently underway between the Han Chinese and the Turkic-speaking Uyghurs over control of Xinjiang, the earliest inhabitants of the region were Scythians, whom most scholars believe were an Eastern Iranian people. Nomadic Persian tribes are known to have migrated eastward and settled throughout the Altai Mountains in northern Xinjiang.

The Scythians reached the zenith of their influence from the ninth century BC until the fourth century AD, and this influence is believed to have extended into central China. Chinese records from the era referred to the Scythians as "Sai" people, and Scythians are also mentioned in the New Testament (see Colossians 3:11). Many of the Caucasian mummies unearthed in Xinjiang are believed to be Scythians. Their nearest relatives today are the Iranian Farsi-speaking Tajik people who are still found in modest numbers in southwest Xinjiang.

The Wusun and the Hun

Another ancient ethnic group that rose to power in Xinjiang was the Wusun who originally settled in southeast areas before relocating to northern Xinjiang in the second century BC. Ancient Chinese accounts describe the Wusun people as being blue-eyed and red-bearded. Wusun power in Xinjiang overlapped with the arrival of the Hun people, who are called the Xiongnu in Chinese history.

The Huns rose to prominence in Central Asia and Eastern Europe after Atilla led a group of Huns on a rampage throughout Europe in the fifth century AD, but few historians record the

Two Tajik women from Xinjiang with green eyes and fair complexions.
Dwayne Graybill

significant contribution the Huns made in faraway Xinjiang at a much earlier time. Around 176 BC, the Huns living on the Mongolian steppes expanded westward into Xinjiang.

The Huns were an Indo-European group, and a Chinese history provides this detailed description of their physical features: "They are short, with a stocky body and a very large round head, broad face, prominent cheekbones, wide nostrils, a fairly bushy moustache and no beard except for a tuft of stiff hair on the chin. The eyebrows are thick, the eyes almond-shaped with a very fiery pupil."[4] One Christian scholar has speculated how the demise of the Hun people around the time of Christ may have blocked the spread of the gospel into Xinjiang by the early Church. If history had unfolded slightly differently, Christianity may have been spread to China by the first Christians:

> Not until 60 BC did China finally gain from the collapsing Xiongnu (Hun) empire firm control of the trade route. . . . Commerce prospered until 6 BC, but just about the time of Christ's birth there came a sharp break in Han Dynasty power. . . . Disorder broke out along the frontier and by AD 16, as recorded in the Chinese chronicles, "the Western Regions were broken up and scattered like loose tiles."
>
> For the next 60 years, until the eighth decade of the Christian era, communication between China and western Asia was broken off, so it is quite true that in the first few decades of the apostolic Church it would have been virtually impossible to reach China by land from Roman or Persian Asia.[5]

At about the same time that Christ's disciples were spreading the gospel throughout the known world, a monumental event took place in Xinjiang which fundamentally shaped the history of Asia. During the reign of Emperor Mingdi of the Eastern Han Dynasty (AD 58–75), Buddhism entered China via the Karakoram Pass between today's Pakistan and southwest Xinjiang. According to some accounts, the introduction of Buddhism occurred after Emperor Mingdi had a vivid dream:

> He saw a golden figure floating in a halo of light across the room. Unable, like Pharaoh, to conceive what meaning to place upon his dream, Mingdi assembled his wise men and astrologers and from them invited suggestions as to its interpretation. . . .
>
> They hinted in reply that the figure seen by the Emperor was probably that of Buddha, and the result of their explanation was the dispatch of a special envoy to India to investigate the truth. After a considerable period of absence the envoy returned, having obtained not only the necessary sacred books, pictures, and images of the new religion, but having also been fortunate enough to persuade some Indian priests [Kasyapa Matanga and Sharmaratna] to accompany them to the home of their ruler.[6]

One Christian author laments,

> Though the Silk Road was open in those critical early years of the Christian Church, it was Buddhist missionaries from India who used it, not Christians from Jerusalem or Antioch; and the missionary faith that flowed along it, putting down deep roots in eastern Asia, was not Christianity but Buddhism. This may be why Buddhism, and not Christianity, is now more often called the "most purely Asian of the great religions."[7]

The new religion quickly gained in popularity and spread throughout China, Tibet, and ultimately to Korea, Japan, and Southeast Asia, so that today many hundreds of millions of people throughout the world adhere to Buddhist teachings and philosophies.

The Tocharians

Later, a group known as the Tocharians emerged in Xinjiang. These people, called Yuezhi by the Chinese, were described as different from other peoples in the region, as their eyes were not

A ninth century cave painting of a Tocharian monk and a Chinese monk

as deep set nor their nose bridges as high as the other inhabitants of Xinjiang at the time.

The Tocharians were originally nomadic pastoralists from western Gansu Province and reputedly boasted an army of 100,000 to 200,000 horse archers. After defeat by the Huns (Xiongnu), a large group of Tocharians moved into northern Xinjiang, while a smaller number relocated to the edge of the Tibetan Plateau in southern Xinjiang. The Tocharians founded the state of Kumul (Hami), which became a key center for Buddhism in China and is where most of the ancient mummies and Buddhist wall paintings and artifacts have been found.

The Han Chinese

For more than 2,000 years, Xinjiang has been under sporadic Chinese control to some degree, but only in 1759 did the region receive its present name and become officially incorporated into

China's territory. Han influence in Xinjiang has ebbed and flowed throughout history, reflecting the rise and fall of the Chinese dynasties.

The first widespread Han influence in Xinjiang occurred in 60 BC when the Han Emperor Liu Bingyi vanquished the Huns, and new Chinese political and military commands were established in the western regions. The Han effectively gained control of the Silk Road, and China began communicating with little

A ninth century wall painting of Uyghur princes wearing Chinese robes, showing early Han influence in Xinjiang

known nations in Central Asia and the Middle East, far beyond its borders.

According to Chinese historical annals, the first contact between China and the "barbarian world" outside the Orient occurred in 91 BC when an embassy was sent along the Silk Road from Xi'an to "Anxi," the Parthian Empire based in modern-day Iran. The King of Parthia dispatched a large calvary of 20,000 soldiers to meet the travelers. Discussions were held, silk was traded, and reciprocal embassies were arranged after the Chinese keenly invited their hosts to come and see the greatness and extent of their empire. The Parthians duly arrived in Xi'an where they offered gifts to the emperor including large birds' eggs while skilled musicians and jugglers entertained the court.

Brisk trade between China and the Middle East continued until the seventh century, when silk-moth eggs were smuggled from China to Syria inside a bamboo cane purportedly carried by a Nestorian merchant. The Syrians soon began to manufacture their own silk, and China no longer had a monopoly on the much sought-after product.

In AD 97, the Chinese emperor sent General Ban Chao from his station near Kuqa (Kuche) in Xinjiang to research the extent of the "Western Regions." Ban and his entourage traveled all the way to Syrian Antioch in the Roman Empire, "reaching the Seleucia Harbor where the Apostle Paul had commenced his first missionary journey 51 years earlier."[8]

For many centuries Chinese influence in Xinjiang declined. Occasional military skirmishes reinforced their authority, including one campaign in 750 when the Tang Dynasty armies drove the Tubo, or ancient Tibetans, out of the Tarim Basin and extended their control as far as the banks of Lake Balkash in today's Kazakhstan.

The ruthless conqueror Tamerlane (also called Timur), the son of a Turkish tribal chief, was born in 1336. From Moscow to the

Ganges River in India, Tamerlane slaughtered entire populations as he spread Islam by the sword and turned fertile lands into desert wastes. After his armies conquered Baghdad, they piled up 90,000 heads, and when Delhi in India fell, a vast number of people were slaughtered, including 100,000 prisoners.

Tamerlane's final goal was to conquer China and to convert the population "from vile idolatry" to Islam. He mobilized a massive invasion force of 1.8 million soldiers to march from Samarkand, in present day Uzbekistan, to China in 1405. But before the campaign commenced, Tamerlane died, and it was called off. Chinese and world history would have been vastly different if he had succeeded in conquering China, where the Ming leaders were still trying to consolidate their rule after the collapse of the Mongol empire in 1368.

For centuries, the Chinese struggled to fully control Xinjiang. But in July 1759, they amassed a huge army and crushed Muslim rebels in the Kashgar area, and for the first time the entire western region was fully incorporated into Chinese territory. Ever since, the Han have viewed Xinjiang as an indispensable part of China. They claim to have ruled the region continually since before the time of Christ. With this unwavering belief, the current leaders of China have few qualms about mercilessly crushing Uyghur dissent and doing whatever they deem necessary to retain complete control over the strategic region.

Recent demographic changes have dramatically shifted the population balance in favor of the Han, with hundreds of thousands of migrants from other Chinese provinces settling in Xinjiang each year. The Han population has increased from just 10 percent in 1949 to almost 50 percent in the latest census, and if the large numbers of People's Liberation Army soldiers and their families are counted, the Han are the majority people in Xinjiang. The population of Urumqi, the capital city, is more than 80 percent Han.

The Uyghurs

Ironically, despite recent claims by Uyghur independence movements that Xinjiang has always been their homeland, the first
ancestors of the Uyghurs were relatively late arrivals in northwest
China.[9] The Uyghurs were originally a collection of Turkic tribes
located to the south of the world's largest body of fresh water,
Lake Baikal, in today's Siberia. But when their grazing lands were

The traditional dress of Uyghur women may have originated with
the Zoroastrian religion of fire worship. When they twirl around
in dance, the patterns are said to make them resemble flames
Paul Hattaway

25

overrun by Kirgiz invaders in the eighth century, the Uyghurs migrated south into today's Xinjiang.

Although the earliest Uyghurs were nomadic, their culture was far more advanced than other tribes, and they possessed their own written language. For centuries the Uyghurs were animists, worshiping a host of nature spirits and consulting with shamans. One legend tells of a gray wolf which mated with a woman, leading to the formation of the Uyghurs. Recently, the totem of the "gray wolf" has been revived as a symbol of nationalism among some Uyghur factions.

Between 1407 and 1415, Xinjiang was led by Mohammed Khan, a fanatical Muslim who forcibly imposed Islam on all his subjects. If his followers came across a man who was not wearing a turban, he might be killed by driving horseshoe nails into his head. At this time, the remaining remnants of Nestorian Christianity in Xinjiang withered before ultimately vanishing from history. The cruelty meted out by Muslims in Xinjiang was such that the European word "ogre" is thought to have been derived from the word for "Uyghur." All communities within their reach dreaded the Uyghurs, and many areas were completely evacuated before their cruel forces arrived.

The Mongols

Next to rise to prominence in Xinjiang were the Mongols who occupied the region in 1228. Rather than attempting to replace the embedded Turkic culture, the Mongols sought to integrate it into their political and economic systems. Many Uyghur officials were given high positions in the Mongol court, and Genghis Khan and later Mongol leaders used Uyghur consultants to establish a civil system to consolidate their rule, which ultimately expanded as far as Hungary in Eastern Europe.

Today, approximately 150,000 ethnic Mongol people continue to live in northern Xinjiang where their history has been an intense struggle for survival. Many Mongols in Xinjiang are from the Oirat tribe, also known as the Zunghar (or Dzungar) Mongols. The Chinese emperors in faraway Beijing grew furious at the constant irritation caused by Oirat rebels, and they launched a series of military campaigns to force the Oirat into submission. A systematic genocide was launched in 1757 during which young men were slaughtered while women and children were taken as the spoils of war.

A Qing scholar named Wei Yuan wrote that about 40 percent of the Oirat were killed by smallpox, 20 percent fled across the border into today's Russia or Kazakhstan, and 30 percent

An Oirat Mongol woman atop her camel
Paul Hattaway

were killed by the army who left no communities for hundreds of miles.[10] By the time the carnage had ended, approximately 80 percent of the Oirat population—or between 480,000 and 600,000 people—had been killed in what "amounted to the complete destruction of not only the Zunghar state but of the Oirat Mongols as a people."[11]

The current protagonists

After millennia of conflict and the rise and fall of many empires, two peoples have emerged as the key protagonists in Xinjiang—the Han Chinese and the Uyghurs. Their battle has been bloody and brutal, and over one million Uyghurs are reportedly being detained in Chinese concentration camps at the time of writing this book.

Also as Islam continued to dominate life in Xinjiang, mass killings of non-Muslims were carried out for generations. One of the worst massacres took place in 1865 when a Uyghur officer named Yakub Beg launched a "holy war" against all infidels in

A banknote issued by the Eastern Turkestan government in 1939

the region. Seven cities in southern Xinjiang were occupied, and every Han Chinese resident of Kashgar was slaughtered. The conflict then moved to Yengisar where a large number of Han soldiers and civilians lived. Qing troops were mobilized to the town, but "when all ammunition and food were exhausted and there was no hope of getting reinforcements, those under siege finally burned themselves to death. Yakub Beg proclaimed himself the new khan and wantonly killed pagans."[12]

This grim episode reinforced the belief that Xinjiang was a place of barbaric cruelty to be subjugated at any cost as a matter of life and death.

During the first half of the twentieth century, popular uprisings by Muslims in Xinjiang led to several factions vying for power. Attempts were made to align the region with the Turkic world by renaming it Eastern Turkestan. In January 1945, a Kazak named Osman led a rebellion in southwest Xinjiang and established an independent Eastern Turkestan Republic. China's Nationalist rulers convinced Osman to abandon the new republic in return for a pledge of real autonomy, but the promise was never kept. Osman was finally captured and executed in 1951.

When the new Communist government established control of Xinjiang in 1949, they ruled the region with an iron fist, crushing all dissent and talk of separatism. A Muslim league that was opposed to Chinese rule emerged in Xinjiang. But in August 1949, the plane carrying the leaders to talks in Beijing mysteriously crashed, and Muslim opposition quickly disintegrated.

At the beginning of 2021 it was estimated that there were 15,000 mosques in Xinjiang. Islam remains at the core of Uyghur identity, despite recent efforts by China's rulers to violently uproot it from society. Han Chinese clearly have the upper hand numerically, and they have economic and military dominance. But in the minds of most Uyghurs and other Muslim inhabitants of Xinjiang, the Han are a foreign occupying force. The resilient and proud Uyghurs mourn the days when they ruled their vast, arid territory.

At the root of ethnic tension in Xinjiang is the fact that Uyghurs and Han Chinese are culturally polar opposites. As one source explains,

> The Uyghurs don't have much in common with the Chinese. The Uyghur religion is monotheistic Islam, their written script is Arabic, their language is closely related to Turkish, and their physical features are basically Caucasian—many could easily be mistaken for Greeks, southern Italians, or other southern Europeans. . . . There is little likelihood of Xinjiang ever achieving any real autonomy—the influx of Chinese soldiers and settlers means that it is almost certainly out of the question.[13]

Nestorians in Xinjiang

Although an unsubstantiated legend exists that the disciples of the apostle Thomas traveled from south India across the Pamir Mountains into Xinjiang between AD 100 and 280,[1] another five centuries was to pass before the first representatives of Jesus Christ entered northwest China. In 635, Nestorian missionaries from Syria are recorded to have traveled down the Silk Road into Xinjiang and onward to Chang'an (now Xi'an), which was the capital of China at the time. The Nestorian historian Malech reports,

> For 150 years this mission was active. . . . 109 Syrian missionaries have worked in China during 150 years of the Chinese mission. . . . The missionaries traveled on foot—they had sandals on their feet, and a staff in their hands, and carried a basket on their backs, and in the basket was the Holy Writ and the cross. They took the road around the Persian Gulf; went over deep rivers and high mountains, thousands of miles. On the way they met many heathen nations and preached to them the gospel of Christ.[2]

A later account of the Nestorian enterprise written between 730 and 790 tells of large numbers of Turkic Christians in Central Asia—the fruit of zealous evangelism by the Nestorian missionaries. These believers, who likely inhabited parts of Xinjiang as well as today's Central Asian republics, reportedly

> had four great Christian kings who lived at some distance from each other. Their names are given as Gawirk, Girk, Tasahz and Langu. . . . They were the heads of the four tribal confederacies of the Keirats, Uyghurs, Naimans and Merkites. The populace of each king is said to have been over 400,000 families. If there were

five persons to a family, this would mean two million per king for a grand total of eight million. If only half that many represented the actual population, it would still represent a Christian

A seventh century wall painting, showing a Uyghur or Han Christian in Xinjiang

community so great it would be a tremendous witness to the zeal of those early missionaries.[3]

An ancient account exists of how the Keirat tribe became Christians. According to a historian, one day the Keirat king went hunting in the high mountains, only to lose his way in the deep snow so that he despaired of ever finding the path again. A man suddenly appeared before him and said, "If you believe in Christ I will show you the way." The king assented and was

> directed on his way. When he reached his camp the king at once sent for certain Christian merchants who were there and asked to be instructed in the Christian faith. He received the gospel at their hands and joined with them in the worship of Christ. He then sent a messenger to the nearest metropolitan asking him either to come himself or to send preachers and teachers to baptize him and his people, adding that there were 200,000 who believed with him.[4]

Between 795 and 798, the Nestorian patriarch Timotheus wrote to his good friend Raban Serbius, informing him that he had appointed a bishop for the Turks and was in the process of appointing one for the Tubo, who are the ancestors of today's Tibetans. In 665 the Tubo had occupied four places in today's southern Xinjiang: Kashgar, Kucha, Hotan, and Karashar (Yanqi). When Timotheus announced he was sending a bishop, the area was still under Tubo control, and the bishop was most likely sent to Hotan.

The fact that a bishop was needed indicates the presence of many Christians at the time. According to one source, by the second half of the eighth century, "the Christian Uyghur Turks were a powerful political force in Eastern Asia. . . . It seems they converted to Christianity at an early date and exerted a strong Christian influence for a long time."[5]

Further evidence exists that Central Asia was once a hotbed of vibrant Christian faith. More than 600 Christian tombstones have been unearthed 100 miles (162 km) north of the Xinjiang border, around Lake Issuk-kul in today's Kyrgyzstan. Dating as far back as 858, most of the inscriptions in the Syriac script reveal a wide range of ethnicities among the children of God. One woman buried there is "Terim the Chinese"; a priest is "Banus the Uyghur," and another is "Kiamta of Kashgar."

The Nestorians ministered in relative peace until 845, when the emperor issued an edict to restrict religion. Although the edict was primarily aimed at reducing the influence of Buddhism, Christians were caught up in the carnage. Approximately 2,000 Nestorian monks and nuns were forced to abandon their spiritual vocation, which dealt a crushing blow to the fledgling Church in China at the time.

After the persecution of 845, the Nestorian enterprise in China faltered, and the faith appears to have been stopped in its tracks. Many Christians sought safety in main centers including Gaochang in northeast Xinjiang. A Buddhist historian named Zan Ning wrote that although Christianity had been suppressed in 845, "the roots . . . were not completely eradicated and in due course they spread and became prolific."[6]

The second Nestorian wave

By the thirteenth century, Nestorian influence had expanded and reached into almost every part of Central Asia. The Kerait people, who had probably converted several hundred years earlier, continued to follow Jesus Christ.

The second Nestorian wave had a different tone from the first, however, and mistakes were made that have harmed the cause of Christ among the people of Xinjiang to the present day. Much damage was inflicted by a fugitive Naiman prince named

Kuchlug who appears to have been a nominal Christian trained in Nestorian culture rather than having a personal relationship with God. Although he was based in the Altai region in northern Xinjiang, in 1211 Kuchlug staged a coup and seized control of Kashgar in the south. He appointed a governor, but this official was promptly murdered by the local Muslims who had grown resentful of Nestorian influence. Kuchlug responded by sending troops and laying siege to Kashgar for two to three years until the residents finally surrendered.

Since he and his wife were Nestorians, Kuchlug decided to enforce his authority by converting the people of Kashgar and surrounding districts. When the chief imam protested, Kuchlug had him killed by nailing him to the door of the Islamic school in Khotan. In many other ways Kuchlug harshly repressed the Muslims, but the more he persecuted them, the stronger they seemed to grow.

Incredibly, eight centuries later when missionaries in Kashgar encountered resistance when they tried to share the gospel with local Muslims, they were told that the people of southern Xinjiang would never believe in Christ because Christians had once brutally slain one of their imams by nailing him to the door of the Islamic school. Memories linger a long time in Xinjiang.

A short time after Kuchlug, in the mid-thirteenth century, Hulagu Khan—who was a grandson of Genghis Khan and a brother of Kublai Khan—conquered much of western Asia for the Mongols. He married a devout Kerait Christian named Dokuz Kathun who famously accompanied her husband on his military expeditions. On one, as tens of thousands of people were being slaughtered during the siege of Baghdad in 1258, she used her influence to have the Christians in the city spared.

Hulagu died in 1265 at the height of his power and was soon followed to the grave by Queen Dokuz. The chief bishop of Persia, Gregory Bar Hebraeus, paid this tribute to the fallen couple:

In the year 1265, Hulagu, King of Kings, departed from this world. The wisdom of this man, and his greatness of soul, and his wonderful actions are incomparable. And in the days of summer, Dokuz Kathun, the believing queen, departed and great sorrow came to all the Christians throughout the world because of the departure of these two great lights, who made the Christian religion triumphant.[7]

Unfortunately, the blessings that came to Christians in Central Asia through Hulagu Khan did not extend to his successor, Ahmed Khan, who converted to Islam after ascending the throne. To prove his zeal for his new religion, Ahmed became a cruel persecutor of Christians and ordered that every Christian be banished from his lands.

Marco Polo arrived in Xinjiang just eight years after the deaths of the Christian king and queen. He found that Nestorian Christianity appeared to be thriving and reported, "There are

A 13th century painting of Mongol ruler Hulagu Khan
and his Christian Queen Dokuz Kathun

36

in the country many Nestorian Christians, who have churches of their own. The people of the country have a peculiar language, and the territory extends for five days' journey."[8] The intrepid explorer mentioned the presence of both Nestorians and Christians during his traverse of Xinjiang in the early 1270s. "The number of Uyghur believers was so great at the time that they were even called a Nestorian state," Polo wrote.

1275—The first Back to Jerusalem mission

In the year 1275, two Uyghurs, a monk named Rabban bar Sawma and his student Rabban[9] Markos, embarked on a pilgrimage from Mongol-controlled China to Jerusalem in what could be dubbed the first ever "Back to Jerusalem" mission by the Chinese Church. The older Sawma tried to dissuade his protégé from going on the trip by telling him how dangerous and long the journey would be and that he would probably never see his homeland again. His warnings seemed only to make Markos more determined, and "at last, having agreed that neither of them would abandon his companion even if he had to suffer trouble because of him, they rose, distributed their rags and common things to the poor, and went to the town to obtain some companions for the journey and to lay up provisions."[10]

The duo was surprised when, the next day, they received a reaction from other Christians to their plans that countless missionaries were to experience in later generations. When a group of believers heard about the intended journey, they hurried to the place where Sawma and Marko were staying to try to change their minds, telling them,

> Do you not know how far away is the country to which you are going? Are you not ignorant of the difficulty of the road? You forget that you will never arrive over there. Stay here. Fight your

battle in the state of life to which you are called. It is said, you know, the kingdom of heaven is within you.[11]

Undeterred, the Nestorian pioneers answered the group as follows:

> We have renounced the world and we regard ourselves dead to it. Fatigue has no terrors for us, and fear does not disturb us. We ask but one thing of you: for the love of Christ pray for us; put aside all skeptical talk and ask God that our plan may be fulfilled.
>
> The Christians embraced one another with tears and sobs. "Go in peace," they said to them. "May our Lord whom you have sought go with you; may He do with you what pleases Him and is good for you. Amen."[12]

Finally, before their trip took them beyond the Great Wall and into the little known realm of the "barbarian tribes," two Nestorian princes summoned Sawma and Markos and pleaded with them to reconsider their plans. The princes reasoned, "Why are you leaving our country and going to the West? We give ourselves great trouble to bring monks here from the West, and how can we let you go?" Rabban Sawma answered them as follows:

> We have renounced the world. As long as we are near our own we shall have no rest. We are bound therefore to flee for the love of Christ who gave himself up to death for our salvation. We have given up all that is of the world. Though your love moves us, we shall go. Your goodness charms us, your kindness is spread wide over us; but if we are glad to stay with you, we are also reminded of the Word of the Lord who said, "What does it profit a man to possess the whole universe if he lose his soul?" and, "What shall a man give in exchange for his soul?" We wish for perfection. All that we can do in our weakness is to remember your kingdom day and night in our prayers.[13]

When the princes saw that their words would have no effect, they offered the Nestorian pioneers gifts of horses, gold, silver, and clothing. When the missionaries resisted the offer, the princes insisted saying, "We advise you not to go empty handed, for you will not be able to reach the end which you set before you." Sawma and Markos, "seeing that they offered these things with a sincere heart, accepted what the princes gave them. They parted one from another with heavy hearts. Tears were mixed with joy when they said farewell to them."[14]

The men continued their journey with abundant supplies for the rigors ahead. When they reached Tangut (probably in today's Ningxia Region of north China), the local Christians put on a display that shows the powerful influence Nestorianism still had at the time. One account says,

> The inhabitants learnt that Rabban Sawma and Rabban Markos were come on their way to Jerusalem. Men and women, young people, children, and little infants went out at once to meet them, for the faith of the people of Tangut was very fervent and their thoughts pure. They loaded the monks with presents and received their blessing, and all followed them weeping and saying: "May our Lord, who has called you to the honor of serving Him, go with you. Amen."[15]

After crossing the Xinjiang desert and arriving in Kashgar six months later, Sawma and Markos found the town "almost completely destroyed by famines and wars."[16] For many months they continued westward along the Silk Road until their journey was cut short by war in Syria. They made a detour to Baghdad where they remained for the rest of their lives. Although he was just 35 years old, and despite his objections that he was unqualified for the office, Markos was appointed Yahballaha III, the Patriarch of the Church of the East, thus becoming the leader of millions of Nestorian Christians.

In June 1287, Sawma visited Rome where he was met in the Vatican by various Catholic cardinals. They proceeded to grill him with doctrinal questions and expressed skepticism that a Christian in his position had come all the way from China. Sawma wisely answered both lines of enquiry by saying the following:

> You must know that many of our fathers have gone to the lands of the Mongols, the Turks, and the Chinese, and have taught them. Today many of the Mongols are Christians; there are princes and queens who have been baptized and confess Christ. They have churches with them in the camp, and show great honor to the Christians, and there are many converts among them. . . . No one has been sent to us Orientals from the Pope. The holy Apostles taught us, and we still hold today what they handed down to us.[17]

In 1288, Markos sent Sawma to visit many European monarchs, including King Philip the Fair of France and King Edward I of England. Sawma returned to Baghdad and died in 1294, aged 74.

Markos, meanwhile, continued to lead the Nestorian Church, although the brutal slaying of millions of believers by bloodthirsty Arab Muslims took a heavy toll, and he grew weary of his calling. Markos, a simple student from China who became the head of the Nestorian Church, died at Baghdad in November 1317, aged 72.

The respected church historian Samuel Hugh Moffett has commented on the extraordinary influence the Nestorian Christians had throughout Central Asia, the Middle East, and China at this time:

> This was the last high plateau in the history of Nestorians in Asia. Their patriarch, Mark (Yahballaha III) exercised ecclesiastical sovereignty over more of the earth's surface than even the pontiff in Rome. . . . The 13th century can be called the years when Christians spread the faith more widely in Asia than at any time in the first millennium and a half of Church history.[18]

The decline of Nestorianism

By the end of the thirteenth century, just after Marco Polo's journey, Nestorianism fell into sharp decline in Xinjiang and would soon vanish from society. By 1349, a list of 25 Nestorian dioceses did not include Kashgar for the first time in seven centuries. The reasons for the demise of Nestorianism after nearly 700 years are not totally clear, but several theories have been offered.

When the Catholic missionary William of Rubruck visited the Orient in the 1250s, he was particularly unimpressed by the moral condition of the Nestorians he met. In particular he noted that not only did Nestorian priests fail to condemn sorcery and divination, but many also practiced it themselves, giving charms to their followers and claiming to heal the sick with ashes. William unflatteringly described the Nestorian leaders as "corrupt, liars, usurers, simoniacs and polygamists."[19]

The Nestorian enterprise also appears to have faltered because of theological compromise. James Legge, an expert on ancient China, claims the Nestorians had become "swamped by Confucian, Taoist and Buddhist ideas, a certain degenerate, nominal Christianity."[20] While many Christians throughout history have quickly dismissed Nestorianism as a heresy,[21] the available evidence shows that Nestorian Christianity was a powerful force for good,[22] especially in the early centuries when countless thousands of lives were radically transformed by the gospel of Jesus Christ.

The collapse of the Yuan Dynasty in 1368 also brought about the end of Nestorian influence in Xinjiang. Without the protection of the Mongols, the Christians were exposed to Islamic violence, and many thousands were butchered or forcibly converted to Islam.

The seeds of Nestorianism did not completely die in Xinjiang, however. Five hundred years later, when Russian soldiers invaded

Ili in the mid-nineteenth century, they surprisingly "came across 300–400 Nestorian believers still living there. The Russians tried to convert them to Russian Orthodoxy but they refused. Nothing is said of their fate afterwards."[23] Today there are still an estimated 80,000 Nestorian Christians in the Middle East, 5,000 in India, and 25,000 mostly Syrian Nestorians in the United States.[24]

Catholics in Xinjiang

A mission to fanatical Muslims

Although the Catholic missionary William of Rubruck first traveled across the Central Asian steppes and entered Xinjiang in the 1250s, there is no evidence that he tried to share his faith or establish churches. Eighty years passed before a Franciscan mission succeeded in planting Catholicism in Xinjiang for the first time, centered in the frontier town of Ili.

In the fourteenth century, Ili was considered beyond the extent of Chinese civilization. Thousands of convicted criminals (including persecuted Christians) were banished there to serve the rest of their lives in exile. An early traveler explained that the journey to reach Ili required

> frightful deserts to be traversed, and . . . mountains and their glaciers to be crossed. These gigantic mountains are, in fact, formed by masses of ice, heaped one upon another, so that travelers can only cross them by cutting steps as they go. . . . It was among the populations of these great valleys that the Franciscans succeeded in propagating Christianity.[1]

After years of struggle, a Franciscan base was established, and Friar Richard of Burgundy was appointed the first bishop of Ili. He handpicked some mature brothers from his order to join him in the remote work. Among them were two monks from Alexandria in Egypt, Francis and Raymond Ruffa, and three laymen: Peter Martel from France, Lawrence of Alexandria, and a black man known as John of India. This small team were pioneer evangelists in the true sense of the word. One source says,

These zealous apostles did not content themselves with residing and preaching in the towns; they were continually traversing the vast extent of Tartary, dwelling, like the nomadic populations of those regions, in huts upon wheels, which carried them across immense tracts of country to wherever the spiritual wants of new converts and the probability of conversions seemed to require their presence.

Having no fixed habitation, they followed these pastoral tribes, and adopted their vagabond way of life; stopping with them at their various encampments, living like them upon milk, and glad to pass their days in their tents, if they were only permitted to preach the gospel to their occupants. What energy and perseverance did these poor monks display![2]

To put their achievements in context, a letter written in 1338 by the Spanish missionary traveler Pascal de Vittoria recounts some of the intense opposition he received from Muslims during his journey through Central Asia:

These children of the devil endeavoured to seduce me by their presents, and promising me voluptuous enjoyments, honor, and riches, all that can be desired of worldly things; they desired to pervert me, and when I repulsed their offers with contempt, they stoned me for two days, singed my face and my feet, tore out my beard, and overwhelmed me with outrage and abuse; but as for me, poor monk as I am, I rejoiced in that the adorable goodness of our Lord Jesus Christ had judged me worthy to suffer these things for His Name. . . .

They often administered poison to me, and often plunged me in the water; they fell upon me, and beat me, and inflicted other evils of which I will not speak in this letter. But I thank God for all, and I hope to suffer more still for the glory of His Name.[3]

Soon after the Franciscans arrived, the prince of Ili fell sick. Francis of Alexandria had some experience as a surgeon, and he succeeded not only in helping the prince recover, but also won the confidence and favor of his father, the khan. For several years the missionaries were granted freedom to preach the gospel throughout the realm. But this freedom came to an abrupt end in 1342 when the khan was poisoned by a Muslim enemy. The murderer usurped the throne and immediately issued an edict ordering all Christians to renounce Jesus Christ and embrace Islam. Failure to do so would result in death. The Christians at Ili, however,

> had the honor and courage to refuse obedience to the tyrant, and took no notice of his menaces. They publicly professed their faith, and continued to celebrate as before the ceremonies of their religion. The usurper, being informed of this noble and holy rebellion, gave orders that the means of seduction should first be tried, with respect to both the missionaries and their converts, but that, should these fail, the Christians should be pitilessly exterminated.[4]

At the time there were seven missionaries serving at Ili. They were arrested, chained together, and made to stand before a furious Muslim mob, who

> struck the missionaries on the head with whips and sticks. Then they stabbed them, and finally cut off their noses and ears; and when they found that neither opprobrium nor torment could shake the constancy of these valiant apostles, whose voices rose high amid their tortures to glorify Jesus Christ, to preach the gospel, and to utter anathemas on Mohammed and the Qur'an, they struck their heads off.[5]

The cruel massacre of the Franciscans at Ili occurred in June 1342. The local Christians—who included Uyghurs, Kazaks, Mongols, Russians, and Han Chinese—refused to flee and were thrown into prison and tortured with barbaric cruelty. Many believers laid down their lives and received a martyr's crown.

Despite being deprived of leadership and direction after the 1342 massacre, the Church in Ili survived against all odds. Remarkably, more than 400 years later, the gospel was still being preached in this remote outpost. In 1771 thousands of Torgut Mongols fled into China from their homeland in Russia, where the Orthodox Church was persecuting them. One source notes,

> When they arrived in the Ili Valley they found another form of Christianity. The Franciscans had established a Christian center there from as early as the 14th century. . . . They had built a magnificent church. Ili later became the Gulag of China, to which criminals were banished and to which Chinese Christians who refused to apostatise were sent.[6]

Bento de Góis

After the massacre of 1342, a veil of silence fell on Xinjiang, and almost all news of Christianity in the region fell silent for the next 250 years. Jesuit missionary Bento de Góis (commonly spelled de Goes in English) was born in Portugal in 1562 and traveled overland to Xinjiang via Afghanistan and the imposing Pamir Mountain Range.

Bento de Góis

After serving at the Jesuit mission in Lahore, de Góis disguised himself as an Armenian merchant and headed north in February 1603, having heard from traders that China could be reached via the city of Kashgar. He waited for three months in Kabul, Afghanistan, for the harsh winter to pass, and there de Góis met Agahanem, the sister of the ruler of Kashgar and the mother of the ruler of the Hotan region in Xinjiang. The connection proved providential, for Agahanem and her traveling companions were returning from a pilgrimage to Mecca, but had run out of money. The missionary lent her some funds, which she generously repaid with jade after he reached Xinjiang.

Part of the road between Xinjiang and Pakistan, which Bento de Góis traveled over more than four centuries ago

A traveling companion of Bento de Góis detailed the exceedingly difficult time the group encountered as they crossed the Pamirs. They were trapped in the inhospitable mountains for six days, during which

> many of the men froze to death, and some were buried beneath avalanches. While making his way along the steep bank of a torrent, the faithful companion of de Góis, Isaac the Armenian, made a false step, and fell headlong into the abyss. . . .
>
> Six horses, belonging to de Góis, perished and the travelers, profoundly dejected, could see only an inevitable death before them, and already the horrors of famine and cold had begun to take effect. de Góis alone was never cast down. Always confiding in divine mercy, he appeared armed with a super-human courage, and kept constantly in the front of his companions.[7]

Having passed the most dangerous part of the journey, de Góis entered Xinjiang and made his way to Yarkant (Shache), which was the capital of the Kashgar kingdom at the time. It was now November 1603, and the journey had taken nine months.

Although the Portuguese pioneer now found himself among fanatical Muslims, he was at peace, and God's favor rested upon him. He was used to evildoers and their schemes. Once when a ruler in Kashmir had threatened to crush him under the feet of his elephants, de Góis smiled and said he would gladly lay down his life for the one true God. The missionary's calm demeanor disarmed the ruler, and he was allowed to live.

Soon the news spread throughout Yarkant that a European infidel had arrived in the town. Men armed with swords tried to compel the missionary to recant and embrace Islam, but he refused. One account says,

> The commotion assumed such proportions that de Góis thought it advisable to pay his respects to the King of Kashgar, who resided in the town. Some presents, among them a watch and

some looking-glasses, but especially de Góis' tactful behavior, so gratified the king that he had him sent for several times, and even invited him to explain the Christian religion in the presence of his court, which gave rise to many a sharp dispute with the mullahs.[8]

The Yarkant Muslim leaders were shocked and "could not understand how an intelligent man could profess any religion but their own. Elsewhere de Góis was treated less civilly, several times barely escaping with his life from the scimitars of fanatics who were determined to make him invoke the name of Mohammed."[9]

On one occasion, Benedict de Góis was confronted by a furious Muslim who burst into the house where he was staying. The man "placed his scimitar against his breast and threatened to plunge it in if he did not instantly render homage to the prophet Mohammed. The courageous missionary calmly looked at him, gently put aside the scimitar, and said, 'Go. I know not who Mohammed is.'"[10]

After he had survived a year in Yarkant, a fresh party of travelers was formed to accompany de Góis across the vast Taklamakan Desert to China. The king of Kashgar appointed 72 men to travel with the missionary and gave them the status of ambassadors. The king also gave de Góis a large sum of money and other gifts to ensure that his journey was successful.

Although de Góis didn't realize it at the time, the king had cleverly enabled the traveling party to gain access to China. An ancient treaty existed that allowed just seven or eight countries the right to pass through the Great Wall and enter China once every five years, but only if 72 people with the status of ambassadors were bringing fitting tribute to the emperor in Beijing. These expensive gifts were carried to the palace at the expense of the state, while the travelers were to be honored and entertained at the imperial court.

Before leaving Xinjiang and entering China proper, de Góis encountered more problems when the fanatical Muslim ruler of one area summoned him. The missionary went and found a group of angry Islamic clerics waiting for him. They strenuously denounced Christianity and extolled the virtues of Islam. But "after a hot controversy they were reduced to silence, and the sovereign wound up the debate with the remarkable declaration that Christians, too, were true believers, followers of a religion which at one time had been professed by their forefathers."[11]

After de Góis was forced to wait several days at Turpan, the local ruler warned de Góis that beyond his territory lay territories inhabited by frenzied Muslims, and that he would be wise to drop the title of Christian if he desired to preserve his life. As this ruler prepared the travel documents for de Góis to proceed, the ruler asked, "Shall I leave out the word 'Christian'?" The faithful missionary, however, cried out, "Write down that I am a Christian; it is a title by which I am honored, that I have always borne, and no danger, not even the certainty of death, will make me give it up."[12]

The party continued their journey toward China, passing the corpses of dozens of men who had been murdered by bloodthirsty bandits. The intrepid Portuguese pioneer desired to reach Beijing and spend time with the great missionary Matteo Ricci, who had been informed of his impending arrival. However after passing the Great Wall into China proper, de Góis was forced to stop for months at Jiuquan in Gansu Province, where his funds began to run out. He was forced to stay in the Muslim part of the town where he was constantly harassed by the sons of Ishmael. A letter was dispatched to Beijing asking for money so de Góis could continue his journey, but by the time Ricci received the letter and sent a man to rescue him, de Góis had fallen gravely ill, and he died on April 11, 1607. Ricci believed de Góis had been poisoned by the Muslims.

Exiled to the realm of the barbarians

For the next two centuries, the only snippets of information to emerge about Christianity in Xinjiang were occasional accounts of martyrdoms as Catholic missionaries continued in their efforts to establish the faith in the staunchly Muslim region. A widespread persecution from 1746 to 1748 saw hundreds of Catholics put to death throughout China. Juan Morao, a Jesuit priest, was exiled to Xinjiang where he was strangled to death.

Banishment to Xinjiang was a favorite punishment meted out to all criminals and suspected insurgents by the Qing Dynasty rulers. To prevent escape, convicts received a black tattoo on their forehead.

In 1785, Adrien Zhu Liguan, a native of Fujian Province, died at Ili in Xinjiang. Zhu and a colleague had been arrested and thrown into prison and then given a sentence considered worse than death at the time—exile beyond the Great Wall into the realm of the barbarians. Zhu and seven other Christians commenced the long journey from Beijing to the hostile outpost of Ili, but the 68-year-old Zhu died from exhaustion after many months of travel and the stress of being under arrest.

In 1786, two more Chinese believers, Cassius Tai Jiajue and Pius Liu Zizhen, perished in Ili after the government wrongly assumed that Christians had participated in a Muslim rebellion that was underway in the northern provinces. Even though the emperor's enquiries found that the Christians were not involved in the uprising, he took advantage of the situation to persecute them. Tai and Liu were sentenced to perpetual exile in Xinjiang, and the journey from Beijing to Ili took more than a year to complete. They made it alive, but hard labor and inhumane treatment awaited them. Both men died not long after reaching Xinjiang.

A prisoner confined in a cangue

In 1805, a special map showing the distribution of Catholics throughout China that had been prepared for the pope was discovered in Guangdong Province. As a result,

> Thirteen were banished to Xinjiang. Two were distant cousins of the emperor; their names were excised from the imperial genealogy. The names of two other bannermen involved in the same case were removed from the banner register. All four were condemned to the wooden frame known as the cangue for several months prior to their exile and were forever banned from returning home. The other nine . . . were sentenced to slavery in Ili after spending three months in the cangue.[13]

One of the next mentions of Catholics in Xinjiang was made by the Church of England missionary explorer Henry Lansdell who briefly crossed the border into Yining during an epic journey through Russian Central Asia in 1876. While visiting the town, he "found 65 Chinese Roman Catholics, who had been deprived of missionary and priestly functions for 17 years. They were still holding on, however, and asked me for a service, which I gave."[14]

The Catholic Church in Xinjiang today

The long but sporadic attempts by the Catholic Church to gain a foothold in Xinjiang had borne little fruit. A 1907 study found that almost 650 years after William of Rubruck first visited the region, the Catholic enterprise numbered just two churches and 300 adherents in all of Xinjiang.[15] By 1922, a survey found that Catholics in Xinjiang numbered 313 church members, with an additional 457 people "under Christian instruction."[16] In 1926 a much higher figure was reported of 13,836 Catholics in Xinjiang.[17]

In the years preceding Communist rule in the region, Christians needed to be fortified so that they could withstand the coming onslaught. But the 1930s saw an outbreak of vicious persecution by Muslim fanatics against all Christians in Xinjiang, and by 1941, the Catholics counted "fewer than 800" believers in the entire vast territory.[18]

These numbers have markedly increased since the 1990s, but only because of the influx of millions of Han Chinese who moved to Xinjiang from other parts of China. The migrant force included Catholics who sought to worship God in their new location. By 1994, a modest total of 6,000 Catholics were reported in Xinjiang,[19] with the number rising to 9,000 in 1997.[20] The most recent estimate for Catholics in Xinjiang was 42,200 in 2010.[21]

Despite a history of nearly 800 years in Xinjiang, today only Tibet, Qinghai, and Hainan have fewer numbers of Catholics among all of China's 30 provinces, municipalities, and regions. Catholics are a miniscule dot on the religious landscape of Xinjiang and are dwarfed by Evangelical Christians who today number approximately twenty times as many church members as their Catholic counterparts.

1890s

Although 1892 is commonly cited as the year when the first Evangelical missionaries settled in Xinjiang, two missionaries had previously traveled through the region in 1888, when Henry Lansdell of the British Bible Society teamed up with George Parker of the China Inland Mission (CIM).[1] The duo traveled as far as Yining near the Russian border. They did some translation work combined with medical outreach before returning to neighboring Gansu Province, where Parker had been working for the previous 12 years.

Henry Lansdell and George Parker

Nils Fredrik Höijer

In southern Xinjiang, the genesis of what would become a flourishing work occurred when Nils Fredrik Höijer of Sweden received a burden from God to take the gospel to the many unreached people groups of Central Asia and the Middle East. Höijer, who was born in 1857, may be a little known name in the English-speaking Christian world. But he deserves to be listed

Nils Fredrik Höijer, a great mission pioneer

among the greatest of mission pioneers in Asia alongside the likes of William Carey, Adoniram Judson, and Hudson Taylor. A summary of his achievements states,

> Höijer, founder of the Swedish Slavic Mission, lived and died to make Christ known among the peoples of the East. His calling was primarily to the Russian Empire . . . then on to the multi-cultured Caucasus, later to the Uyghurs of China, and all the way to Alaska and Siberia.
>
> Linguistically gifted and fearless, he continually broke new ground among Russians, Armenians, Kurds, Uyghurs and other peoples. The seemingly impossible did not deter him. . . . Nils Fredrik Höijer was often ahead of his time, a visionary who set his sights to reach the unreached peoples of the East.[2]

In 1891, Höijer was burdened to start a work in the ancient city of Kashgar in Xinjiang which for millennia had been a key stop on the fabled Silk Road. Many church leaders tried to discourage him, saying northwest China was too far away and too dangerous. But such warnings only served to motivate the courageous apostle, and he started out on the long and difficult journey to Kashgar accompanied by three Christians from Turkey, Persia, and Russia.

When they drew near to the border between Russia and China, the party was informed that there was no chance they would be permitted to enter Xinjiang. Höijer laughed and confidently told the Russian governor, "If I can get past the Russians, surely I can handle the Chinese."[3]

To enter Xinjiang, the men faced their greatest challenge and had to ride horses for 280 miles (454 km) through the snow-capped Tianshan Mountains. They prepared thoroughly and bought as much sugar as they were able to carry after Höijer received a tip that the Kirgiz nomads on the Xinjiang side of the border loved sugar and considered it as valuable as gold. The small group purchased enough provisions for 14 days and hired six horses and two men. Cold, hunger, wild animals, and brigands were the dangers they could face, with cold and hunger being their greatest enemies. . . .

One night they came to a large Kirgiz tent village at 6,500 feet [1,981 meters] above sea-level. It was freezing and they suffered greatly from the cold. Some Kirgiz helped them gather wood, water and hay, and they spread the hay on the frozen ground. As a fire began to burn in the center of the tent, a long line of big, strong men gathered around it.

The two men Höijer had hired signalled to say they were brigands who intended to cut their throats. Höijer then brought out his secret weapon, the sugar. The faces of these swarthy men lit up as the lumps of sugar were passed around. It turned out that with sugar as payment, they had all the help they needed.

Crossing the Terek Davan Pass was a sore trial. The cold set in and the wind blew the snow up in swirls, making it hard to breathe. The air was thin and the horses slipped several times.[4]

Despite having made it to the border between China and today's Kyrgyzstan, Höijer and his companions were far from their destination, and a local official refused to let the men cross the border and arrested them. By divine intervention, the group was released and entered Xinjiang, finally arriving at Kashgar after enduring many more days of hardship.

As soon as they arrived in Kashgar, while they were still covered in dirt and sweat, a huge Cossack soldier rode up at full gallop and ordered Höijer to immediately appear at the Russian consulate. After Höijer was led into a large room adorned with portraits of the Russian Tsar, the consul interrogated the missionary to discover the motives of his visit. In the end, "the consul was very positive to him and promised to give what protection he could to the Swedish missionaries who would later come."[5]

Although his stay in Kashgar was brief, Höijer felt he had achieved the purpose of his visit. He commenced the long journey home again in February 1892, after leaving the Turkish Christian Johannes Avetaranian with instructions to prepare the way for the arrival of more Swedish missionaries. Avetaranian remained alone for two years until the first Swedes, Lars and Sigrid Högberg, arrived in Xinjiang.

Höijer died in 1925, aged 68, while visiting Seattle in the United States. His passion for taking Christ to the unreached was unrivaled, and a great ministry emerged that has continued to serve Jesus Christ among the vast unevangelized regions of Central Asia to the present day.[6]

Johannes Avetaranian

In an era when the British or Americans tended to be the first Evangelical missionaries in most locations around the globe, the honor of being the first Evangelical to reside in Xinjiang aptly belongs to an ex-Sufi Muslim named Johannes Avetaranian, whose family claimed to be directly descended from the prophet Mohammed.

Born in Turkey as Muhammad Shukri Efendi in 1861, he became a dervish mullah and was highly respected by his people. One day, however, the direction of Avetaranian's life was upended when he read a Gospel booklet. The message burned in his heart and mind, and after obtaining an Armenian New Testament, he gradually began to doubt the Qur'an and the religion he had been brought up in. Avetaranian recalled the moment when he passed from spiritual death to life:

> I read the Gospel from beginning to end for the second time and then carried on with the Epistles. I cannot describe what joy and love filled my heart as I read the first chapters of Romans, because through them I became completely convinced that Jesus is the Son of God. Indeed, if many clever and learned men would have tried to convince me, it would have been impossible for them to

affect me as profoundly as the words of Romans. . . . I pressed the book to my lips, kissed it again and again, and opened it up, reading what was in it over and over. . . .

I believed everything from my heart; it was so new and unexpected. It was the first time I received an impression of the glory of God, and my heart spoke, "O Lord, my Creator, now I believe You have loved me, for You have given me this book. . . . I want to follow You alone, O Jesus, Son of God, whatever may happen."[7]

When the Turkish mullahs discovered that one of their own had become a Christian, they vowed to kill him, but he escaped by fleeing across the border. On February 28, 1885, he was baptized at Tbilisi in today's nation of Georgia, and was given the new last

Avetaranian in 1900

name Avetaranian, meaning "son of the gospel." At the time he was engaged to a Muslim woman, but she was unable to accept his new faith, and the engagement was called off. Avetaranian completely saturated every part of his life into Christ Jesus, and his zeal to honor the Living God in all things consumed him. Once, after attending a church service, he said:

> The Lord had given me such a love and fervency that I feared nothing. I was still in my mullah's garb and came to the church meeting dressed that way. . . . When I went to the bazaar . . . the Muslims gave me dirty looks from every side. As soon as one of them addressed me, I used the opportunity to preach the gospel. . . . I was so taken up by it all that I thought neither about life nor about danger and death. I saw nothing but Christ and His love.[8]

In 1891 after Avetaranian had been a Christian for three years, a Swedish missionary asked him to consider relocating to faraway Kashgar in northwest China where help was needed to set up a new mission station to reach the Turkic Uyghur people. Unsure about what lay ahead, Avetaranian committed to living in Kashgar for one year, and he traveled there with Nils Fredrik Höijer. Upon arrival, he bought a set of local clothes so he would blend in with the people. He recalled,

> The Kashgaris soon came to see me and were very curious to learn what had led me there. At first it was hard for me to understand their language, but I soon learned it since Kashgari is closely related to my mother tongue, Osmanli Turkish. . . . I brought along two large chests of Bibles in Chinese, Arabic and Persian and set them up at my home. I told the Kashgaris that these books were translations of the Old and New Testament: those holy books the Qur'an states are from God.[9]

Avetaranian saw that there was a desperate need for Scripture in a language the people of Kashgar could understand, so he began to translate the New Testament. He soon discovered that two dialects were spoken in Kashgar, one by the local Uyghurs and another harsher dialect spoken by immigrants from Andidjan in Uzbekistan.

The Turkish disciple of Christ soon made friends with many local men who visited his home to listen to Bible reading and to ask questions. They told him, "It is just as you preach, but we have not seen any Christians. The Europeans who have been in Kashgar for the most part have not believed in God at all, nor in an afterlife. Rather, they have ridiculed all religions. We have seen no trace of what you have read to us from the Gospel."[10]

Omar Akhund

God's Word slowly began to wield its powerful influence, and before long Avetaranian's servant Omar Akhund, who may have been a Kirgiz or a Kazak, wanted to be baptized. When Omar was asked how he knew about baptism, he replied, "You read in the Acts of the Apostles that if someone believed in Jesus, he was baptized. I now believe Jesus is my Savior, and that is why I would like to be baptized." When Avetaranian warned him that baptism would lead to persecution from the Muslim leaders and possibly death, Omar stated, "I am not worth more than the first Christians. They too were persecuted and killed."[11]

Omar Akhund was duly baptized by Avetaranian in the Tumen River, becoming the first Evangelical Christian in Xinjiang. Thus the torch of Christian faith that had first been lit by the Nestorians more than a thousand years earlier but appeared to have been completely snuffed out was reignited.

At his baptism when Omar was asked if he wanted a Christian name, he replied, "I would like to be called Lazarus, who loved Jesus and who rose from the dead."[12]

When Omar's wife learned that her husband had become a Christian, she betrayed him to the mullahs who threatened to kill him if he would not renounce his new faith and return to the mosque. Their threats only seemed to strengthen his faith, however, and on many occasions he shared the gospel with the infuriated clerics. One day Omar was ordered to attend a gathering of 50 mullahs. After binding his hands and feet,

> They placed a rope around his neck and threatened to strangle him immediately if he spoke about Jesus and the gospel. Although Lazarus was a strong young man, he did not defend himself; rather he declared to the mullahs that he would die for Jesus. When they saw he was not afraid of death and noticed that the Chinese government did not comply with their wish to punish him because of his conversion, they began to torment him anew during the month of Ramadan.[13]

In February 1897, Johannes Avetaranian left Xinjiang for a visit to Europe to oversee the printing of his Uyghur New Testament. But linguists found fault with many of the words and expressions used in it, and the project was postponed. Although he had intended to return as soon as possible, Avetaranian never set foot in Xinjiang again. Instead, he began working with the German Orient Mission in Bulgaria, and he became the editor of a Turkish Christian newspaper which was distributed in Turkey and throughout Central Asia.

In June 1900 Avetaranian married Helene von Osterroht, a German believer, and together they worked on many translation projects to increase the availability of God's Word in the Turkish-speaking world. Finally in 1914, after many delays because of the First World War and after numerous revisions, news that the Kashgari Uyghur New Testament was ready to be printed brought great joy to Avetaranian's heart. He wrote, "We have prayed day and night that God would open a way to send God's Word to Kashgar and have learned that He will do it."[14]

Johannes Avetaranian continued to serve the Lord Jesus Christ until his death in Germany in December 1919, at the age of 58. He has gone down in Christian history as the first Evangelical missionary to live in Xinjiang, and before his death he was greatly encouraged to hear reports of breakthroughs and conversions among the Uyghur people.

Swedish recruits

A trickle of missionaries from the Swedish Mission Covenant Church arrived in Kashgar throughout the 1890s, and the mission became the main light for the gospel in Xinjiang in the twentieth century. Over time schools and chapels were built, and many Muslims converted to Jesus Christ and joined the family of God.

One of the more interesting of the early Swedish missionaries was Anna Nyström who had served in today's Iran and the Caucasus region before she moved to Xinjiang in 1894. The

Avetaranian and his wife engaged in Bible translation

following year she married a Persian doctor, Josef Mässrur, and they served Christ together in Yarkant where they made many friends and were highly respected by the Uyghur people.

Anna had been weakened after contracting cholera during an epidemic that swept through Persia. After the couple spent nearly 20 years serving among Muslims, they returned to Sweden in 1913 where Anna's health was found to be broken beyond repair. She was immediately hospitalized but died a short time later.

Yarkant later developed into one of the main ministry centers of the Swedish Mission in Xinjiang, but the 1890s had been a long and intense struggle as they tried to gain a foothold in the region. The missionaries reflected on the period from 1892 to 1900 as "years of insecurity," when

> Local Muslims were infuriated that there was a Christian presence in their sacred territory, and they refused to allow the mission-aries to rent any residence. For an extended period they had to live in a garden area, and even then several riots occurred. Finally the Muslims, together with the Chinese authorities, incited a riot during Easter in 1899. The mob threatened to tear down the newly rented dwellings of the missionaries and to topple the young mission.[15]

The nineteenth century came to a close. Although Christian work was in its infancy, a solid foundation was being laid that prom-ised future growth for the kingdom of God in Xinjiang.

1900s and 1910s

The Boxer Rebellion plagued the missionary enterprise throughout China and resulted in the slaughter of thousands of Chinese Christians in the summer of 1900. However it barely touched distant Xinjiang, not only because of its geographic isolation, but also because so few Christians resided in the massive territory at the time. This situation slowly changed throughout

In an era before international banking, money to run the mission arrives from Sweden

the first two decades of the twentieth century as the Swedish mission in southern Xinjiang began to grow, one new worker at a time.

The China Inland Mission pioneer George Hunter began the century based at Lanzhou in neighboring Gansu Province. From there he made several long trips into Xinjiang, distributing gospel literature to people in numerous languages along the way. He relocated to Urumqi in 1905 where he rented a shop that sold Christian literature to passers-by. On certain days, the shop was used as a chapel for preaching the gospel to all interested people. In the winter of 1907–08, Hunter reported,

> I made an effort to sell books and tracts to the people gathered from all parts of the district so as to spend the winter months in Urumqi. With the aid of a mimeograph I was able to print about 1,000 Chinese calendars, which the people bought readily. I also printed quite a large number of Turkish tracts, and sold a number of Gospels in Chinese. . . . I had some scrolls nicely written, with Scripture texts in Chinese, Arabic and Turkish, and pasted them on the large doors of the shop. This caused quite an attraction. Many came to the shop, and there were good opportunities for preaching.[1]

It is difficult for people today to comprehend the loneliness and endurance that Hunter and other pioneer missionaries experienced in the vast region. Despite their many years of faithfully sowing God's Word, in 1911 a missionary magazine reported, "The number of communicants reported in 1911 for the province of Xinjiang is two."[2]

Gospel literature distribution continued to be the dominant characteristic of George Hunter's ministry in Xinjiang, and many of his reports detail the quantity and variety of Scripture he sold or gave away to people and their responses to it. In August 1909, he shared about some of the dangers he faced while traveling across the desert to southern Xinjiang:

George Hunter with Chinese enquirers at Urumqi (1913)

I disposed of about 200 tracts and preached on the street. . . .
From the bazaar we started for Pialma, where we hoped to arrive
before dark, but the darkness overtook us when we were about
10 or 13 miles from Pialma, and soon we completely lost our
way in the desert.

I tried to use my compass, but this could only be done by
lighting matches, which were often blown out by the wind. We
wandered about for some time, but soon got hopelessly lost. At
last we heard people shouting and talking in the distance. We
were very glad, and ran to the place where we heard the sound.
We soon came to a caravan of men, women and children, only
to find them hopelessly groping for tracks in the sand, as they,
too, had lost the way. . . .

There was nothing for us to do but to lie down and try to rest,
hungry, and especially thirsty, as we were on the dry sands of the
Taklamakan. I tried to sleep, but could not. I thought I could hear

the sound of a running stream! . . . Early in the morning we heard the voices of travelers in the distance, and in going in that direction we were soon on our way to Pialma, where we purchased a musk melon, and thus moistened our parched mouths.[3]

Two lone lighthouses

As the 1910s progressed, Evangelical work in Xinjiang continued to be dominated by the Swedish Mission in Kashgar, while around Urumqi and northern parts of the region, the CIM duo of George Hunter and Percy Mather reached out for Christ like two lone lighthouses amid an ocean of darkness.

Throughout the decade, reports from Hunter continued to give insights into how the gospel was slowly being disseminated. In a 1910 report he said,

> Urumqi, the capital, makes a good center for preaching the gospel, especially so during the winter months. When the cold weather comes, many of the laboring classes are glad to go to Urumqi, where they can buy ten pounds of coal for about one cent, and are thus enabled at least to keep themselves warm during the long, cold winter. At such times we have only to open the street chapel door in order to secure a good audience. When the warm weather comes the people are drawn from the city to the country districts, and thus we find that season more suitable for itinerating work.[4]

The challenges of remote ministry in Xinjiang meant that the missionaries were cut off from the rest of the world for long stretches of time. Letters usually took six months or more to reach them, if they arrived at all. This report reveals the incredible isolation the pioneers were called to endure:

> The station at Urumqi is some two or three months' journey from Kashgar on the one hand; two month's journey from Lanzhou, the nearest station, on the other, which is again more than two months' journey from Wuhan. Thus to reach their nearest

neighbors to the east or west would necessitate from 60 to 90 days' traveling.[5]

George Hunter's evangelistic ministry touched people from more than a dozen different ethnic groups, and a report he wrote in August 1910 gives insights into the challenges of outreach among several minority groups:

Hui

We have done a good deal of work among these people. They often visit the preaching chapel, are represented in nearly every street audience, and sometimes come to the Sunday services. Although fond of argument, often only to show off their superior knowledge, they are nearly always polite. The Arabic Scriptures prepared by the British and Foreign Bible Society are especially suitable for this class. Those of them who can read Chinese buy the Chinese portions. Like all Muslim work, this is exceedingly difficult; still the door is wide open.[6]

A Kirgiz family in southern Xinjiang after hearing the gospel for the first time

Kirgiz

The only gospel work that I know of among this tribe is in the mountains near Kashgar. There at first they were very shy of foreigners, but owing to the kindly visits of the Swedish missionaries (who often spend a hot summer month in these mountains), prejudice is completely broken down. Last year Miss Nordquist and Miss Swanson, of the Swedish Mission, visited some of these tribes in the mountains between Kashgar and Yarkant, and they were encouraged to find that the gospel message was gladly received. The writer spent two nights in Kirgiz tents in these mountains within Russian territory. Uyghur Gospels in the Kashgar dialect were readily received and read. . . . This field seemed to me to be especially suitable for hardy, enterprising married missionaries.[7]

Uyghur

Work among the Uyghur people is very hard indeed. The mullahs as a rule are especially opposed to the gospel. I have taken several journeys among these people and have done some evangelistic work among them. Last year (1909) in a journey as far as Hotan, 72 stages from here, some bitter opposition was shown, particularly in the large and degraded cities. In some of the country villages the people listened exceedingly well. The medical, school, and gospel work of the Swedish Missionary Society in Kashgar and Yarkant has done much to break down opposition, and they have gathered a few Christians around them. Workers among the Uyghur Muslims must not have such a word as "discouragement" in their dictionaries.[8]

Kazak

I do not know of any gospel work being done among this large tribe. A few years ago the writer visited some Kazak tents on the way to Ili, and the Uyghur Gospel portions were readily received and read by them. They are Muslims, but of a very peculiar type. . . . These people, dwelling on the Altai Mountains, speak a very peculiar kind of Turki, and I do not know of any books written in their vernacular.[9]

Mongols

Last year I sold quite a number of Mongolian and Tibetan Scriptures to the Mongols in the district of Karashar [Yanqi]. Several years ago I also sold a number of Mongolian Gospels to a small tribe. . . . Mongols seldom speak any other language but their own, so that learning Mongolian would be the first duty of the missionary who has grace enough to give up all and go and live among these degraded people. . . . One of the Mongolian princes called for me last year while in Karashar and bought a Gospel.[10]

Xinjiang, meanwhile, was experiencing an influx of Han Chinese immigrants, the first trickle of what would one day become a roaring stream of millions. Hunter shared his thoughts on most of the Han he had met in the region:

Many of the Chinese are settled in this land in small groups, and can only be reached by a great expenditure of time. . . . Almost all Chinese settlers long to return to China proper. Those who are not banished by the government are either runaways or such as hope to make a fortune. Very few of the former manage to pay their way back again, because they usually squander what money they get. Those who come on business return as soon as they have made enough money. The answer one gets from almost all of them, if you question them about returning, is: "I would go tomorrow if I had enough money."[11]

The Swedish Mission expands

In southern Xinjiang, the Swedish Mission continued to attract many Uyghurs and Kirgiz people to the faith. Over time the mission expanded their influence through schools, orphanages, and hospitals, enabling them to reach tens of thousands of people from every walk of life. While ministering to people's physical needs, the missionaries were careful not to neglect their spiritual needs also, and the gospel of salvation was proclaimed at every opportunity.

A succession of new missionaries joined the effort, some of whom were forced to leave Xinjiang after a short time due to the hardships they encountered. When the mission wanted to expand their work in Kashgar to better reach the Han Chinese residents of the city, they recruited Albert and Maria Andersson because Albert already spoke Chinese.

The Anderssons traveled from Sweden in 1900 but were delayed in Central Asia due to the ravages of the Boxer Rebellion. They finally crossed the border and reached Kashgar, but in 1902 they lost their ten-month-old daughter, Mia. The grief caused by Mia's death deeply impacted Albert and Maria, and in 1906 they

Swedish missionaries and patients at the mission hospital

returned to Sweden for an extended time of rest. The following year they returned to Xinjiang where they attempted to soldier on. But Albert's health gradually deteriorated, and a further crippling blow occurred when their six-year-old son, Göte, died in Kashgar.

Heartbroken and feeling crushed, the Anderssons returned to Sweden in 1911 where doctors declared that Albert's days were numbered and he would soon die. He lived another four years, however, before going to his eternal reward in March 1915, aged 50.

The crucial printing press

One of the major turning points in the success of Christian work in Xinjiang was the arrival of a printing press in 1912. The press was painstakingly transported from Sweden across Russia before being broken into small pieces and carried on the backs of mules across the mountains into Xinjiang. This printing press proved to be a crucial weapon in the struggle to spread the light of Christ among the darkness of Xinjiang.

Over the years, an estimated 60,000 to 70,000 books of Scripture and other Christian publications were printed in Kashgar and distributed over a vast area of Xinjiang, which both exposed unbelievers to the gospel and counteracted Muslim leaders in their efforts to discredit Christianity. The impact of the printing press was immense, and one missionary remarked, "Whereas people used to tear up the Gospels they were offered, or throw them in the fire, they now receive them gratefully, yes, and are even happy to buy them. They are also showing them the same respect a Muslim usually shows to other holy writings."[12] Distributing the Word of God among Muslims in Xinjiang was not without challenges. One man, a teacher, visited the Kashgar mission station and bought a Gospel of Matthew, which he took home and shared with the leaders of his mosque. The first few chapters were accepted and discussed, but when they read the last verse of the third chapter which says, "This is my beloved Son," consternation reigned among the mullahs. Referring to Jesus as the Son of God was, and still is, considered blasphemy by Muslims, so when they read this,

> The men simply erased the word "Son" from the Bible portion. As they continued to read they were also shocked when they came across the word "Father," so it too was erased. When they reached the 11th chapter where "Father" and "Son" appear several times together they realized how dangerous the book really was. It was decided the only thing to do was to burn it, but one of the mullahs intervened, saying, "We cannot do this! We ourselves confess that the Gospel has come from God." They mocked the man, but he was able to hide the book, and after some time he went to the mission station with his "edited" copy and received a new one in return.[13]

The printing press continued to pump out large quantities of Scripture in the languages of Xinjiang until it was taken over by the Chinese authorities who used it to produce propaganda material.

One of the many Uyghur Christian books that were printed in Kashgar

A Kazak influx

The history of the Kazak people in Xinjiang has been marked by brutal oppression. Between 1916 and 1920, more than 100,000 Kazaks crossed the border into China after the Russian government imposed conscription on them. The intrepid George Hunter wrote about some Kazaks he encountered in the summer of 1917:

> A Kazak mullah came to our tent and took away books, and asked many questions. . . . Quite a number of men and women came in. They boiled us some milk. I told them I belonged to the people of the Holy Prophet Jesus, that He came down to earth and died for us all, and that just before He ascended to heaven He told His people to go into all the world and preach the gospel to all people, and that was what I had come to do. I feel the Holy Spirit blessed the words spoken. . . .

> I preached to a Mongol and a Kazak man from the story of the "Rich Man and Lazarus." When I had finished, the men explained it to each other. While doing this they both laughed, one so much that I believe I saw the tears coming out of his eyes. I fear that these men suffer much at the hands of rich men.[14]

At the start, Hunter was alarmed by the bloodthirsty reputation of the Kazaks, and he was warned not to pass through their territory. Over time, however, the missionary won their trust and came to appreciate them, so that a colleague said,

> Now he finds them most kind and hospitable, and feels far safer among them in the mountains than when he is on the plains among the Chinese or Hui Muslims. When left to themselves they do not show hostility to the gospel, nor do they burn or destroy the books as the Uyghurs do. They also seem to be healthier than, and morally superior to, the other Turkic races, and are mostly free from the use of strong drink, hemp, and opium.[15]

Hunter, with the help of a converted mullah, translated the Gospel of Matthew into Kazak, which was the first Scripture translation the Kazaks of Xinjiang ever had in their language.[16] Thousands of copies were distributed over a wide area, exposing multitudes to the life and teaching of Jesus Christ for the first time.

George Hunter

George Hunter, who was later dubbed the "Apostle of Turkestan," was born in Kincardineshire, Scotland in 1861. His mother died when he was an infant, but he grew up and went on to spend 57 years of his life in northwest China, mainly ministering to Muslims. At the time of his death in 1946, few Christians around the world had ever met Hunter or knew much about him. He was a mysterious figure to many—a man who shied away from the spotlight and preferred obscurity. In 1945 a missionary colleague provided this summary of Hunter's life and service:

George Hunter, the "Apostle of Turkestan"

Many Christians who have closely followed the progress of the gospel in inland China will be familiar with his name, but very few will have had any personal contact with him. The reason is easily explained. One afternoon I asked him when he had last visited England. He laughed for a moment and remarked slowly and with some relish, "Well, it was in the last year of the reign of Queen Victoria (1900)!" . . . He has not been to the Chinese coast since 1932. . . .

George Hunter's way of life and the remoteness of his field has made him an exception to many rules. He does not (so far as I know) write circular letters and his long absence from this country has greatly reduced the number of his connections here, so that many people do not know much about him.[1]

After God saved him, Hunter applied for overseas missionary service, but his application was rejected. He engaged in local Christian work in Britain with the YMCA and other organizations before reapplying to join the China Inland Mission. This time he was accepted, and he departed for China in February 1889. Hunter had his one and only furlough back in Britain in 1900—after 11 years in China—and only because the Boxer Rebellion had forced the compulsory evacuation of all missionaries. Remarkably after returning to the deserts of Xinjiang, he happily spent the remainder of his life in northwest China—46 more years—without a break and without ever seeing the land of his birth again.

Unsurprisingly, Hunter never married, and the only mention of any romantic affection was his love for an Aberdeen lass named Jessie, to whom he was engaged to marry before she tragically died from an illness at the age of just 22. He never discussed how her death affected him, although when he visited her grave in 1900, he placed a granite heart over it because her family would not allow him to erect a tombstone.

During his time at language school in eastern China, Hunter was shocked when some of his fellow missionary students married and began families. He lamented, "With wives and families, how can they go from here to preach, suffer, and maybe die for Christ in some distant, unevangelized part of China? They are already sidetracked!"[2] George Hunter vowed to remain single his entire life so he could fully devote himself to serving God.

A unique personality

Many Christians who are unfamiliar with life on the mission field may develop a false impression that all missionaries are sociable, outgoing people. The reality is often quite different, yet God is able to use both the strengths and weaknesses of His children for His glory. Hunter was a man who appeared to thrive on loneliness and isolation, and God used those traits to achieve much for His kingdom in Xinjiang.

Decades after the end of Hunter's career, missiologists were still debating the impact he had in Xinjiang and whether or not he was helped or hindered by his black-and-white personality. Author Ralph Covell described Hunter as follows:

A man of violent likes and dislikes, who found it difficult to tolerate younger missionaries. If they wished to relax with some table tennis, he felt this was too light-hearted an attitude for missionaries who were faced daily with issues of life and death. . . .

Hunter had a violent dislike for Roman Catholics. On one occasion he had accepted an invitation from the provincial governor of Gansu to attend a feast, but dismissed himself early when he found that a Dutch Catholic was present. Religious holidays, such as Christmas—he called it Chris Mass—or Easter, were anathema to him. . . . He was very disciplined in his daily lifestyle. What Hunter ate never varied—morning porridge, boiled mutton and rice at noon, and leftovers from noon in the evening.[3]

In 1907 Hunter was asked to travel to Shanghai to attend a major mission conference and to present the claims of the unreached peoples of Xinjiang. He reluctantly made the long journey to the coast,

> but no one there seemed interested in the wealth of information and experience he possessed about the unevangelized regions he represented. Two weeks in Shanghai after the close of the conference were enough of civilization for him, and he returned to his lonely outpost from which he didn't emerge again until 1931.[4]

George Hunter thoroughly disliked traditional mission stations where foreign believers were often surrounded by high walls and servants. He felt that such a model was a major hindrance to the advance of the gospel. Instead, his passion for contact with remote, unreached people "drove him to seek them out in their desert encampments or among the folds and valleys of unexplored mountains, where they hid themselves with the skill and cunning of wild animals."[5]

Known as an austere and reserved individual, Hunter was described by one colleague as "a dour man with a character compounded of severity, sternness and obstinacy, but he was sterling to the core and showed occasional facets of faithful affection and even tender-heartedness." And, "He was simple, unpretentious, unassuming."[6]

The pioneer's biographers added this blunt assessment:

> Hunter's nature lacked the gift of drawing people to himself or even of attaching them to each other. He was truly the messenger of the Lord to them, but he took no personal interest either in the hearers or in their families. No one who believed through his ministry would ever say that George Hunter had won him by his genial and warm disposition, yet he prayed earnestly and with unfailing regularity for them all.[7]

On the field, Hunter lived a very simple life. Even though he only returned to his homeland once, he remained thoroughly British—during his entire career he used a Union Jack as his bedspread. A fellow missionary observed,

> He was British in all his sympathies as well as by nationality, and nothing which Britain did was allowed to be adversely criticized in his presence without the speaker receiving a strong rebuke. The Britain he knew was pre-eminently the Britain of the Victorian days, and to him she stood for the land which displayed the flag of liberty, the land which had freed the slaves, and the land to which in a special way had been committed the gospel of Jesus Christ for transmission to the whole world, and which therefore had become the center of the great missionary societies.[8]

Although he rarely spoke about himself, occasional glimpses of Hunter from fellow missionaries provide precious insights into his way of life. David Bentley-Taylor wrote,

> Having for decades lived a life of isolation and loneliness and become inured to months and months of gypsy-like existence, the amenities of civilization and the constant presence of missionaries seemed to him unnecessary. He preferred to carry on in his own way and be free to live as he had become accustomed. Every night he had a little Bible class there in his room by the uncertain light of an oil lamp. Not very many attended and yet it was surprising the people who did drop in now and then—leaders in the church, soldiers, students, non-Christians as well as Christians.[9]

A friend of many peoples

During his long span of more than half a century in northwest China, Hunter came into his own as a gifted linguist. He was able to preach in seven languages—Uyghur, Kazak, Chinese, Manchu, Arabic, Mongolian, and Nogai, a Turkic language spoken in Russia. It was said that

He attempted to learn an adequate amount of all the local languages such that he could converse simply about the gospel with whomever he met. The surrounding languages and dialects of Urumqi were numerous. . . . He learned the language from the people on the street and the nomads on the steppe. He was a self-taught, need-to-know linguist.[10]

The British and Foreign Bible Society worked closely with Hunter during his entire career, providing thousands of Bibles and Scripture portions for him to distribute. The Manchu New Testament had been translated in 1835, but had sat, unused, on a shelf in London for almost 80 years as the Manchu dynasty collapsed and the language became practically obsolete.[11] Then one day a letter arrived from Hunter in Xinjiang reporting how

His long itinerating travels had brought him to a very distant oasis of the Gobi Desert. This had been given over to faithful Manchu troops who had fought in battles during the reign of the Qianlong Emperor [1735–96]. These troops took their Manchu tongue with them to the territory, and continued to use it even when it had ceased to be spoken elsewhere. . . . Soon the parcels arrived in Urumqi, so that the next time George Hunter visited that oasis he added Manchu Gospels to the load of books in many languages which he always carried.[12]

During countless thousands of miles of difficult travel—often through bandit-infested territory and across vast barren wastes where massive sandstorms cut his face like a dagger—George Hunter's meticulous journal entries revealed that the local people generally received the gospel gladly, although he was often threatened by mullahs, robbed by evildoers, and attacked by wolves and wild dogs. The extent of Hunter's sufferings over more than half a century of ministry will only be fully revealed in heaven because with his understated manner he left few clues about the severity of the many attacks he endured. As a typical example, in one report he simply mentioned that the mullahs in one location had been "rather rude." It was later revealed by a colleague that Hunter's life had been in grave danger after the Muslims of that town took blood oaths to kill him.

The dangers that George Hunter faced were far outweighed by the joy he felt when people heard the gospel for the first time. In 1907, for example, the mullah of a mosque near Turpan bought an Arabic New Testament from Hunter, and "immediately buried his face in it and kissed it, and in other ways evidently tried to express his love for it."[13]

Hunter firmly believed that the living Word of God would lodge in the hearts of those who read it, and that it would bear fruit in due season. He was constantly challenged, however, by the struggle to obtain Scriptures in the remote northwest. On one occasion he was ecstatic when a caravan of camels arrived carrying eight boxes of Gospel tracts in various languages. The

Hunter starting another long journey on horseback

shipment had taken two years to arrive from Shanghai because it had been delayed by civil unrest and other troubles along the way.

George Hunter's ministry was largely a thankless one of much faithful sowing of seed but little evidence of people turning to Christ. In 1908 he baptized two people, but there was no subsequent mention of more converts. He found that the intense pressure on both former Muslims and Buddhists to recant was so great that many new believers failed to go on in the Christian faith. As a result, "he feared new converts would backslide, disgracing the Name of Christ, so he did not keep any baptismal records. Evangelism was his passion."[14]

At times the atmosphere in Xinjiang took a turn for the worse, and though he was an extremely courageous man, Hunter knew his life could easily be taken at any moment but for divine protection. On one occasion he wrote from his base in Urumqi,

> In the various cities that I have visited I find doors are open among the Chinese, especially those who know something about us; and they are quite ready to buy books, etc. But this cannot be said regarding the Turkic Muslims of Xinjiang.
>
> Indeed, there is a well-organized and universal opposition to everything that has the name of "Christian." The Muslims of Xinjiang in general are the very opposite of those of China proper. If they had the power, I fear that even our lives would be in great danger. Indeed it looks to me, as this opposition has been going on long, that they prefer God's judgment to His Grace, and cruel war to peace in Christ.[15]

Heaven sent co-workers

Despite Hunter's preference for his own company, God decided to send a small team of colleagues to join him in his great endeavor, even though the veteran missionary had not requested any help. In 1914, Percy Mather arrived in Xinjiang from his former base in Anhui Province. Hunter had been isolated for so long that he was beginning to lose some of his English vocabulary, but from the start a warm friendship was forged between Hunter and Mather. The latter wrote,

> He looked tired and worn when I first met him, but has brightened up wonderfully since then. He keeps saying: "Oh! It is grand to have you young folks here. It does my heart good just to see you and hear you talking." Dear old man. I've taken him to my heart and feel I have had two fathers now. It is a great privilege and honor to be with him.[16]

The ministry of Hunter and Mather was greatly enhanced when a Mongol assistant, Nimgir, was given to them by a Mongolian living Buddha. For many years Nimgir formed an excellent partnership with the missionary duo. Together "they crisscrossed Xinjiang. . . . Hunter witnessed to the Central Asians in general, and Mather to the Mongols. Nimgir was their adjutant, translator,

Nimgir, Hunter's long-time Mongol assistant

manager, dresser and administrator, as well as their protector and horse-minder. Together they distributed thousands of Scriptures throughout a huge area."[17]

God has a way of encouraging His servants when they need it most. In 1914, when two other missionaries were feeling particularly discouraged that so few people had been showing an interest in the gospel, they stopped at a village where a Chinese man appeared at the door and asked to be instructed about Jesus Christ. The man said,

> Seven or eight years ago a foreigner passed through our village. I had been working at the farm and was returning home late. While crossing the street this foreigner called me and gave me a book, saying, "Old gentleman, I want to give you this book. Take it home and read it. It contains the true doctrine!"
>
> He was an elderly man with a beard and I have never seen him again, but I took the book home and as I read its pages I destroyed my idols, I tore the household gods off the door and burned them, and I severed my connections with the three secret societies to which I belonged. Since then I have worshipped the God of that book.[18]

Needless to say, the missionary who had handed the man the Gospel was George Hunter.

The years passed, but Hunter's passion to share Christ with the lost remained undiminished. In 1921 he gave insight into the variety of ethnicities he impacted as well as the unique payments he received for gospel literature in a region where bartering was still the main type of transaction. Hunter reported,

> By July 12th we left the burning plains and were high up in the cool mountains. We visited a Kazak tent and found the only inmate was an old woman, her only son having gone to visit some friends. We gave her matches and needles in exchange for milk. We then visited some Mongol Kalmyk tents and gave Gospels and tracts in exchange for milk and butter. Next day we met a Halh

Mongol lama doctor who was greatly reverenced by the people. He could read Tibetan and Mongol, so we gave him some Gospels and he gave us butter and cheese.

We visited some tents of the Olot tribe of Kalmyks. One man could read, so we left a Gospel with him. Several Kazaks visited our tent. We preached to them and gave Gospels to those who could read. In the evening a Mongol gave us milk in return for eye medicine.

Hunter in 1919

On our way to Kobdo, we drew near to the camp of one of the most popular Kazak chiefs in Altai. We were met by one of his officials, who requested us to call and see the chief who was ill. When we reached his tent we were welcomed by a mullah. I was glad to see him. He speaks perfect Chinese and some years ago helped me with the translation of the Kazak Gospels.

Finding the chief suffering from heart and lung trouble, we gave him some medicine but feared there was little hope of his recovery. They were very kind to us and gave us boiled mutton and milk. We then continued our journey.[19]

Soviet torture

Hunter was shocked by the sudden death of his younger colleague Percy Mather in 1933, but he didn't let it slow him down. He plunged further into the work God had called him to do. That same year, a Chinese warlord named Sheng Shicai seized control of Xinjiang, which he ruled with an iron fist until 1945. In a foreshadowing of later developments in the twenty-first century, Sheng killed or imprisoned at least 100,000 Uyghurs, and the political landscape in Xinjiang lurched significantly toward the Soviet Union, which viewed the British as a key rival for control of Central Asia.

Trouble soon came to all foreigners in Xinjiang. The authorities didn't believe the motives of missionaries could be anything but political, and Hunter was suspected of being a British spy. All missionaries were ordered to leave Xinjiang, but George Hunter refused to go. He was duly arrested and detained in a Soviet prison in Urumqi for 13 months, during which he was frequently tortured by two Russian agents in a bid to break his spirit. Constant interrogations took place late at night to weaken the missionary through sleep deprivation. Tellingly, Hunter was given injections that deadened his mind. The great pioneer later wrote,

The injections, which were given in order to reduce my will-power, told upon me and made resistance more difficult. Had they continued much longer I might have said that I was a spy. . . .

Do what you can to make the Church at home understand that this has nothing to do with the severities of normal imprisonment, but is based on profound understanding of demoniacal psychology. Long after you are released you still hear their voices taunting you, and for longer still you feel that they are after you, seeking to hurt and destroy you.[20]

Just before Hunter's 79th birthday, he was put on a plane and deported to Gansu Province. For the next four years he lived in the city of Lanzhou, but he constantly longed for an opportunity to return to his beloved Xinjiang. After his awful torture experience, one source said,

He emerged triumphant, but broken. He had come to know the power of God in a new way, but he had lost his nerve, and on the few occasions when he allowed himself to speak of the incidents of his imprisonment he would drop his voice to a whisper and look around furtively as though he felt himself surrounded by enemies and spies.[21]

In 1945, Hunter was able to get halfway back to Xinjiang by traveling to Zhangye, but "there, in increasing weakness, he spent the last two years of his pilgrimage—alone. When he died in December 1946, the nearest foreign missionary was 250 miles [405 km] behind him."[22]

Ironically for someone who spurned publicity his whole life, in 1932 Hunter was awarded an Member of the British Empire (MBE) by King George VI for his services in Central Asia. Mildred Cable comments,

The cruelest blow to George Hunter was that on being expelled from the country he was never allowed to revisit his home or even to collect his valuable books or manuscripts. Where they have been scattered no one knows. He died as he lived, a lonely man, far from his fellow countrymen, and during his last illness he was nursed by Chinese Christians. He was one of the last great pioneer missionaries.

It is regrettable that he has not passed on more of the accumulated knowledge which he possessed; but his is the honor which he most coveted; not the MBE which the King was graciously pleased to grant him, but that of being a translator of the Scriptures into the language of some remote tribes which otherwise would have not yet had them.[23]

Percy Mather

Born in the English county of Lancashire in 1882, just seven years before George Hunter commenced his ministry in China, Percy Mather was 21 years younger than the veteran pioneer. But the two men complemented each other and became such close friends and co-workers for the gospel that the two names of Hunter and Mather have been paired together ever since when Christian work in Xinjiang is discussed.

Percy Mather

Mather surrendered his life to Jesus Christ when he was 21 and sailed to China seven years later, ultimately joining Hunter and becoming the second CIM missionary in Xinjiang. After several years living in a mission compound in eastern China, Mather felt uncomfortable and was convinced that he was participating in an unbiblical model of outreach. He felt deeply stirred whenever he read George Hunter's reports from Xinjiang, and he longed to break away from the confines of the mission compound and share Christ in wide open spaces. Mather was convinced that God wanted him to relocate to the vast northwest. Hunter, however, had not requested a co-worker and was such a unique individual that few people thought it possible that anyone would be able to work with him.

Percy Mather was a sensible man who carefully weighed up the cost of the call before committing to serve in one of the most remote and inhospitable places on earth. After wrestling in prayer, he wrote, "Great is the need in darkest Xinjiang. I feel I must be where the need is greatest and the work hardest. Not only is it my desire . . . but I feel absolutely certain that God has called me, and that I am in line with His will."[1]

When his mother asked Percy if he had any plans to get married, he told her, "Mother, I would never do any woman the wrong of taking her as wife into such conditions as exist in Central Asia."[2]

When he first traveled to Urumqi in 1914, Mather knew he needed to find favor with the veteran pioneer, so he wisely took 5,000 Gospel booklets with him to replenish Hunter's supply. The two bachelors immediately struck up a good friendship, and other missionaries noted,

> The tone of George Hunter's reports was subtly changed, and unconsciously to himself they now revealed the happiness which had become possible, even in the same arduous conditions when shared, as they now were, by a young, congenial, spiritually keen

and mentally resourceful companion. By himself he had been a lone wanderer, but now the two formed a team, and viewed their commission as a joyful adventure in which each was a faithful partner, bound to the other by the indissoluble tie of Divine appointment.[3]

Drawn to the Mongols

Not long after arriving in Xinjiang, Mather found himself drawn to ministry among the Mongols, even though they were not the most numerous people group in the region and reaching them posed a serious challenge due to their nomadic lifestyle and widespread distribution over hundreds of miles. Some of the Mongol customs were also unique among all of China's peoples, such as their practice of "burial in the fields," where a corpse was placed on a wooden cart which was pulled furiously by a horse until the body fell from the back of the cart. Wherever it fell, it was left to be devoured by beasts and birds of prey.

Mather wanted to learn the Mongol language, but there were no study books available at the time. He could speak Chinese but was unable to find anyone in Urumqi who spoke both Chinese and Mongol until he heard of a recently convicted criminal who was fluent in both languages. The governor would not let the prisoner out to teach the missionary, however, so Mather asked to be locked up in the man's cell every day. This unconventional method caused much laughter throughout the city. But it helped Mather achieve his desired outcome, and he became fluent in Mongol.

Percy Mather's biographers explored the deep affinity he felt with the Mongols and explained that in 1915, just a year after he first set foot in Xinjiang,

> Mather had lost his heart, and had lost it to the Mongols. Ever since his first contact in Urumqi he had an impulse of friendship towards them. He loved their spontaneity, their hospitality, their

simplicity and their child-nature. . . . They loved him and he loved them and soon became fast friends.

He instinctively knew the best way of approach to primitive folk and when he walked into an encampment, fiddle under his arm, there was immediate response and mutual understanding. Among the Mongols he became a Mongol. . . .

To the Mongol, Mather always showed himself the friendly man, helpful, capable, approachable, eminently understandable and obviously without guile. From the first moments of contact they recognized in him one who would never take advantage of their simplicity. If in the country, he was their guest, and in town he became their helper in all manner of ways, and would go with them to shops to show them where and how to buy, entertain them in his house, and, what they liked best, to escort them to a photographer to have a portrait taken. . . . At the mention of his name the Mongols raise both thumbs in the highest expression of praise they know.[4]

Percy Mather's hard work in Xinjiang produced a prodigious amount of literature. Among his completed projects were

A Manchu dictionary, grammar, and a small book of proverbs. He also finished a small Tatar dictionary and one in Kalmyk or western Mongolian. As if this were not enough, he found time as well to help Hunter complete a dictionary in another Kalmyk dialect. All of this foundation work was necessary for the translation of numerous tracts, booklets, or Scripture portions in these several languages, all of which were then used in the wide itineration done by these two stalwarts.[5]

Apart from his linguistic skills, Percy Mather was also a rudimentary doctor and a musician. He often played the fiddle and mouth organ to attract a crowd, and Hunter would preach while Mather treated the sick and injured.

In 1927, Mather grew concerned about the prevalence of eye disease among the Mongols, and he wished he had the skill to help them. He traveled to Britain to take a medical course before returning to Xinjiang with the necessary knowledge and ophthalmic equipment. News of his healing abilities quickly spread, and a host of people with eye diseases lined up at his door. After church one Sunday morning, he wrote,

> I had to attend to 80 patients after I had taken Sunday service; so many people came to us for medicine. A Mongol has just been in with trachoma and ulcers on his eyes. He paid with 3 pounds of lump sugar, a 2 pound box of biscuits . . . 70 large tomatoes, 10 pounds of potatoes, 6 huge watermelons, 20 cayenne pods and 4 large cabbages.[6]

In 1931 Mather traveled by himself to Tacheng in the extreme northwest of Xinjiang, adjacent to the Soviet border. He went there to work on a Manchu dictionary for he desired to share

Percy Mather in 1928

the Word of God with the tens of thousands of Manchu and Xibe people in the region. He filed this report from the remote outpost:

> Although Tacheng is such a large city, there is no dentist here, so that the Russian doctor sent round and asked us to extract teeth for some of his patients. Through the medical work we have been in touch with the heads of the mosque and their wives and families, and also with the family of the head military man, with policemen, soldiers, civilians, Chinese, Russians, Tatars, Hui, Kazaks, Uyghurs, Manchus, and Mongols of different tribes. Many of the nomads have taken Gospels back with them to their tents in the lonely mountains, where we trust they are even now reading the wonderful story of the Cross.[7]

Muslim work

When he was home in Urumqi, Mather also reached out to Muslims in the city, although their response was often less than ideal. In April 1915 he recalled,

> Yesterday a Uyghur called me across to his shop and wanted to look at some of my books. He bought two tracts, and immediately passed them on to a mullah, who pulled out a box of matches and burnt the tracts publicly in the middle of the street. The young merchant laughed and tried to draw my attention to the burning tracts, but I took no notice.[8]

Later, Mather was distributing gospel literature in the Muslim section of the capital when a Uyghur "took a Gospel of Mark to look at and when he thought I was not looking he stole off with it. I took no notice, as he is evidently badly in need of it, and I trust he may soon find out what a treasure he has got."[9]

In 1919, when a Kazak headman refused to let Mather and Hunter pass through his territory, Hunter wrote that the man "gathered the neighboring Kazaks, seized us both, and bound

Mr. Mather with ropes, and proceeded to do the same with me. We did not struggle in any way, and on our consenting to go we were loosed."[10]

Among the Tatars

By 1930, Mather had developed many strong relationships with leaders of the Tatar people who are one of the smallest of China's 55 official minority groups today, with a population of just 4,889 people recorded in the 2000 census. Mather wrote of the Tatars:

> I have now been in Tacheng more than 15 months, and I like the place very much, and think it one of the most interesting cities

A young Tatar woman from northern Xinjiang
Paul Hattaway

of the land of China. Never in any place in China have I found the people friendlier and more open to the gospel.

The Tatars are exceedingly kind and the finest Muslims I have ever met. Many of them are merchants and comprise the wealthiest class here. They are very intelligent, and about 80 percent of them can read. Many of them also read and speak Russian, and are well acquainted with the latest news and science. . . . Their houses are spotlessly clean. They wear overshoes and take them off before entering the house. It is a treat to see the washing hanging out in their yards. It seems almost as white as snow. I have made many friends among them, who welcome me into their homes just like one of themselves.[11]

The late China expert Ralph Covell summarized Mather's influence among the Tatar people by remarking, "He sang at their festivals, and lived a similar life to them, and helped their sick. . . . He spent much time in the city of Tacheng and his name was widely regarded among Russian, Tatar, Chinese and Mongolian sections of the city."[12]

Slaughter and disease

In January 1933, George Hunter traveled to the Chinese coast to meet and bring six new missionary recruits back to Xinjiang. Soon after they arrived a storm of discontent burst, and Urumqi was attacked by 10,000 Muslim fighters in what came to be called the Kumul Rebellion. A terrible slaughter ensued, and the city "was shut up for six weeks. Thousands were said to be killed, and the battlefield outside the town was a sight never to be forgotten."[13]

The shell-shocked new missionaries were ordered to tend the wounded, and all public buildings in Urumqi were used as makeshift hospitals. The atmosphere was so tense that no prayer requests or other communications could be sent back home, lest the writer be charged with spying. Because of the conflict there was a scarcity of goods in Urumqi, so Mather often risked his life by visiting surrounding villages to buy grain, vegetables, and meat from people he had met during his 23 years of service.

One day Mather came home from the hospital feeling sick. He immediately laid down in bed, and his good friend George Hunter tended to him, expecting he would soon recover as he had on several previous occasions. This time, however, the Living God was calling His servant home, and on May 24, 1933, Percy Mather died of typhus. He was 40 years old.

The normally unflappable Hunter became sullen for some time after the death of his close colleague, and said, "I cannot tell you how much I feel this great loss. Our brother was so well equipped with languages and also beloved by all the various tribes in Xinjiang. He has not died in vain."[14]

Years later when George Hunter was being tortured in prison, he often dreamed about riding his horse across the great grasslands of northern Xinjiang with his dear brother in the faith. These were the happiest times of Hunter's life. He had never imagined that his invaluable co-worker—who was more than 20 years his junior—would die first. Hunter led the funeral for his departed friend and recruited a Russian Baptist choir to sing at the service.

Australian missionary Aubrey Parsons wrote this tribute to Percy Mather:

A better man one could not have met, and the grace and Christian character that he showed on all occasions pointed him out as a man who knew his Lord intimately. . . . On all occasions he was ready to give a helping hand to those in need, and his thoughtfulness was very much appreciated by everybody. It could be truly said of him that he gave his life for the people here. . . . It did not matter where one went, in the city, in the country, or through the mountain passes, Mr. Mather was there known and respected; he was worth ten men.[15]

1920s

—•◆•—

Turmoil and triumph

The early 1920s saw the completion of a huge project to quantify the size of the Church in China and to identify the challenges it faced in evangelizing the nation. A ground-breaking, 600-page book edited by Milton Stauffer, *The Christian Occupation of China*, was published in Shanghai in 1922. Although data from Xinjiang was extremely scarce, Stauffer summarized recent outreach which showed the great ethno-linguistic diversity in the region:

> The CIM missionaries in Urumqi have made extensive itinerating trips distributing Christian literature in a variety of

The church at Yarkant (Shache) was built in 1923

101

languages. During a recent trip, Gospel portions and tracts were sold or distributed as follows: 326 Chinese Gospels, 4 Genesis, 25 Catechisms, 57 Kazak Gospels, 5 Uyghur Life of Abraham, 5 Uyghur Genesis, 10 Uyghur Samuel, 90 Uyghur Scripture tracts, 12 Manchu Gospels, 20 Mongol Gospels, 2 Kalmyk Gospels, 21 Tibetan Gospels, 1 Russian Gospel, besides a quantity of Chinese, Dungan, Mongol, and Tibetan tracts.[1]

Although no estimate of the number of Evangelicals in Xinjiang at the time was provided, Stauffer notes, "To be a fully equipped missionary in Xinjiang one needs to be well acquainted with Islam, and to be able to read a little Arabic, so as to acquire Muslim theological terms. It is also desirable to be able to speak both the Chinese and the Turkish languages."[2]

In the same survey, Catholics in Xinjiang were found to number just 313 church members, with an additional 457 people "under Christian instruction."[3] The entire region was served by just four foreign priests at the time, and no Chinese priests. However, another publication in 1926 gave a much higher figure of 13,836 Catholics in Xinjiang.[4]

A comprehensive strategy

In the 1920s a general belief existed in Christian circles that it was impossible to proclaim the gospel in the Muslim world and that the kingdom of God would need to be established through good deeds. The Swedes in Xinjiang did not adhere to this opinion, however, and Rikard Nyström wrote in 1921, "We are now able to preach to great crowds of Muslims in this country, Sunday after Sunday, year after year, in churches and, when possible, in bazaars, without being hindered."[5]

The Swedish Mission adopted a comprehensive strategy to reach the lost during the 1920s. Key components of their work in Xinjiang were schools, orphanages, and medical facilities where physical help for the sick and injured was always accompanied by the sharing of the gospel. In 1926 alone, more than 28,000 people were treated at the mission's medical centers that for most of the time were led by a small team of just eight missionary nurses and one doctor, Gösta Raquette. In addition to their medical work, the Swedish missionaries

> gave food in the time of famine, provided clothes for the naked during the cold winters, and gave training in weaving as a means of providing work and compensation for the poor. The women missionaries also helped brighten the lives of the local women, who faced many tragic difficulties from divorce and polygamy in their Muslim households.[6]

The missionaries were so encouraged by progress in southern Xinjiang that John Törnquist noted in 1921,

> Several years ago each station received a set of cups for the Lord's Supper. This could easily have been taken as an ironic reminder of how things ought to be as opposed to how things really were. At that time there were no churches here. Now the sets of cups

A Swedish missionary preaching to Muslims in Xinjiang

are regularly used for Communion. We thank God for this with all our hearts.[7]

Later in 1928, Törnquist shared the following upbeat report during the Swedish Mission's 50th anniversary celebrations:

The general situation in Xinjiang for our Mission has never been better than it is now. The work has been quite successful; more so than what was dreamed of just a decade ago. The Mission has, by God's grace, become one of the most important missions in the Muslim world. The whole missionary world acknowledges the importance of our lonely outpost in the fight for the kingdom of God.[8]

Other Swedes experienced tragedy in Xinjiang. Among them, John Norstedt—who had served eight years on the mission field—died of typhoid, and Lisa Gahns perished just a few months after her marriage to missionary Carl Persson. A newly recruited couple, Petrus and Ingrid Kangstrom, endured many difficulties. On the journey to Xinjiang, Ingrid suffered a serious injury. As she was not able to obtain adequate treatment in Kashgar, they were forced to return to Sweden so she could recover. Then on their return journey to China, Petrus fell seriously ill, and they were forced to again return to Sweden.

Friction on the field

Because of the missionaries' sacrificial service, the locals in southern Xinjiang gained a deep respect for these Swedes. During a time of unrest in Kashgar in 1923, Oskar Hermansson was nearly seized by the authorities, but the people formed a protective circle around him and prevented his arrest.

The following year saw strong persecution break out against the Christians, resulting in "a Swedish missionary and one of his converts being beaten and dragged through the streets of

Yarkant."[9] One difficulty the Swedes had as they attempted to establish the kingdom of God in the midst of millions of Muslims was the question of how to structure local church services in a culturally relatable manner. One missionary noted,

> The format of a Christian service was something new and unusual to a Muslim, as neither songs nor preaching were incorporated in their own style of religious services. There were, however, many positive things to be found in a Muslim church attendee. For example, it was easy to achieve stillness and a spirit of worship as Muslims were used to taking part in prayer in the mosques, and when the pastor lifted his hands to pray, everyone did the same.[10]

Over time internal problems arose among the missionaries, and interpersonal relationships were stretched to the limit. Most reports of conflict seemed to involve John Törnquist who was the longest serving Swede in Xinjiang from 1904 until his death in 1937. He was unique among the Swedish missionaries in Xinjiang in that he specifically focused on reaching the Han

Five new Uyghur and Kirgiz believers at their baptism in the 1920s

Chinese, whereas all the others were sharing Christ with the Uyghurs, Kirgiz, and other Muslim groups.

Törnquist's main antagonists were Lars Högberg and Gösta Raquette, whom the mission leaders in Sweden consulted whenever questions arose about the work in faraway Xinjiang. This practice irritated Törnquist who bluntly informed the mission leaders in 1924: "We refuse to accept Högberg and Raquette as our authorities."[11] Tension between some of the strong-willed missionaries continued for years, and Gunnar Hermansson told the mission board that "he felt persecuted both by the missionaries in Xinjiang and by the mission leaders in Sweden. If they didn't apologize, he threatened to expose publicly the difficulties within the mission. In carrying through his threat, he created further problems for the mission leaders."[12]

Despite the conflict, John Törnquist was a dedicated follower of Christ, and two years before his death he had written in his diary,

> If God the Father suddenly spoke to me in a human voice and said, "You have 30 years to live on earth, provided you stay in Europe. If, however, you prefer to go to Asia, you will only have ten years," I would then gladly accept the ten years and continue on my journey to the field.[13]

Occasional signs of cheer

For many years, vast areas of Xinjiang remained completely untouched by the gospel, and few recruits were found who were willing to spend their lives for Jesus Christ in the sandy wastes of northwest China.

Despite the hardships and extreme isolation, missionaries in Xinjiang were greatly cheered by occasional signs that the Word of God was touching and changing people's lives. On one occasion, missionary Hans Döring met a Han man named Wan who professed to be a follower of Christ. He was found to

A young Uyghur Christian family in Xinjiang

have a sound knowledge of the gospel, having first encountered Christianity when he received a copy of the Book of Acts seven years earlier. Döring wrote,

> The little book, outwardly insignificant, and rejected by its first owner, had been to Wang for seven years a well from which he had drunk living water. . . . When he invited me to sit down he took the book down from the nail on which it hung on the wall. Its original cover had been replaced by a new one on which he had rewritten the title.
>
> The smoke of his small mud hearth had turned the book to a gray-black color, but the inside gave evidence of much reading and of rent pages carefully patched. He had kept this copy of the Scriptures in as prominent a position as his neighbors kept their idols. . . . He bought three New Testaments, one for himself and one for each of his two assistants.[14]

Bakhta Han

As the message of eternal life in Jesus Christ continued to slowly spread among the Muslims of Xinjiang, small numbers of men and women opened their hearts to the Holy Spirit and repented of their sins. One recipient of God's grace was Bakhta Han who was born into a desperately poor family in 1891. Her mother died, and her father was blind, so from a young age Bakhta was required to join him on the side of the road to beg for food and money.

One day Bakhta's father was told about the mission hospital in Kargilik (Yingjisha), and that perhaps the foreigners there might be able to restore his sight. Hoping for a miracle, the old man made his way on foot to Kargilik with his daughter holding one end of a long rod to guide him along the way.

Little Bakhta was amazed when a tall, blonde Swedish doctor, speaking their language, told her father that indeed his eyes could

Bakhta Han and her son in the early 1920s

be healed, and that they were welcome to stay at the mission station during the surgery and for several days afterward. Bakhta was loved and accepted by the missionaries who gave her a new, clean dress and allowed her to eat all the food she wanted. She had never been treated so kindly in all her life.

Finally, the day came when the bandages were removed from the old man's eyes, and he wept for joy when he realized he could see! He beheld the rustling trees outside his window and marveled at the beauty of nature. Best of all, he saw his daughter for the first time!

The time came for Bakhta and her father to return home, but both had heavy hearts. Bakhta had enjoyed every moment of her time with the kind missionaries and dreaded the thought of returning to her tiny, dark room. Her father, meanwhile, was distressed because the foreigners had done a great deed to him by restoring his sight, but he had nothing to pay them. After thinking about it overnight, he took Bakhta by the hand and told the missionaries,

> May God give you long life and multiply your fortunes a thousand-fold. You have removed the veil from my eyes and restored

Staff and a large number of patients at a Xinjiang mission hospital

my sight, but I have nothing to pay you with. Everything I own in this world is in this child. Show me your goodness by accepting her and letting her grow up with you.[15]

The missionaries knew that accepting Bakhta Han would add to their workload and bring extra expense, but they could not refuse this precious gift. They also knew they would be rescuing her from a life of evil, as almost all unmarried women ended up trapped in prostitution. Bakhta remained in Kargilik, and her father returned home. The villagers mocked him for "selling his daughter to the foreigners," but he remained steadfast in his conviction that the missionaries were good people who would bring no harm to his precious child.

Bakhta was convicted by the message of two converted Muslims and was impressed by their boldness. By this time she was not the only Uyghur child at the mission station. Three other girls from poor families had been accepted by the missionaries, and soon four boys joined them.

Many Muslim families in the area secretly desired to send their children to the mission school where the students learned at twice the rate than at the madrassa (Islamic school). But most parents were not willing to risk the wrath of the mullahs. As a result, it was usually the most impoverished families who sent their children to the mission school because they had nothing to lose.

Sometime later, the population of Kargilik was abuzz with news that two men had converted from Islam to Christianity and were proclaiming the Injil (Gospel) to all who would listen. Hundreds of people flocked to the meeting hall to witness this extraordinary sight, but the Muslim leaders were angry and plotted how they could put an end to the two men's "virus" before it spread to others.

The now 13-year-old Bakhta and three orphans publicly confessed their new faith and were baptized in the river. She cultivated a deep affection for her Savior, and she loved to worship Him with all her heart.

As the influence of the mission in Kargilik spread, a piece of land known as Beshisht Bagh (Garden of Paradise) was purchased and became the site of a home for boys and a home for girls. The boys were taught a trade, and those found to be gifted in evangelism were trained at the mission Bible school. The girls, meanwhile, were taught how to run a household and care for children.

In Xinjiang, many girls married at a young age, in keeping with the actions of the prophet Mohammed who according to Islamic scholars married a six-year-old girl and consummated the union when she was nine. The people of the town wondered if the Christian girls would marry, as they were considered relatively advanced in age by their teen years. The joyous day came when Bakhta married Samuel Ahun, and two of her friends married other young Christian men who had been raised at the mission station.

Samuel Ahun (left) with Christian workers at the mission hospital

111

Bakhta's husband, Samuel Ahun, worked for the mission hospital as a nurse's aid. Together they had five children, but the two smaller ones died in their infancy.

In 1937, a violent Muslim uprising almost wiped out the Church in southern Xinjiang, and Samuel Ahun was one of many Uyghur believers put to death by the Muslim leaders who sought to wipe out Christianity once and for all.

It was assumed that Bakhta Han had also earned a martyr's crown. However after nearly half a century of silence, news emerged in 1984 that she had recently passed into the presence of Jesus Christ. Despite the risk, a friend of Bakhta knew the old missionaries would want to know, so she wrote a letter to Sweden, saying, "We gathered around her weeping and praying. We could do nothing else."[16] Bakhta Han, who had once led her blind father along the road to the mission station at Kargilik, had died at the age of 93.

Bakhta Han's daughters Mariam and Mehnisa in 1933

French Ridley

In 1926, British missionary French Ridley, who had served among the Tibetans and Hui Muslims in Qinghai Province since 1890, surprised many when he was assigned to Xinjiang, even though he was 63 years old at the time. He willingly accepted the new post, but Ridley privately expressed his disappointment that no younger man had been prepared to serve in the remote region. After settling into his new home in Urumqi, Ridley wrote,

French Ridley

It is hard ground when we come into contact with the Muslims. They are very much like the Pharisees in the New Testament. . . . How necessary then it is for us who are dealing with Muslims to be gentle with them, and through the Scriptures only, looking up each verse. . . .

Sometimes when beginning to open the Bible to answer them, they will put their hand on the Book and say, "Don't look at the book, you tell us." They do not like the Bible unless they are really anxious to know the truth. They are afraid of coming to the Light, lest their sins be revealed. Quite a few of them drop in again and again, to hear the Words of Life.[17]

In 1929, Ridley undertook an extensive six-month journey through the towns bordering the Taklamakan Desert where he encountered much hostility from fanatical Muslims. The veteran missionary filed this report:

We went to a city bordering on Lopnur. . . . After a little refreshment we went on the street. At first there was a rush for the books, and when the excitement cooled down, I found a good stand well above the people. We had not been speaking long when a young Uyghur mullah brought near to my feet a Gospel of Mark half-burnt and still burning. There was a laugh till I reminded them that it was their "letters" they were burning, not mine, which stopped their laugh for the time.

As I continued preaching, a piece of mud was thrown at me, then another and another. I kept on till I had finished my subject, and then got down, when the young folks began to hiss and shout and crowd around me.[18]

A few days later Ridley was passing through Turpan when he again ran into trouble from angry Muslims:

In the afternoon some youngsters began to hoot, but some Hui checked them. A Gospel was torn to pieces and sent back to me. I had a very quiet audience in the evening, preaching from the temple steps. In the afternoon we went outside the West gate and had a very quiet, attentive audience, till a long white-bearded teacher with one eye came along from his school at the mosque and cursed me.

My audience stood still, and then he cursed them and told them to go. Some slunk away but still some remained, which so enraged the old man that he ordered his scholars to pelt me with mud. They began in earnest, so I slipped into a nearby shop. An old man wearing a turban came along and said he would see me into the city, but as soon as I got on the street, he left me and the scholars began to pelt again. . . . I shall not easily forget my trip.[19]

It appears Ridley was genuinely shocked at the treatment he encountered on this journey, which was unlike anything he had experienced in his long career. The veteran wrote,

I have now spent 38 years among Muslims. However much the Muslims in Xining may have hated the gospel, outwardly they were always very courteous. . . . On this visit to Turpan I had a different experience. First tracts began to be burnt, then mud began to be pelted when speaking, and on two occasions broke out into hooting and howling, pelting mud, rotten fruit, etc. . . .

Never once in 38 years had the Muslims molested me in any way. Nevertheless, in my five week tour I met many who have been very friendly, and I was able to sell all my books. A little dispensing of medicines seems to me will be the best and easiest way to reach these people, backed by the prayers of God's people.[20]

The long journey across Xinjiang appears to have exhausted Ridley, and in 1931 he remained in Urumqi for an extended time of rest. He didn't recover his strength as expected, however, and the following year French Ridley retired to the peaceful countryside of Northumberland, having spent nearly four decades of his life in China. He died in 1944 at the age of 82.

By the end of the 1920s, the situation seemed to have somewhat calmed down in Muslim areas of Xinjiang, with one missionary noting, "Even though less than 100 people are

Christians, a couple of hundred people gathered for the services in both Kashgar and Yarkant."[21]

Overall, Christian work in Xinjiang remained incredibly difficult, as indicated by this sober evaluation by missionary Gottfrid Palmberg:

> I am sorry to say that in accordance with my knowledge of conditions I cannot pretend this field to be ready for harvest; however, the need of "sowing" is utterly pressing. Workers intending to scatter the gospel seed in this country ought to know beforehand that their task is not to gather the harvest in joy but to sow in tears.[22]

The Trio

In 1926, many people in Xinjiang were shaken by the arrival of three single, female British missionaries who traveled 800 miles (1,296 km) overland from Gansu Province through bandit infested territory and across the Gobi Desert.[1] Their caravan consisted of three carts—carrying a total of eleven people in their party—including five church members from Gansu, two men to take care of the animals, and a cook. One cart carried nothing but Gospel literature in eight different languages, which they gave or sold for nominal sums to people along the way.

Eva French, Francesca French and Mildred Cable

Selling "provided them with some ready cash. In the absence of banks, and the presence of robbers, carrying money was always a problem. Paper money could only be used in the town where it was printed, and travelers on remote roads were easy targets for thieves."[2]

Sisters Eva and Francesca French and Mildred Cable had already gained great notoriety among Western Christians for their gripping reports from the mission field. But few people in Xinjiang had ever seen a Western woman before, so their presence created a stir wherever they went.

The women—who at the time were 57, 55, and 48 years old respectively—had an unexpected welcome when they entered Xinjiang. The reclusive George Hunter had heard about their journey and decided to travel three weeks from Urumqi to welcome them. When the Trio first met Hunter on the road to Hami, however, they were unsure if the tall, blue-eyed man dressed in typical Uyghur garb was in fact the veteran missionary. When they were convinced it was him, they climbed down from their cart and shook his hand. Their first meeting was said to have been

> rather awkward, and not only because the women were initially confused by his clothes. Hunter was not a gregarious man. Even his relationship with fellow worker Percy Mather seemed to be based on mutual but distant admiration rather than warm personal regard.
>
> Over his many years of service in Xinjiang, Hunter rarely interacted with women, and it had been years since he had spoken with any Europeans besides Mather. Perhaps that was why he was uncomfortable and stiff upon meeting the ladies. He began their acquaintance in silence, with a bow, and then, after the briefest of introductions, he bowed again, retiring to his own wagon for the rest of the journey into Hami.[3]
>
> . . .

118

Hunter did not actually remain with the women and the party. He and his servant, a Mongolian named Nimgir, traveled well ahead of them. His cart, the women explained, was faster and, therefore, he was able to make better time than they could. Perhaps because of his unease at being around women, he only rejoined the ladies when their carts and mules needed attention.[4]

Because all travelers stopped at the same places along the way, the Trio found themselves mixing with all segments of Xinjiang society—wealthy merchants, brigands, escaped convicts, and Russian spies. The searing daytime heat made travel almost impossible when the sun was out, so they often got up at two o'clock in the morning to start the day's journey and set up camp by noon.

At night, groups of unruly men gathered around the campfires to gamble, fight, and curse. Not missing an opportunity, the French sisters and Mildred Cable got their organs out and held morning and evening services with singing and preaching. Each night, "a motley crowd gathered, glad of the diversion, and curious to see the first foreign women to pass that way. Some of them stayed on afterwards to talk at a much deeper level."[5]

After arriving at Urumqi, the Trio sold the animals that had carried them across the Gobi Desert, except for a mule they called Molly, which had become their pet as much as a draft animal. Hunter agreed to take care of Molly until the women returned to claim her.

They filed this report back home:

Being the first women missionaries who had ever traveled by this road, our presence created quite a sensation, far more from the fact of our being women preachers and unmarried, than by reason of our foreign nationality. In such a cosmopolitan centre, where Chinese, Uyghur, Parsee, Mongol and Tibetan jostle each other in the street, we were generally accepted as Chinese from a very distant province.

As we went in and out among these Muslim women, we realized that the satanic method, by which the Muslim has abrogated
to himself all religious rites, leaving the women untaught and
despised, has created an opportunity for the gospel in his own
harem. Never did we fail of a cordial welcome, and a great sphere
awaits the woman missionary who will master the Uyghur language and move about in these places.[6]

During two later trips to Xinjiang in 1928 and 1932, the Trio
once again based themselves in Urumqi where they found many
opportunities for effective ministry among the women of the
city. They also found Molly the mule alive and well nourished.

The Trio's visit to Xinjiang in 1932 also created a stir, but by
this time they were more experienced with life in the region and
were more aware of the people's spiritual needs. They formulated
a plan of action, saying,

We conferred as to the best means of reaching the women of
Urumqi with a definite gospel appeal. After consultation, thought

The Trio with their adopted Chinese daughter Topsy in Xinjiang

and prayer we decided to hold a three days' mission. The town was posted, and preparations were made for large meetings. . . .

The response was beyond our expectations, and each day the church was filled with eager listeners and the Good News was proclaimed. We were all much encouraged by the response, and we believe a real and lasting work has been done. There is now in Urumqi that which has been prayed for, for years—a band of Christian Chinese women workers.[7]

After attending the Trio's meetings, Percy Mather wrote to his sister, "It was fine to see the church crowded every midday, and

Mildred Cable talking with a Kazak woman

to watch some 300 women listening to the gospel message. Our Sunday services are now a great sight and at last the women's side of the church is filled as well as the men's."[8]

During their later visits to Xinjiang, the ladies' presence attracted unwanted attention from Muslim men. At one meeting they were harassed and shouted at by a group of troublemakers, and when they stopped at a small town near Turpan, they wrote, "Our dramatic appearance collected a large hostile mob of bold Muslim schoolboys who were only kept at bay by the inn-keeper and a horsewhip which he freely used. Not daring to come near, they vented their feelings by reviling the band of Christians who had dared to enter their precincts."[9]

In one place Mildred Cable was kicked in the head by a donkey, and the tough pioneer observed that the donkey's owner "appeared to care nothing for the accident, merely seeming to view an infidel's head as the legitimate kicking ground for a donkey privileged to belong to one of the 'faithful.'"[10]

The Trio's long third journey through northwest China took 16 months, and the gospel was shared with many along the way. When they later tallied some of their accomplishments, they found "they had visited 2,700 homes; conducted 665 meetings; and distributed or sold 40,000 portions of Scripture."[11] One benefit of the Trio's journeys to Xinjiang was that for the first time, local Christian women saw how a Christian woman should be. Hunter and Mather were two diehard bachelors, so the feminine touch and strong, courageous faith of the British ladies greatly encouraged the local Christian women.

The Trio returned to England in 1937 where they lived in a small cottage for the rest of their lives, apart from their many missionary journeys around the world through which they inspired many believers to serve God wholeheartedly. The queen of England also honored the Trio by inviting them to Buckingham Palace in 1938.

Perhaps the greatest contribution these courageous single women made to the missions effort in Xinjiang occurred when Francesca French and Mildred Cable teamed up to write the posthumous biographies of Percy Mather (published in 1935) and George Hunter (1948). For the first time, multitudes of Christians read about the lives of these pioneers, and much prayer and effort for the evangelization of the unreached peoples of Xinjiang went forth as a result of their brutally honest portrayals of the uniquely gifted men.

1930s

The failed dream of East Turkestan

By the early 1930s, the desire of Xinjiang's Muslims for their own nation reached a climax. They repudiated the atheism of both the Soviet Union and China and decided to establish a new country to be called the Republic of East Turkestan, which was later changed to Islamestan. Although there was much enthusiasm and support for the concept of nationhood, various Muslim factions were never able to agree on a united way forward, and the

Missionaries and their friends at Kashgar in 1935

Chinese authorities, despite being in disarray and engaged in a brutal civil war, were determined to ensure the concept never gained traction.

Undeterred, a king of East Turkestan was appointed. Bertram Sheldrake was a British-born son of a wealthy merchant who had made a fortune importing condiments, with Sheldrake's Pickles growing to become a well-known company. Bertram, who was raised a Catholic but converted to Islam at the age of 15, had spent his fortune doing all he could to spread Islam around the globe.

A delegation from Xinjiang asked Sheldrake to head the new Islamic kingdom, to be based at Kashgar. A prime minister and minister of defense were also appointed, and envoys were dispatched to key nations in an attempt to garner support. Alas for the Muslim dream, no other governments would support the initiative, and it soon withered on the vine of history. By June 1934,

Newspapers were reporting that Islamestan had "hit a snag." Rumors swirled that Sheldrake was becoming king only to steal all of Xinjiang's considerable deposits of jade; that he was a British spy; and that, if he assumed the throne in Kashgar, then Islamestan would become a British-controlled kingdom.

The Chinese, naturally, complained to London; London assured Nanjing that it would not tolerate a British national attempting to rule "any form of independent regime within Chinese territory". . . . The shaky coalition in Kashgar started to fall apart, factions split, and fighting broke out across Xinjiang. Two Chinese warlords fought each other as well as any forces either once or still aligned to the East Turkestan Republic. But it was probably the Soviet Union's hostility that finished off the Islamestan dream. . . .

Bertram Sheldrake returned to England in 1944 and died in 1947, still technically the exiled king of a state that had ceased to exist 13 years earlier, and had hardly existed at all.[1]

Emil Fischbacher and the new recruits

Apart from the successful Swedish Mission in southern Xinjiang, few Evangelical missionaries had established themselves in the region, though George Hunter and Percy Mather dominated work in the northern areas. Overall it was fair to say that the China Inland Mission work in the region had been disappointing. One report stated that by 1937, "when Xinjiang boasted three mission stations and seven CIM missionaries, the total number of converts officially reported was just 19 (since the opening of the region in 1904 by Hunter)."[2]

One of the new missionaries, 29-year-old Emil Fischbacher of Scotland, was raised in Glasgow, the sixth of eight children in his family. He was baptized at the age of 12, and when asked what he wanted to do when he grew up, he immediately replied, "Be a missionary." In 1929, Fischbacher had been contemplating his future plans when he read an appeal in the CIM magazine for 200 new missionaries.

Emil Fischbacher

Fischbacher contacted the CIM and offered himself for service as a medical missionary to China. He wrote, "I constantly rolled over in my mind this question: Did I study medicine in order to preach the gospel or to be a physician? . . . There was no way I could not go."[3] Fischbacher entered the CIM training school and discovered that he was the 200th new recruit to answer the appeal. He sailed for China on the last day of 1931, one of six new missionaries assigned to work in Xinjiang.

When fighting between the Communists and Nationalists made it impossible for the six recruits to reach Xinjiang by the normal routes, the veteran George Hunter devised a plan. Despite being in his seventies, he traveled to Shanghai and met the six workers—Fischbacher and his fellow Britons Raymond Joyce, George Holmes and William Drew; the American Otto Schoerner; and Aubrey Parsons from Australia.

Together they traveled north to Tianjin, where Hunter purchased two new 1.5-ton Ford trucks. Finally, on September 13, 1932, they set out on their long overland journey, traveling across Inner Mongolia for 1,800 miles (2,916 km), often in places where there were no roads. They evaded sandstorms as they crossed the vast Gobi Desert, and had to dismantle parts of the vehicles and their provisions and have them carried across a river by seven camels. The camels then towed each truck through the water, and the trucks were reassembled on the other side. The group finally entered Xinjiang 34 days later, and the six new recruits were placed under the supervision of Percy Mather.

War had broken out in Xinjiang, and when the fighting was at its fiercest, hundreds of wounded soldiers were put under the care of Fischbacher and the other new missionaries. Although they worked from dawn to midnight each day, Fischbacher found time to write to his sister, saying,

This is a chaotic war region, but God brought us through with His marvelous protection. . . . Although we are in a storm of shot and shells, we are not at all afraid. . . . At the request of the former provincial governor, I promised to perform major emergency operations on men with sword and bullet wounds, yet other wounded soldiers were continuously brought in. . . . Think about it—more than 300 men with major and minor wounds, many of them not having yet been attended to. The whole hospital is really dirty, the smell is awful. . . . I am incredibly busy, with no medical instruments and even no medicine. Perhaps I have to learn how to perform faith healings![4]

George Hunter (right) and the six new missionaries who drove to Xinjiang in 1932 (above); and one of the trucks that nearly fell into a river (below)

Months passed, with the situation becoming even more dire. Another letter to his family hinted that Fischbacher was at the point of collapse:

> When I got home, I didn't feel quite right. I have been working non-stop, with insufficient sleep. There are over 400 wounded soldiers in the hospital, and in my ward there are 125 in critical condition. Many have not taken a bath for two or three months, and are awfully dirty. They have insufficient nutrition and there aren't enough staff to care for them, with the result that most of the burden falls on us overworked foreigners. The past three months have plunged me into the real conditions of the people, but we may have to wait many years before seeing such an opportunity for the gospel again.[5]

Just days after writing his last letter, Emil Fischbacher was exposed to a patient with typhus. He too contracted the fever, and his immune system was too depleted to fight it. He died in the morning of May 27, 1933, just three days after Percy Mather had passed away.

After hearing of his brother's death, Theodore Fischbacher immediately applied to join the CIM. He married and had children in China, serving there 15 years before being expelled by the Communists in 1949. More than half a century later, Leslie Lyall wrote of Emil Fischbacher's brief but lasting impact in Xinjiang:

> The young doctor, after less than two years in China, contracted the disease from his soldier patients and died; whereupon his younger brother in Scotland immediately volunteered to fill his place. Over 50 years later and 30 years after the Communist Revolution, grateful local Christians continued to care lovingly for the doctor's grave and headstone. And in contrast to that year of 1934 there is, half a century later, a large, thriving church in Urumqi, and there are thousands of Christians in the province, showing that the labor and sacrifice of the pioneers were not in vain.[6]

Revival in Kuwo

A missionary identified only as "Webb of Swindon" wrote to revival historian J. Edwin Orr in 1934, telling of a visitation of the Holy Spirit that had broken out at Kuwo in Xinjiang.[7] Webb had returned to Xinjiang in 1933 and began praying for co-workers to help him hold an evangelistic tent campaign. The tent was set up in the center of the district, outside the south gate of the city. A week after Webb experienced a personal breakthrough in his prayer life, local workmen visited the Sunday worship service. The missionary spoke with them privately, and they came under deep conviction of sin. The men all fell to their knees and

> burst out crying, sobbing out their confession of sins to God. Five or six got converted on this occasion, and two were filled with the Spirit. The blessing next overflowed to the three sons of the house and the father went to the meetings . . . and came back filled with the Holy Spirit. The father was so on fire for God that at his own expense he organised a week's meeting.[8]

Unbeknown to Webb at the time,

> The whole row of houses immediately opposite them were brothels. One of the sins aggressively denounced was the sin of prostitution, and many of the young men who got converted used

The Kashgar Mission station in its final days, containing a church, hospital, and mission homes

to frequent those establishments. After a two month campaign, preaching twice a day, there were 120 professions of faith, but much of it proved to be "shallow soil" as many quickly withered under persecution. All the houses of ill repute were mobbed by the locals . . . and it was not long after this that the city magistrates arrested the occupants and closed the places. Webb wrote: "We heard to our joy that it was all the doing of the Jesus religion."[9]

The sun sets on the Swedish Mission

For years tensions had risen in southern Xinjiang, and although the Swedes continued to make inroads into the kingdom of darkness, the missionaries sensed that their time was short. In 1931, Gustaf Ahlbert wrote,

> These last few years here have been by far the most laborious and trying years of my life so far. But I dare say, they have also been my happiest years. Never during the last thousand years has the Christian mission in Xinjiang been so successful and promising as it is now. During the first three quarters of this year more than 30 Muslims have confessed their faith in Christ and been baptized. The converts have still to suffer much for their faith and go through many persecutions from their relatives and neighbors.[10]

By 1932 the church in southern Xinjiang boasted 163 members—mostly Uyghurs and Kirgiz. In addition to evangelism and medical work, the Swedish Mission ran at least ten schools for children of all ages, with classes in both the Uyghur and Chinese languages. Two orphanages, one for boys and the other for girls, helped take care of the most vulnerable members of society. A detailed analysis of the influence of the Swedish Mission at its strongest point said,

> Between 1928 and 1932, 86 people had been baptized. At the beginning of 1932 church registers showed that there were 56 members in the Kashgar church, 29 in Hancheng, 65 in Yarkant

and 13 in Yengisar. Altogether there were 163 members who were regularly partaking of Communion, 22 missionaries on the field, and approximately 30 national workers including both Chinese and Uyghurs.

Sunday school statistics show that 170 children were being taught the Scriptures, and in the day schools the attendance records show almost 300 students.

The hospital work was very encouraging too, providing a natural contact with people from all walks of life. During 1932, a total of 13,228 patients were treated and about 50 major operations performed.[11]

During the entire 46-year span of the Swedish Mission, it was estimated that 400,000 patients received treatment through the ministry. As three or four family members and friends often accompanied each patient, the number of people exposed to the gospel of Jesus Christ probably numbered in the millions. They returned to their home villages, often weeks away, armed with Gospel literature and telling others about the good Christians they met at the Mission hospital.

Overall, the hostilities that had greeted the early years of the Swedish work had died down over time as locals came to realize their motive was one of love and sacrificial help. Although the stricter Muslims remained antagonistic to any Christian presence in Xinjiang, many locals developed a deep love and respect for the missionaries.

Vendla Gustafsson reported that for years the Christians in Kashgar had been praying for a spiritual revival, which "had begun in the hearts of the Christians and then moved into the community around them. When the Spirit began to work, some of the Christians confessed that they had, in secret, visited the mosques. In services people were openly testifying and confessing sin."[12]

Tearful good-byes

In 1933, a tidal wave of violence broke out across southern Xinjiang, and the Swedes struggled to continue their work in increasingly difficult circumstances. For months they were confined to their homes, and no one was allowed to sell them food or firewood. Some Muslim friends threw vegetables over the wall of the mission compound at night to help the missionaries, but access to water and sanitation services were cut off. Faced with the reality of grim conditions and with no ability to share the gospel with people, it soon became apparent to the missionaries that there was no point staying.

In September 1937, a special farewell service was held in Kashgar for the departing missionaries. Many tears were shed by both the Swedes and their local friends. Before they came to Xinjiang in the early 1890s, the gospel had not been proclaimed in the region since the Nestorians many centuries earlier. But the brave ambassadors for Christ could now leave Xinjiang with their heads held high, knowing they were leaving behind a few hundred strong and dedicated followers of Jesus Christ.

At the farewell service for missionaries at Kashgar in September 1937

Most of the missionaries returned to Sweden via Russia, while others traveled across the Karakoram Pass into today's northern Pakistan. Finally in August 1938, the last three Swedish missionaries were escorted to the border by armed Chinese soldiers. After 46 years of faithful and effective service, the Swedish Mission in Xinjiang had come to an end.

The great Swedish missionary effort in Xinjiang had concluded, but their influence continued on for many years. A Christian native of Xinjiang, Mark Chuanhang Shan, commented on the influence of this unique mission:

The soldiers who escorted the last three missionaries to the border in 1938

The success of the Swedish missionaries was indeed amazing. For one thing, their approaches were proper with extreme kind-heartedness and excellent lives; also, the very first Uyghur converts from Islam to Christianity won the respect and praises from their own nationality, thus influencing and guiding many of their friends and relatives to accept their new belief. As a result, the first local Uyghur church was soon set up and developed quickly and grew strong. There were more than 30 Swedish missionaries then. From 1919 to 1939 the number of adult Uyghur Christians in the church who had a firm faith increased to over 200. If teenagers were added, there were about 500 members.[13]

Slaughter in the Desert

The high point of the Swedish Mission in Xinjiang could be dated to 1932, but in a region plagued by death and destruction for millennia, Satan's response to the growth of the Church was a full-blown attack designed to obliterate the followers of Jesus Christ once and for all. Muslim warlords began decimating the Church in 1933, which led to the expulsion of the last Swedish missionaries five years later. Once they were out of the way, the slaughter of local Christians was fully implemented.

One of the first signs that a huge storm of destruction was gathering on the horizon occurred when two Chinese Seventh-Day Adventist evangelists were killed at Hami in January 1933. After spending almost two years in Xinjiang, Bei Jinzhen and Zheng Xiangpu started the long journey back to their homes in central China. It took them 18 days to cross the desert from Urumqi

Believers outside the church at Hancheng (left),
and the church after its destruction (right)

136

to Hami, and they were unaware that Muslims in the city were preparing to massacre every Han Chinese person. Two days after Bei and Zheng arrived in Hami, 1,700 Chinese residents were horribly slaughtered, and not a single man, woman, or child was left alive. Bei and Zheng were among those caught up in the diabolical massacre.

In Urumqi, missionary Raymond Joyce was deeply disturbed by the spiritual change he saw sweeping across the region. He wrote,

> Truly the whole province lies in wickedness. We have seen to what lengths the unregenerate can go, whatever be his color, tongue, or religion. Hatred, murder, and lust just seem to have run loose. The dark places of the earth are the habitations of cruelty. What a privilege it is to be here at such a time. May we indeed be as lights shining in a dark place.[1]

Trouble in the south

By April 1933, a Muslim faction from Hotan had seized control of Kashgar, Yarkant, and the other towns south of the Taklamakan Desert. Hundreds of Chinese men were butchered while their

Christians at Yarkant

137

wives and daughters were captured and used as sex slaves or forcibly married off to the deviant attackers who gained control over most of Xinjiang. A total of 266 Han people in Hotan were forcibly converted to Islam.

One of the primary objectives of the Muslim rebels was to get rid of all Christian influence in Kashgar, Yarkant, and the other places where the gospel had taken hold.[2] On April 27, 1933, the Uyghur emir of the short-lived Republic of East Turkestan, Abdullah Bughra, ordered the Swedish missionary Rikard Nyström to appear before him. Nyström was in charge of the mission's medical dispensary that had benefited thousands of people in Yarkant and the surrounding districts. Nyström went to see Abdullah with his colleagues Arell and Hermansson. After being forced to wait a long time at the governor's mansion,

> The Emir himself came into the room, holding a handkerchief to his nose (to filter the air contaminated by Christian breath). He began to ask such questions as "Did you intend to use these poisons [medicine] to harm me and my followers?" Then he yelled, "It is my duty, according to our law, to put you to death because by your preaching you have destroyed the faith of some of us! Out with you—bind them!"[3]

After Nyström was tied up, the cowardly emir—whose bodyguards were elite assassins from Afghanistan—personally struck the defenseless missionary. A group of soldiers armed with rifles, swords, and clubs told the three missionaries to prepare for death. Abdullah raised his sword and was about to start the slaughter when an Indian aide sprang forward and begged for the missionaries' lives. They narrowly escaped death.

After dealing with the missionaries, the cruel tyrant focused his wrath on the local Christians, demonstrating a particular hatred toward all who had converted from Islam. The male Christians were beaten and thrown into prison at Yarkant and

Kashgar. Some were beheaded while others perished from the terrible tortures inflicted on them. At least 100 Christian men suffered martyrdom for their faith in Jesus Christ.

The female Christians—including girls as young as 11—were forced to marry Muslim men. One of these girls later said,

> We were called unbelievers, dogs, birds of ill-omen, scum, swine, a shame to our people and accursed. . . . They said, "You must realize that this is being done to save you from damnation. Now say that you will leave your rebellious ways and come back to the faith which was yours in the cradle and which you should never have left."⁴

The terrorized Christian girls didn't utter a word, and none renounced their faith.

Meanwhile, the imprisoned Uyghur and Kirgiz Christians

> were interrogated under the drawn sword that was lifted over their heads. They had to choose between Islam and death. . . .
>
> Joseph Johannes was sentenced to death by crucifixion. He was to die a similar death to the Lord whom he loved and had faithfully given witness. . . . He had to spend that night, standing tightly tied to a pillar. When he stood there in the night waiting for death he was filled with a heavenly peace and blessing in his soul, so much so that he could not remain silent. Loudly he started to praise and worship God. . . .
>
> In all the ways they could think of they made him suffer, trying to make him turn back to Islam. If they succeeded their victory and triumph would have been greater than to take his life.⁵

Although they were still under arrest themselves, the missionaries were allowed to see Joseph. They reported,

> His feet were locked in heavy irons, his face was badly disfigured, and his body was covered in bruises, black and blue after the beatings and abuse. As he slowly dragged the irons into the room, the missionaries stood up with their guards. The officer

commanded them to sit down, but they stood for a long time in this way to honor a prisoner for Jesus Christ. Despite his bonds, Joseph looked more like a king than a prisoner.

A few months later Joseph was released from prison, but he was a shadow of his former self, and his strength had been taken away. Still, he had not denied Jesus Christ and remained a brave and devoted Christian.[6]

After the initial killings of Christians in the spring of 1933, there was a pause in the persecution as the rebels became deeply engaged in the civil war. A remarkable turnaround in the fortunes of the missionaries occurred after the Muslim leaders realized they could use the missionaries' medical skills to treat their wounded soldiers. For several years the mission work continued, during which more Muslims made professions of faith in Christ.

Numbered among those who paid the ultimate price for their love for Jesus was 20 year old Hassan Akhond of Yarkant. A

The church choir at Yarkant in happier times

Muslim friend of his was later released from prison and told how Hassan's soothing voice had calmed the nerves of the other prisoners at night as he sang hymns to his Savior. One night they heard him "faintly singing 'Loved with Everlasting Love,' in Uyghur. The next two nights Hassan's chain dragged, but after that there was silence, and they concluded he had died of starvation."[7]

Almost all of the Christians imprisoned at Kashgar perished. The list of martyrs included an evangelist named Khelil Akhond, the principal of the Chinese school Liu Losi, and many others. The Christians were herded into groups and then crammed into small, unventilated cells not large enough for each man to even sit down, so that

> They all spent day and night in a half-standing, half-crouching position. The few who survived said they got aches and swelling in their knees and then in the upper part of their calves and thighs. Mortification usually set in and death followed. The unheated cells were bitterly cold, especially for prisoners who had not been allowed to bring more clothing than those they were wearing when arrested.
>
> Some believers had been sent to prison only half-clad. Others were subjected to unmentionable tortures. Apart from those who were executed, prisoners died almost every night, and sometimes four or five corpses were taken out of the cells in the morning. After several years' imprisonment, when all the leading Christians had perished, the half dozen survivors were admonished with threats and released.[8]

Ali Akhond

Ali Akhondwas raised in a dedicated Muslim family.[9] He faced Mecca and prayed at the five prescribed times each day and was careful to obey the teachings of the mullahs and imams. One day Ali rode his horse into the market at Kashgar where he overheard an old Swedish man in a dusty grey coat telling a group of students that he would never die. Ali thought the man was crazy. But he was strangely drawn to the man's claim that he would never die, and Ali thought about it often.

Ali later obtained work at Kashgar, leaving his wife back on the farm. He intended to use his time in the city to attend lectures on Islam. But instead he came into contact with the Swedish Mission and often went to listen to their singing and preaching. One night, a missionary stood up and read the words of Jesus

Ali Akhond (left) with another Christian at Kashgar

from the Bible, "Very truly I tell you, whoever obeys my word will never see death" (John 8:51). Remembering the time he had heard the same words in the market, Ali decided to find out what the Christians meant by this saying.

Ali accepted some Gospel literature and took it home to read, but a friend threw it into the fire, warning Ali that if he read the material he would become an infidel. He returned to the mission and was given the same books, but this time another friend tore them up before Ali had a chance to read them.

Undeterred, Ali Akhond secured yet more Christian literature, and over the following months he closely observed the lives of the missionaries and their converts. What he saw impressed him. Whereas many marriages among the Uyghur people ended in divorce or discontent, the missionaries seemed to have genuine love for one another, and all of the Uyghur Christians appeared to have an inner peace and joy that he longed for but which Islam was powerless to provide. A few years passed, and by this time Ali had taken a second wife. One day,

> It began to occur to Ali Akhond that the Swedes' successful married life, their unselfishness, truthfulness and honesty might be due to obeying the teachings of Christ; so he began to try to follow that teaching himself. . . . About a year later he realized . . . for certain that Christ was alive and that Christ was God. He saw the terrible thing that faced him. If he believed, he would be cut off by his own people. But even so, he decided that he must throw in his lot with the despised Nazarenes. He parted from his secondary wife, making provision for her and undertaking to support their little son who stayed with his mother. Then he asked to be baptized.[10]

The missionaries were shocked by Ali Akhond's conversion, and one of them remarked,

The long and varying battle, which finally led to his conversion, could be compared to the conquering of a citadel, where one fort after another must tumble, until the citadel surrenders. At one point he had heard of the invitation to a baptism service at Hancheng, where four Chinese and two Muslims gave their confessions and were baptized. He was completely gripped, and afterwards he had a hard time holding to his old position. He didn't take his final step until after several years of battle, and he made the decision at an extremely hard time for all of us, when missionaries barely expected any victories. His conversion, which many had long waited for and prayed for, almost came as a surprise.[11]

After his public baptism, everybody in Kashgar knew that Ali Akhond had turned his back on Islam and embraced the "religion of the Crusaders." Ali returned to his first wife, and after a few years she also repented and became a new creation in Christ. The transformation in Ali's life was startling, and he could not keep the message to himself. In the mid-1920s, he was appointed as a fulltime evangelist by the church in Kashgar, and he led many Muslims to embrace Jesus Christ.

These breakthroughs did not come easily, however, and Ali was constantly harassed and threatened by his fellow Uyghurs who considered him to be an infidel. Whenever Ali preached in a church service,

There were always many more Muslims than Christians present, and when he preached on the story of the Prodigal Son, he could make everyone see the handsome young boy in a striped silk coat, white turban and crimson leather boots riding away from his father's house on a fine stallion. . . . At Christmas there were often congregations of 200 or 300 for the early morning service.[12]

When the persecution of 1933 broke, there was nowhere for Christians to hid—certainly not someone with such a high public profile as Ali Akhond. He was one of those who gained a martyr's crown at Kashgar. The honest Ali Akhond, who had found God after seeking for Him with all his heart, finally discovered the true meaning of what the missionary had taught years earlier. He had kept the words of Jesus, and as a result he gained eternal life. Ali's decayed body was returned to the earth, but his spirit had already soared into the arms of Jesus who had purchased Ali with his own precious blood.

Habil and Hava

Growing up in Yarkant, a young Uyghur boy named Mohammed and his sister, Hava, lived next door to a school run by the Swedish missionaries. When Mohammed was ten years old and Hava (Eva in English) was four, their mother suddenly died. This sad event threw the family into turmoil because the father was heavily in debt to a Chinese opium smuggler. Two years later, in 1926, more heartache was added to the children when their father died. That same night the opium smuggler appeared, intending to use Mohammed as a forced laborer and to use Hava as a sex slave in payment for their father's debts. The children ran to the school and begged the missionaries to save them.

The Swedes did not have the amount of money owed to the creditor, but they devised a plan to protect Mohammed and Hava. Mohammed had attended classes at the mission school for a number of years, but his father had not been able to pay the fees. The missionaries wisely lodged a legal claim, telling the magistrate that the mission was owed a sum of money for unpaid fees, and if they were granted guardianship of Mohammed and his sister, the mission would consider the debt paid in full. Because of his illegal dealings, the opium smuggler did not dare contest the claim in court, and the children were rescued.

Over time, the grief-stricken children grew to love the Swedish missionaries. Mohammed enjoyed playing soccer and watching birds. Little Hava especially adored Gerda Andersson who was in charge of the girls' home.

In 1931, a 26-year-old evangelist named Yusuf Khan[13]—the son of a famous mullah in today's Pakistan—came across the border to live in Yarkant, and revival broke out among the Muslim population. As Yusuf was a British citizen, the local Muslim leaders were hesitant to persecute him. A missionary described Yusuf as "the most successful national. He was the first to succeed in discovering acceptable approaches in witnessing to Muslims. He made Christianity Eastern."[14]

Habil at the age of 12

Yusuf Khan wrote this about the revival in Yarkant:

> Many, who say they want to become Christians, or are nominal Christians, do not leave their old way of life. They still visit the graves of Muslim saints or sit at the feet of the Sufi leaders. Now a new period is coming, especially among the young men who have been brought up by the Mission. Their lives have now been filled by God's power and they have been delivered from old Islamic beliefs. They burn with the desire to preach the Word to their Muslim brothers and sisters.[15]

Because of Yusuf's preaching, several of the young men connected with the mission put their faith in Christ and were baptized, including Mohammed. At his baptism, he put aside his Muslim name and took the new name Habil (Abel in English). Habil knew that baptism would cost him his friends, reputation, and possibly his life, but he didn't care. All he wanted to do was follow Jesus.

The missionaries were greatly impressed by Habil's zeal and hunger for God, and in 1932 he was invited to become the assistant principal of the mission school at Kashgar, even though he had only just turned 19.

The following year a jihad was declared, and the rebels decided to annihilate all "pagans," including Uyghur Christians. Yarkant was overrun by the rebels on April 11, 1933. Just before the road between Kashgar and Yarkant was cut off, Habil had returned to Yarkant to take care of his sister, Hava, who was then 13. Many young girls and women were being raped and carried off by the wicked men.

One source lamented, "A tragic and miserable fate befell the children of the orphanage, too. They were seized by the rebel troops and locked together with other Christians. The girls were humiliated and some older ones were forced to marry Muslims."[16]

147

Sensing the extent of the demonic onslaught that had come upon them, Habil "wept and prayed for courage to be faithful to his Savior in life and death, like Stephen."[17] Suddenly, as the Christian boys sung a hymn together, a shout went up to run. Soldiers had surrounded the building, and only one boy managed to escape.

Habil and the other Christians were roped together and taken to the governor's mansion where the diabolic Emir Abdullah Bughra struck Habil over the head and screamed, "Shoot them all!" It was decided that one of the boys should be killed first to make the others fearful. A soldier separated Habil from the others and untied him. The brave young Christian then

Habil and Hava in 1932

knelt down and looked up to heaven with the serenity of one of the ancient martyrs. Then he looked across at his friends as if to bid them goodbye. The order was given, "Fire!"—Habil fell to the ground . . . and the Emir said, "Finish him off with your sword."

Then they began to thrash the other prisoners until two of the boys called out, "Shoot us, too, and put us out of our pain." When he had wreaked his anger on them, the Emir sent the Christians bound to prison, and ordered that Habil's body be thrown out for the dogs to eat. When it had remained untouched for three days, however, some kindly Muslims buried it, for they took that as a sign from God.[18]

Another account of Habil's martyrdom says,

He fell on his knees, closed his hands, and looked toward the sky. No worry, fear, or prayer for mercy was spoken to the executioners. His face, turned upward, shone. The young Christians who were there will never forget what they saw in Habil's last moment on earth. They did not see death or fear, but a young man, who with eyes shining like stars seemed like he was looking into the open heaven. Then there was a shot and a cutting executioner's sword. The righteous Habil had his victory.[19]

About a week later Abdullah summoned Hava to the governor's mansion. The believers prayed for the pretty 13 year old, afraid the wicked emir planned to vent his lust on her body. Just after sunrise the next morning, Hava returned to the school and sank down on the floor. After wiping the tears from her eyes, she bravely recounted what had happened the previous night.

The evil man had locked the door and told Hava, "Now, you shall be mine!" Hava begged to be killed so she could join her brother in heaven. Abdullah Bughra was surprised to hear that the young girl was the sister of the man he had shot dead. Somehow her plea managed to touch even his hard heart, and he allowed her to go free as long as he was provided another Christian girl in her place. That dreadful experience fell to a young lady named Buve Khan, who was engaged to Habil at the time of his martyrdom. She was forced to become one of Abdullah's wives.

A short time later, Hava and the other Christian girls were forcibly married off to Muslims. The man Hava was forced to wed suffered from advanced syphilis, and she soon contracted the disease. She also fell pregnant, but the baby died at birth. Missionary Gerda Andersson was still in Yarkant at the time, and when she heard what had happened to the beloved girl, she sent a cart to Hava's house and collected her at the point of death. Andersson gently placed Hava in her own bed and nursed her day and night until she recovered.

The rebels were later defeated, and Hava's husband fled Yarkant and later sent her a letter of divorce. Having suffered the deaths of her mother, father, brother, and newborn baby, young Hava's heart had been crushed by the evil she had been forced to endure.

*The wicked Abdullah Bughra, who orchestrated the
slaughter of Christians in southern Xinjiang*

Through the love and tears of the other Christians, Hava continued to walk with the Lord, but several years later, "after the strain she had gone through, she died before she was 20."[20]

Abdullah Bughra, meanwhile, experienced the justice of God. One year after he oversaw the slaughter of God's children in southern Xinjiang, he commanded Uyghur and Kirghiz forces during the Battle of Kashgar when Hui Muslims loyal to the

This photo of two Christian families captures the tragic demise of the Church in Xinjiang. The men were killed and their wives were forced to marry Muslims. It is not known what happened to the children

Chinese government were mobilized to fight against the Turkic Muslims. Abdullah was killed by Chinese troops at Yarkant in April 1934. His head was cut off and put on display at the Id Kah Mosque in Kashgar as a warning to all other potential rebels.

The body of Christ had suffered a dreadful blow in Xinjiang. After the persecutions of the 1930s, the few surviving ex-Muslim Christians faced the horrors of the Second World War, followed by more than half a century of Communist rule. To the present day, there has never been another wide scale turning of Muslims to Christ in Xinjiang as there was when the Swedish Missionary Society was ministering there.[21]

1940s

The Communists take over

The 1940s began with God's people in Xinjiang few in number and scattered across a vast area. Fears were held that the tiny remnant would be unable to withstand the new Communist regime. Evangelical churches had been devastated by the mayhem of the 1930s, and the Catholics also suffered heavy losses so that "fewer than 800" believers counted for the whole of Xinjiang in 1941.[1]

Xinjiang remained in a state of turmoil throughout the 1940s, caught up in the political arm wrestling between China, the Soviet Union, and other nations that plunged the region into chaos. Regular insurrections and bloodbaths also continued as the long struggle between the Han Chinese and Uyghurs showed no signs of subsiding.

A Xinjiang Christian family in 1943

In November 1944, an armed insurrection by Muslims occurred at Yining. Countless Han men were killed, and the women were raped. Some 10,000 survivors retreated to Yanqi in the Tianshan Mountains where another slaughter took place that left just 30 refugees alive.

Any chance that the 1940s was going to be a relatively quiet time for the Church in Xinjiang was quickly shattered. All foreign missionaries were expelled, and Christians were brutally persecuted by both Muslim leaders and the Communists who gradually rose to prominence throughout the region before they finally gained power over the whole country at the end of the decade.

Despite the bleak conditions, occasional glimmers of hope emerged. Missionary Raymond Joyce in northern Xinjiang reported a new openness to the Bible among the Hui Muslims:

> During the last few days before Otto Schoemer and I finally left Kucheng [now Qitai], we sold several Bibles to Chinese Muslims. This sudden request for Bibles came as a pleasurable surprise to us, for during our four years there we had not formerly sold more than one or two to any of these people in Xinjiang. We had distributed many Scripture portions to the Uyghurs but had found the Hui much less approachable. . . .
>
> We were encouraged to believe that in the hearts of some of these proud followers of the Prophet exists a hidden interest in the Christian Scriptures and message, so that they could not let pass what to them may be their last opportunity to procure copies of the Bible. We can but pray that God's Word may do its mighty work and bring light to some souls in the increasing darkness of Xinjiang.[2]

The obstinate horse

The Spirit of God continued to move in people's hearts in mysterious ways throughout the region, and stories emerged which displayed God's grace and saving power. Grandfather Ma, a Hui Muslim, was the proud head of a wealthy family in a district that suffered terribly during the Muslim uprisings of the 1930s and 1940s.

His eight-year-old granddaughter, Ma Lingmei, had been allowed to attend a Christian school and had come to truly love the Lord Jesus Christ, much to the dismay of her staunchly Muslim parents and grandparents. Her grandfather grew furious whenever he heard mention of the Name of Jesus, and he forbade Lingmei from praying aloud in the house. On several occasions the old man flew into a fit of rage, beating and kicking the young girl. Despite her sufferings, Lingmei continued to pray for her grandfather, hoping that God would somehow soften his stubborn heart.

One day terror struck the community when they were told that the same rebels who had previously ransacked the town were returning with an even larger force to loot and murder at will. As he owned one of the wealthiest homes in the town, Grandpa Ma knew they would be targeted first, and everything he had worked so hard for would be plundered.

Beset by stifling anxiety at what lay ahead, he suddenly remembered little Lingmei. Didn't she claim that God answered her prayers? Racing home, he grabbed her by the arms and shouted, "If you have ever prayed in your life, pray now! Those soldiers are coming back and will soon be here. You say your God answers prayer. Go into that room and pray that they will not come to our house!"[3]

After being roughly pushed into an empty room, Lingmei calmly called upon her Heavenly Father for help. She prayed: "I am so happy and thankful because Grandfather has told me to pray. Lord Jesus, now is Your chance! Please show my Grandfather that You do answer prayer. Please don't let the soldiers come to our house, I ask this in Jesus' Name."[4]

The rebels entered the town and rode their horses straight down the street where the Ma family lived. The leader stopped outside their courtyard and directed his horse to go through the gate, intending to loot their home. Suddenly, however, a strange thing happened. The rebel leader's horse refused to enter the gate. The obstinate beast then

> backed and kicked; it shied this way and that, and nothing would make it go in. The officer beat it and dug his spurs into it, but it was no use. It would not go in. Then the officer turned to his men and said, "Why, this courtyard must be full of demons; we cannot see them, but the horse can. Not one of you is to go in there, not one!" And he turned his horse and led his men to another part of the town.[5]

Shocked by what had happened, the next day Grandpa Ma went to the mission house, and with a deep sense of humility the aged Muslim said, "To think that all the while that little granddaughter of mine was right, and I was wrong. Teach me about the God who answers prayer like that. Please teach me to pray."[6]

The indestructible seed

After most of the missionaries were expelled from southern Xinjiang, many assumed the fledgling believers would not survive. But against all odds, the seed that had been planted deeply in many lives began to sprout. This summary of the Evangelical work in southern Xinjiang—which at the time was considered the most effective Christian outreach to Muslims anywhere in the world—reveals that the kingdom of God not only survived the onslaught but had begun to thrive by the end of the 1940s:

> The first two baptisms came in 1907, and by 1914 the number had risen to 15. The largest number of baptisms at one time came in

1932, when 14 members, 10 Uyghurs and 4 Chinese, were added to the church community in Kashgar. By 1933, the total number of baptized Christians was 163, mostly Uyghurs and Kirgiz, but some Chinese. However, after a protracted period of persecution when Christians were imprisoned and tortured, the number dwindled, only to reach a new high of 200 after the missionaries were forced to leave.[7]

Although it was almost always reported that the last foreign missionaries left southern Xinjiang in 1938, one Christian couple, the Selveys, were permitted to remain in Kashgar five more years due to Dr. Selvey's skill as a medical practitioner. While living inside the compound of the British consulate, they kept in touch with the surviving Christians in the area and did everything they could to quietly encourage them in the faith. Ingrid Selvey's letters home were closely monitored by the authorities, but she was able to offer glimpses of hope to the departed missionaries.

While many Christians had been martyred, others were among the estimated 5,000 Uyghur and Kirgiz refugees who fled across the border to British India. Using supplies and money left behind by the expelled Swedish missionaries, the Selveys helped arrange travel for children to join their families, including the children of the evangelist Yusuf Khan, who escaped across the border after being arrested, tortured, and sentenced to death by furious Muslim clerics.[8]

It seems that a number of people in Kashgar had been secret believers in Jesus Christ during the years of the Swedish mission and had escaped persecution because they were not outwardly identified with the Christian community. For example, one woman, completely veiled, had attended the church services each Friday, and she never attended the mosque with her Muslim husband. She sat in the same place each week and soaked in the teaching of God's Word but never publicly professed to being a Christian, even though her life had been changed by God's grace.

In another sign that the seed of the gospel had not perished, one day a Uyghur evangelist was riding in the countryside when he came across a group of Muslim men resting on the side of the road. He was surprised to see them reading a New Testament, and one of the men told the evangelist: "We know that the new regime is an enemy of yours, and it will surely . . . kill some of you. Do not fear, we will continue the mission work. We are gathered here to read the New Testament and to pray in the Name of Jesus, because we are fed up with Islam."[9]

In 1939 thieves had ransacked the old Mission buildings and sold whatever they could at the bazaar. The property was later taken over by the Chinese military. Some of the former Swedish missionaries, meanwhile, planned to move to north India to continue their work among the Uyghur and Kirgiz refugees.[10]

In the end, it was decided not to establish a new Swedish mission in India because British control was beginning to wane and the type of Islam practiced in Kashmir was at least as fanatical and anti-Christian as it had been in Xinjiang.

In 1947, the following report by two former Swedish missionaries on the state of the Church in Kashgar makes for grim reading as it closed the curtain on the missionary era in Xinjiang:

Some of the hundreds of children cared for by
Swedish missionaries in Xinjiang

The congregation has almost entirely disappeared. Most of the older and more active Christians have been murdered. An official report names 15 who have been executed. The same thing has happened to some of the younger Christians. Many who had been influenced by the Mission and then closely associated with them have suffered or been killed. With few exceptions those who have been allowed to have been forced to renounce their faith. One survivor wrote in a letter: "All our dear friends were tortured to death in the winter of 1937."[11]

Evidence exists, however, that the deep planting of God's Word among the Muslims of southern Xinjiang was not in vain. Tens of thousands of people had heard the gospel, and hundreds of children who were educated in the mission schools were deeply exposed to Christianity. As late as 1980, a letter reached Sweden from someone in Yarkant who requested a Uyghur Bible, and notes: "Quite often we gather to pray and sing with our friends from the Mission in Yarkant."[12]

The founding meeting of the Hami Christian Church in 1947

The foreign missionary era had come to an abrupt end in Xinjiang, but God began to reveal that it was time for the baton of the gospel to be handed off to the Chinese Church. The foreigners had played a crucial role, but now it would be left to the Han Christians to carry the gospel throughout northwest China.

In 1945, a key event in the history of Christianity in Xinjiang took place when the first Chinese house church was established in Urumqi. A group of vibrant, witnessing believers founded the Hami Christian Church in 1947, and additional fellowships sprouted in other towns and cities, from Altay in the extreme north of Xinjiang down to the deep south.

For decades it was commonly assumed that the level of racial prejudice between the Han Chinese and the Uyghurs was so great that Han Christians could never successfully propagate the gospel among Muslims in Xinjiang. As the 1940s came to an end, however, mounting evidence suggested that assumption

Some of the surviving pioneers who met together in 2005 to celebrate the 60th anniversary of the Chinese house church movement in Xinjiang, which started in 1945

was wrong. Despite chronic instability disrupting life in Xinjiang, promising signs were seen for God's kingdom in many places, with one account stating,

> When the war ended, thriving churches were found in all the main towns of Xinjiang—living churches which Muslims could observe for the first time since the days of the Nestorians. The postmaster of Urumqi and his wife were active Christians. So were two high government officials—both generals. The Urumqi church, consisting of 40 baptized members, was invited to meet in the hall of the Party headquarters.[13]

The Back to Jerusalem Evangelistic Band

The Back to Jerusalem Evangelistic Band. Back row: Fan Zhijie, He Enzheng (Grace He), Wei Suxi, Lu De (Ruth Lu), Li Jinquan; Front row: Zhao Maijia (Mecca Zhao), Ma Peixuan (Mark Ma), Dai Yanzhong (Timothy Dai)

A heavenly vision

Right at the time when many of the expelled missionaries who had labored in Xinjiang were feeling at a low ebb due to the grim prospects faced by Christians in the region, startling news emerged that the Holy Spirit had moved on the hearts of Chinese believers in other parts of the country, calling them to missionary service in Xinjiang and beyond. At least five separate groups of believers received a vision to reach Muslims in northwest China.

One of the missionaries who played a key role in the early days of the Back to Jerusalem Evangelistic Band was Helen Bailey, an American Presbyterian who had lived in China for quarter of a century. She lived on the premises of the Northwest Bible

Institute and was deeply loved by the students whom she nurtured and encouraged to pursue God's call on their lives. Bailey was invited to join the Band, but she wisely declined, believing it was a call to the Chinese Church and should therefore remain an indigenous mission movement.

Bailey promoted the vision in newsletters which were circulated among Western Christians in North America and Britain. In her first newsletter, she called the group the "Back to Jerusalem Band," and ever since it has been known by that name in the English-speaking world, but not among the Chinese Church.[1]

On May 23, 1943, the Back to Jerusalem Evangelistic Band was formally established at the Northwest Bible Institute in Shaanxi Province, under the leadership of the school's vice-principal, Mark Ma Peixuan. The actual Chinese name adopted by the group that day was the "Preach the Gospel Everywhere Band."

Ma, a native of Henan Province, recalled how the Lord gave him a vision for pioneer work in the vast, unreached Muslim world. He said,

> On the evening of November 25, 1942, while in prayer, the Lord said to me: "The door to Xinjiang is already open. Enter and preach the gospel." When this voice reached me I was trembling and fearful and most unwilling to obey, because I did not recall a single time in the past when I had prayed for Xinjiang. Moreover, it was a place which I had no desire to go. Therefore I merely prayed about this matter, not even telling my wife.
>
> After exactly five months of prayer, on Easter morning, April 25, 1943, when two fellow workers and I were praying together on the bank of the Wei River, I told them of my call to Xinjiang, and one of the fellow workers said that ten years earlier she had received a similar call. I thanked God that He had already prepared a co-worker. When I returned to the school I learned that on that same Easter Sunday at the sunrise service eight students had also been burdened for Xinjiang.[2]

The Easter morning service in 1943 to which Ma referred was to prove the genesis for a chain of events that drastically changed the lives of many people. The impact of that prayer time is still felt in the Chinese Church today. One attendee described the pivotal meeting as follows:

> Under the tall trees whose thick boughs spread a leafy shelter overhead, a map of China had been outlined in whitewash. The students stood around, looking at it. They had been hearing again of the needs of the great provinces to the North and to the West. . . .
>
> A solemn moment arrived, which brought with it an almost breathtaking hush. "Let those who have received the Lord's commission leave their places and go and stand on the province to which God has called them." . . . There was a stir among the group of students. Cloth-soled feet moved noiselessly as one, then another, walked across the courtyard to the map. And as the sun rose over the distant horizon, eight young people were seen standing quietly on the patch that was marked with the word XINJIANG.[3]

These were the students who joined Mark Ma in his divine call to the Muslim world. His own account continues with a vivid description of the long dialogue he claimed to have had with God:

> On the evening of May 4th we held our first prayer meeting, and there were 23 present. . . . On May 11th we received the first offering for our mission, amounting to $50. . . .
>
> The Lord said, "Since the beginning at Pentecost, the pathway of the gospel has spread, for the greater part, in a westward direction; from Jerusalem to Antioch to all of Europe; from Europe to America; from southeast China to the northwest; until today from Gansu on westward it can be said there is no firmly established Church. You may go west from Gansu, preaching the gospel all the way back to Jerusalem, causing the light of the gospel to complete the circle around this dark world."

I said, "O Lord, who are we that we can carry such a great responsibility?"

The Lord answered: "I want to manifest My power through those who of themselves have no power."

I said, "That section of territory is under the power of Islam, and the Muslims are the hardest of all peoples to reach with the gospel."

The Lord replied: "The most rebellious people are the Israelites; the hardest field of labor is my own people the Jews. . . . Even you Chinese, yourself included, are hard enough, but you have been conquered by the gospel."

I asked, "O Lord, why is it that missionaries from Europe and America have established so many churches in China but are still unable to open the door to West Asia?"

The Lord answered me: "I have kept for the Chinese Church a portion of inheritance, otherwise, when I return, will you not be so poor?"

When I heard the Lord say that He had kept for us a portion of inheritance, my heart overflowed with thanksgiving. I stopped arguing with the Lord.[4]

The danger of someone claiming to have had direct, two-way communication with God is highlighted by Mark Ma's testimony, because even though it contains interesting information, historically the claim that the gospel has generally spread in a westward direction around the globe is not true. Apart from the apostle Thomas who took the gospel east to India immediately after the resurrection of Jesus Christ, as this book details, the Nestorians spread the Christian message eastward in the first millennia of the Christian era, and millions of true believers inhabited the areas of the Middle East and the Central Asian steppes, including parts of Xinjiang. Nestorian influence spread as far east as the Korean Peninsula, Japan, and the Philippines.

Almost a century after Mark Ma's claims of divine inspiration regarding the global direction of the gospel as a core foundation for the Back to Jerusalem Movement, critics have pointed out that using this concept as a pillar for an entire mission movement is shaky at best, and potentially dangerously ill-informed.

Like Moses who led the children of Israel to the promised land without ever crossing into it, Mark Ma was God's spokesman to his generation for the evangelization of Xinjiang, but he personally never stepped foot in the region. Nevertheless, Ma received harsh treatment for his faith. He was thrown into prison in Chongqing in 1967 where he was tortured and beaten for four and a half years. He later resurfaced as a vibrant figure in the Chongqing churches before going to his eternal reward in September 2008 at the impressive age of 102.

It was the policy of the leaders of the Back to Jerusalem Band not to solicit finances in any way but to pray and trust God to provide for all of their needs. Donations started coming in from all over China, however, from believers whose hearts were touched by the vision. Helen Taylor notes,

> In a remarkable way money came into the treasury almost entirely from Chinese sources, and they felt they must use up what was sent in and trust God to send more. Chinese Christians from many places, hearing of this work, sent generous offerings. It was manifest that the movement was God-inspired.[5]

The first team, consisting of three women and two men, were finally sent to Gansu Province in 1944. Mark Ma and He Enzheng later explained that the delay in launching the mission occurred after "the top China Inland Mission leaders firmly opposed the Chinese Back to Jerusalem Band's evangelization plan and threatened to cut off funding. . . . Finally, the Band refused to wait any longer and embarked on the road to the west without any thought of returning."[6]

In 1945, another two workers were sent to preach the gospel among the Hui Muslims in Ningxia, and the following year the

Lord called two men, Mecca Zhao and Timothy Dai, to long-term service in Xinjiang.

Now that the vision was becoming reality, officers were elected and a constitution was adopted which defined the target area of the Band as

> The seven border provinces of China; and to the seven countries on the borders of Asia: Afghanistan, Iran, Arabia, Iraq, Syria, Turkey and Palestine. . . .
>
> In pioneer districts we plan to establish churches according to the example of Scripture. In places where churches already exist, we plan to serve such churches. We look to the Lord alone for all financial supplies.[7]

Five brave sisters

When news reached the Christian world that five women had departed for dangerous Muslim territories, much concern was expressed for their safety, and the wisdom of the plan was questioned by some. Realizing the dangers and hardships ahead of them, one of the women courageously declared, "We may not reach there, we may die on the way, but we are willing to shed our blood on the highway to Mount Zion."[8]

He Enzheng (Grace He) was a member of the second group of Back to Jerusalem missionaries. At birth she was dedicated to God by her mother, and in her early twenties she received a clear call from the Lord to take the gospel to Xinjiang, and ultimately all the way back to Jerusalem. A detailed account of her solemn call says,

> She was attending an evangelistic meeting, and as the congregation rose to pray, she received a vision from the Lord. Her immediate surroundings faded, and she seemed to be standing alone in a vast, bright wilderness plain. In the distance she heard a voice—a voice full of sorrow, painfully crying for help. She looked

but saw no one, only the horror of darkness, from whence the sound of great anguish came. As she gazed, another voice spoke, a voice from heaven, deep with mercy and compassion: "The people dwelling in darkness have no one to preach the Good News to them." Greatly moved at the sound of that voice, the tears springing to her eyes, she replied, "O Lord, here am I."[9]

Lu De (Ruth Lu) hailed from Henan Province. After meeting Christ, she developed a great passion for lost souls, and while studying at the Northwest Bible Institute, she recalled,

One day as I knelt in prayer the Lord called me by name and in a vision showed me the desolate, pitiful spiritual condition of the northwest. I saw a multitude of lost souls in a mountain valley crying for help to save their lives. Having gone astray, they did not know how to find the True God who could save them. The

The second Back to Jerusalem team at their farewell meeting, alongside a table of gifts which included a wash basin for each missionary. Left to right: Fan Zhijie, Lu De (Ruth Lu), Wei Suxi, Zhang Moxi (Moses Zhang), He Enzheng (Grace He), Li Jinquan

voice of God asked me, "My child, are you willing to go and save them?" When this voice pierced my heart, without hesitation I replied, "O Lord, your handmaiden is willing to obey Your will."[10]

Li Jinquan was born into a Muslim home. Her parents died while she was young, and she was raised by her grandmother. When Li Jinquan was just 12 years old, she ran away from home and fell into a life of sin. At the age of 20 she heard the gospel of Jesus Christ for the first time. She believed and was saved, and in 1941 she enrolled to study at the Northwest Bible Institute.

Three years later, in 1944, Li went on a short-term outreach to a Tibetan area of Gansu Province. After returning to the Bible school, she testified, "The Lord suddenly touched my heart to see the pitiful need of the Tibetan people. At that time I did not have the courage to respond to God's call, but the appeal constantly presented itself before me, and I could not but accept

He Enzheng and Li Jinquan outside their mud home at Ulan in 1947

this challenge from God. . . . The Lord put the burden of Tibet deep in my heart."[11]

In March 1947, Li Jinquan joined the other Back to Jerusalem missionaries and headed west. She based for a considerable time at Ulan in today's Qinghai Province, where she and other workers reached out to Tibetans and other needy people groups.

Mecca Zhao

Zhao Majia (Mecca Zhao) was also born in Henan Province, but when he was a child, his family fled to Shanxi to escape famine. When Zhao was in his late teens, he met Christ and was radically transformed. He was so deeply touched by the love of God that he unreservedly promised to go wherever the Lord would lead him and to do whatever He required.

A short time after he met Christ, Zhao had a powerful encounter with God during a prayer meeting. He later recalled the events of that evening:

> I resolved to pray all night, asking God to show me the way. . . .
> Immediately I broke out in perspiration although it was in the
> dead of winter and the ground was covered with snow. I prayed
> for a long time, the words just flowing out. After a short silence
> there appeared before my eyes a strip of white paper on which
> was written the word "Mecca." I knew this was a new name God
> had given me which embraced His plan for my whole life—but
> at that time I had no idea what "Mecca" meant. I rose from my
> knees with great joy.[12]

Several years later Zhao finally had the mystery of the word "Mecca" solved for him when Mark Ma told him of the commission he had received to preach the gospel in the Muslim world, including to the city of Mecca in Saudi Arabia.

When Mecca Zhao heard about the vision God had given the leaders of the Northwest Bible Institute to take the gospel back to Jerusalem, he was amazed to find it exactly matched his own call. He enthusiastically enlisted in the mission and became one of the pioneer members of the Back to Jerusalem Evangelistic Band. As Mecca Zhao and other team members prepared to set out, many prayers went up before God's throne for the success of the venture and the protection of those involved. The Anglican Bishop Frank Houghton remarked,

> The Church in China has been stirred through the going forth of a group of Chinese workers from the Northwest Bible Institute. . . . They are planning to go forward into Xinjiang, and thence— eventually—to carry the gospel through Central Asia "back to Jerusalem!" They show the marks of a Divine call in their fervent abandonment to His will and equally in a sensible, practical atti-tude which reminds one of Hudson Taylor.[13]

In obedience to his call, Mecca Zhao traveled 265 miles (429 km) on horseback in a westward direction. He suffered terribly from neuralgia and reported that at one stop along the way he was "very miserable, and only able to go to the school and a medicine shop and talk about the gospel a little with the teacher and the shopkeeper."[14]

The difficulties of the journey can be seen from Zhao's letter to Mark Ma:

> All along the way are the pasture grounds of the wild Tibetans, Mongols and Muslims, who live in tents. There are no inns. There are high mountains of grassy deserts, packs of wild animals, man-eating Tibetan dogs and murderous bandits. . . .
>
> Along the road there were many bodies of those who had starved to death or been killed. . . . Every night I looked carefully to see there was no one in sight, and then quietly went into the thick grass hidden from the road. There I took the pack off the horse, and slept under the open sky. I didn't dare make a sound for fear of attracting robbers. Sometimes along the road I heard firing, but I was quite at rest, and in fact I did not encounter any

danger. Travelers all carry guns; my gun was prayer. . . . God let me prove the strength of a "Hallelujah" to scare away robbers and wild beasts, and meet every difficulty.[15]

Some months later the rest of the Back to Jerusalem team caught up with Mecca Zhao, and they prayed together for the best strategy to continue their push into Xinjiang.

Finding that travel by camel was cheaper and far less dangerous than bus travel, they decided to purchase camels. The locals found the sight of Chinese preachers trying to buy camels humorous, and the Band was delayed for two weeks while they negotiated a fair price with the local Muslims.

In July 1947, the Band set out again on their long journey westward, anxious to reach Xinjiang before the summer ended and winter snowfall made progress impossible. The first stage of 90 miles (146 km) across swampy marshes and high mountains took them six days. When they finally reached the Xinjiang border, they were detained for several days while their passports were certified by officials. Permission to proceed was finally granted, and the small team of gospel warriors crossed "into the lion's mouth."

The vision God had given Mark Ma, Mecca Zhao, and the others was finally being fulfilled in Xinjiang. The team made their way into the Muslim world with the fire of the Holy Spirit burning in their hearts. For the next month, they traveled through desert wastes with few signs of human existence except an occasional oasis settlement. Drinking water was scarce, so wherever they could they filled their containers. But many days passed between opportunities to refill.

One month into their journey, the Back to Jerusalem Band's camel train was met by government officials who informed them that permission to travel further had been withdrawn due to new political developments in the region. Despite their pleadings, the officials said it was unsafe and foolish for a group of youngsters, especially women, to travel through the Taklamakan Desert. Since "no amount of persuasion on their part could convince the officials that theirs was not a political mission and that they were not afraid of the dangers en route, it was necessary for them to retrace their steps back to Qinghai."[16]

After prayer, they decided to spend the winter in Qinghai, after which they would attempt to re-enter Xinjiang by another route. In the spring of 1948, Mecca Zhao and Ruth Lu hitched a ride in the back of an oil truck and crossed into Xinjiang sitting atop empty oil barrels. At stops along the way they boldly shared the gospel, and many people were won to the Lord.

Ultimately, Zhao made it all the way to the town of Hancheng (Shule) near Kashgar. After the brutal persecutions and the expulsion of the missionaries in the 1930s, the church in Hancheng had struggled. One source notes, "Before his arrival there was a small number of Han Christians who had not gathered for worship in a long time."[17]

In October 1949, all of China came under Communist control, but the work continued in Xinjiang. Zhao reported the following in late 1950: "Missionaries with the Back to Jerusalem Evangelistic Band and the Northwest Spiritual Band are evangelizing at every large bazaar. They have spread the gospel to Yarkant and Hotan and some Han Chinese and Uyghur people have accepted the gospel."[18]

In June 1951, Mecca Zhao married fellow missionary He Enzheng, and they moved to Yarkant to continue their service for God. Not long after, the extreme anti-religious policies of Mao's China spread even to the farthest corners of Xinjiang, and for a generation all open Christian work came to a halt. The authorities finally made their move against Zhao in 1957, while his wife was away visiting her parents in Shanxi Province. He was arrested and publicly denounced for his counter-revolutionary "errors," and he suffered terribly for his faith in Jesus Christ.

Emerging from the furnace

As the months of persecution and hardship rolled into years, and years into decades, the vision of the Back to Jerusalem workers began to fade. All seemed lost. Like the Israelites who were so close to the promised that they could behold it with their eyes, the Back to Jerusalem vision of the 1940s and 1950s was taken back into the wilderness to await a time when the workers would be better equipped to handle the great task before them.

To the human eye, the Back to Jerusalem initiative had failed. But God knew the dedication of His children and the purity of their commitment. Although the vision was buried for a time, it did not perish. God was faithful, and even though many years of prison and deprivation awaited the Back to Jerusalem pioneers, most emerged decades later from the furnace of affliction alive and well and serving Jesus Christ in Xinjiang.

On March 7, 2007, Mecca Zhao Maijia went to be with the Lord. He had served in Xinjiang for over 60 years. Two years later

He Enzheng and Mecca Zhao at their home in Kashgar in 2001

his wife, He Enzheng, also received her eternal reward. Although they are recognized as key figures in the overseas missionary vision of the Chinese Church, neither Zhao nor He ever left China. A visitor to He Enzheng near the end of her life commented as follows:

> For over 60 years she has knelt down to pray every single morning for China, Jerusalem, and the vision to send missionaries out of China into the Middle East. She has become something of a legendary figure among the Chinese house churches. Those who want to visit have to pass through three levels of house church security because she is under such close surveillance from the Public Security Bureau. . . .
>
> Even after all these years, her mind is incredibly sharp and her memory of the vision is crystal clear. . . . She spoke of how in the 1940s those early pioneers made their way on foot into Xinjiang.

Ruth Lu and Fan Zizhou in 1988

They didn't carry any provisions with them, but simply trusted that God would provide their needs along the way.

On one occasion she was hungry and had asked God to give her some food. All of a sudden she came across a loaf of bread that had been left at the side of the road. Giving thanks to God, she and her friends shared the bread and continued on into the local village to preach the gospel. The following day she discovered that the bread had actually been poisoned by the locals as a trap to kill wild dogs! The missionaries had eaten it and miraculously suffered no ill effects.[19]

Ruth Lu, meanwhile, moved to Aksu in western Xinjiang and married Fan Zizhou of the Northwest Spiritual Band. They eventually moved to Urumqi and faithfully served the churches in Xinjiang's capital for decades. When she was pregnant in 1953, Ruth dedicated her baby to the Lord and asked the Holy Spirit to fill the child with wisdom and grace. Decades later, Fan and Lu's daughter, Fan Chenguang, became a pastor of the Minde Road Church in Urumqi, continuing the rich spiritual heritage that had been handed down by her parents.

Fan Zizhou died in Urumqi in 1995, and Ruth Lu De went to her eternal home in December 2006, aged 84. Many people in Xinjiang believed in Christ because of their witness.

The Northwest Spiritual Band

The missionaries with the Back to Jerusalem Evangelistic Band were not the only Chinese believers whom God called to minister to the Muslims of Xinjiang, as several smaller initiatives were formed in the 1940s. Some reached into Tibetan areas, others to the minority groups of southwest China, and still others went boldly into Muslim regions. Despite their different origins and spheres of work, all of these groups considered themselves to be part of the larger vision to spread the gospel among unevangelized people groups all the way back to Jerusalem.

Phyllis Thompson, a CIM missionary based in Chongqing, remarked in 1949:

> The thing that has impressed me most has been the strange, unaccountable urge of a number of different Chinese groups of Christians to press forward in faith, taking the gospel towards the west. I know of at least five different groups, quite unconnected

A Chinese evangelist preaching to soldiers in the 1940s

with each other, who have left their homes in east China and gone forth to the west, leaving practically everything behind them. Some are in Xikang [now western Sichuan], some in Gansu, and some in the great northwestern province of Xinjiang.

It seems like a movement of the Spirit which is irresistible. The striking thing is that they are disconnected, and in most cases seem to know nothing about each other. Yet all are convinced that the Lord is sending them to the western borders to preach the gospel, and they are going with a strong sense of urgency of the shortness of the time, and the imminence of the Lord's return.[1]

A church network called the Jesus Family was founded in 1921 in Shandong Province by Jing Dianying. Its members sold all of their possessions and distributed their wealth among family members and the poor. They then made their way to towns and villages, preaching the gospel as they walked from one place to another. Their example of communal living and their deep Christian love amazed many onlookers and attracted those who were searching for answers to life as well as the homeless, destitute, and despised. Many blind people and beggars joined the Jesus Family and found eternal life in Christ.

After a time, the Jesus Family lost their direction. A split developed, and a new group emerged known as the Northwest Spiritual Band. By the mid-1940s, God had raised up a new generation of believers who were willing to forsake everything to see Christ glorified among all peoples.

In August 1946, the group's leader, Zhang Guquan, delivered a message entitled "Back to Jerusalem Evangelism" in his home province of Shandong. The believers present were deeply affected by the message, and two single ladies—Liu Shuyuan and Zhang Meiying—resolved to go to Xinjiang, even though they knew little to nothing about the region at the time. These two young women became the first cross-cultural missionaries of the Northwest Spiritual Band.

The strategy of the Northwest Spiritual Band was simply to preach the gospel while believing that Jesus would soon return. Later Chinese missionaries who arrived in Xinjiang also spent little time establishing local congregations but concentrated solely on evangelism. In His mercy, God established many new believers in the faith, and much good fruit remains to this day. They won people to Christ among many ethnic groups including Uyghur, Hui, and Kazak Muslims.

The Northwest Spiritual Band was far from being a large spiritual army marching across the region. The leadership consisted of just four or five individuals plus a few dozen other workers. Despite their small numbers, they proved effective because their vision was so focused. One scholar summarized their work this way:

> The Northwest Spiritual Band would stop at towns and villages along the route and hold evangelistic meetings for a few days before moving on. They had no fixed itinerary, but rather a general sense of going to northwest areas, and they claimed to rely on the guidance of the Holy Spirit. Most of them experienced many hardships yet, from their hymns, they regarded suffering as something that they were proud of, and a necessary cost to pay in order to save souls for God.
>
> There was no specific goal or direction, except a vague sense of evangelizing the whole world by pressing westward. Few, if any members, knew what lay beyond the next town, much less beyond the border of China, as none of them carried any map![2]

The first workers with the Northwest Spiritual Band arrived in Xinjiang in 1947, where they successfully won Muslims to Christ. Zhang moved to the town of Hami, which became the movement's base to reach into other parts of Xinjiang. A chapel and nursery were established, and a small Bible school opened. In the summer of 1948, four members of the Back to Jerusalem Evangelistic Band passed through Hami, and the Northwest

Spiritual Band workers warmly welcomed them. Two evangelists were sent to Barkol (Baikun) where they boldly proclaimed the gospel. God opened the hearts of some of the locals, and by March 1949, a small church of 20 or 30 believers had emerged in the town.

In June 1949, a powerful conference was held by the mission in Hami which was attended by many Christians. Believers were trained to evangelize according to the pattern in the Book of Acts, and they were formed into small teams and dispatched to numerous places throughout Xinjiang. Although some locations saw a lukewarm response to the gospel, Karashar (Yanqi) County—which was inhabited by many Hui and Mongol people— saw a wonderful response, and six months later more than 160 people attended the Christmas services at the new church.

Zhang Guquan

Zhang Guquan was acknowledged as the leader of the Northwest Spiritual Band. A native of Shandong Province, Zhang graduated from seminary and sought the Lord as to what direction his life should take. On one hand,

> He was very much impressed by the communal life-style of the Jesus Family, where the members contributed all their individual possessions and held all things in common. On the other hand, he admired the Little Flock for their study of the Bible and their way of penetrating the depth of the Word. In his time of indecision, he seemed to hear a voice speaking directly to him: "My child, neither of these is the road you should take. I have something special in mind for you."[3]

This new direction led to the emergence of the Northwest Spiritual Band whose leaders said, "Let's rise to our feet and carry the cross to the nations where God is not known. Let us go forth in Jesus' name, giving up everything we have, even our very lives if necessary, so that the Name of Jesus will be glorified among all Gentiles."[4]

The work progressed until persecution struck in March 1951, and Zhang and many of his co-workers were arrested and thrown into prison. Others were ordered to return to their home provinces. For four years nothing was heard of Zhang Guquan, but it was later reported that

> Zhang died in prison in 1956 when he was in his early 30s. Other leaders also died for the Lord. Quite a few who survived the long trek from Shandong to Xinjiang could not stand the test and wavered from the faith, speaking against Zhang and the Band. Later they were sent back to Shandong. Those who kept their faith and stayed behind faced a very bitter life. . . . They had become the refuse of the world. They were wilfully wronged, suppressed, persecuted, insulted and beaten. . . . For the sake of the Lord, they were publicly exposed to abuse and affliction.[5]

Although it was no comfort to him, in 1980 the government reversed Zhang Guquan's sentence, announcing he was not a

Zhang Guquan

criminal and that his "political rights" had been restored. This was an admission by the government that they had killed an innocent man, but by then Zhang had already been in the arms of his Savior for 24 years, having received his reward as one who was faithful even unto death.

Zhang's wife, meanwhile, continued to live many years in Xinjiang, and just before she was called to her heavenly home in 2008, she was moved to tears as she prayed for a group of Chinese house church leaders as they passed through Xinjiang on an overland journey from China to Jerusalem.

The faithful postmaster

The job of postmaster general was a high-ranking government position in those days, and the Urumqi postmaster Li Kaihuan and his wife, Zhai Mingxia, were committed Christians who doubled as missionaries. After requesting a transfer from Yunnan Province to Xinjiang in 1945, Li and Zhai eagerly spread the gospel of Jesus Christ and emerged as key Christian leaders in the churches of Urumqi and the surrounding areas.

For years Li faithfully performed his important job and also used his authority with other government leaders to benefit the body of Christ. He advocated for Christians whenever they were in danger of persecution, and believers in Urumqi deeply loved and appreciated the devoted couple. The following was said of them:

> The Lis were devout Christians. Only one week after their arrival in Urumqi, they had an announcement published in the Xinjiang Daily, saying: "Every Sunday there will be a gathering in Li Kaihuan's home on Tianshan Road. We are calling local Christians to come for worship." After the announcement appeared in the newspaper, veteran believers attended consistently.[6]

The number of people who gathered to worship God quickly outgrew Li's home, so a large meeting room was rented, paid for by the Christian governor of Xinjiang, General Zhang Zhizhong. The first official Chinese-led Evangelical church in Urumqi was established in 1945, which believers consider to be the start date of house church Christianity in Xinjiang.

A congregation of 40 members formed who boldly shared the gospel with Han people in the city as well as Uyghurs and other ethnicities. When floods and other natural disasters afflicted central China, thousands of families were resettled in Xinjiang. Li and his fellow believers worked hard to help the refugees, and many were led to Christ.

Every Tuesday, the Urumqi church members conducted street evangelism with a raised banner and a megaphone, and the number of converts gradually increased. Before long there were 97 church members, and another ten waiting to be baptized.[7] Some of these new believers had the seed of the gospel first planted in their hearts by George Hunter and other missionaries decades earlier.

The influence of Li Kaihuan's work expanded to other parts of Xinjiang, and fellowships were established in several towns including one of 50 Christians at Hami. By 1949, the church in Urumqi had grown significantly, with about 500 people attending Sunday services. All of the church members were reportedly Han Chinese, "except for Mahmud Khan, a Uyghur and former member of the Kashgar church who had fled from southern Xinjiang."[8]

In 1950 the movement was described by an American missionary in glowing terms: "They are very closely associated with Mr and Mrs Li, whose ministry at Urumqi will, we believe, if ever it is published, prove to be one of the most glorious chapters in the history of the Chinese Church. . . . They are a group of fine consecrated men and women."[9]

Li Kaihuan eventually resigned his post office job so he could concentrate on fulltime ministry. He and his wife, Zhai Mingxia, ran a Bible school to train leaders, and they also printed a small periodical called "Streams and Rivers" which was read by Christians throughout China.

Communist aggression continued to spread across Xinjiang, and by 1953, all of the churches under Li's leadership were closed down. Church properties were confiscated, and Li was persecuted for his faith.

Li Kaihuan suddenly died of a heart attack in 1955, and his passing was met with deep grief by all who knew him. Li's life was a prime example of how believers can use their vocation for the glory of God, and the body of Christ in Xinjiang benefited greatly from his ministry to the Lord.

The funeral of prominent Christian leader Li Kaihuan in 1955

Decades later, testimony continued to emerge from Xinjiang of the lasting impact made by members of the Northwest Spiritual Band. One man named Wang recalled that while he was employed as a truck driver in 1948, he heard the gospel for the first time at street meetings led by the Chinese evangelists. He immediately accepted the Lord and was baptized, and for the next 28 years he drove trucks across Xinjiang and as far as Lhasa, Tibet, taking every opportunity to share his faith with people in those remote regions. The following was said of Wang:

> He was a vine that produced grapes, and the truck he drove was a gospel truck. Of all the people who traveled in his truck, no matter whether they were Tibetan, Han or Uyghur, one-third became Christians. . . . What he enjoyed most was the opportunity to witness to hitch-hikers. After 28 years, those who accepted the gospel from this traveling pulpit kept meeting in secret, even in the most adverse situations, scattered all over the vast plain of Xinjiang.[10]

The end of an era

The original Northwest Spiritual Band missionaries continued to impact Xinjiang until July 2017, when Li Daosheng, the last remaining member of the Band, died at the age of 94. Li, a native of Liaoning Province, had made his way to Xinjiang in 1946 in one of the first teams sent by the Band. During more than seven decades of faithful service—three of which were spent in prison—Li led countless people to faith in Jesus, and he founded the Qiyuan Lake Church in Turpan.

About 500 people attended Li's funeral, and Christians from across Xinjiang and other parts of China offered their condolences. A fellow pastor gave this tribute to his fallen colleague:

> It has been 71 years since the Northwest Spiritual Band started the Back to Jerusalem movement in 1946. Li Daosheng said, "I

only pray to be the Lord's witness while I'm alive." The prayer he repeated the most while he was in a prison labor camp for three decades was this: "Lord, don't let me die in poverty or sufferings. Let me experience You by death." . . .

Having accepted the vision of preaching the gospel back to Jerusalem at 21, Li went to Xinjiang and planted churches in Turpan. He dedicated his life to the Lord, engaging in evangelism for almost seven decades. He had no children, but many Chinese pastors and Christians honored him.[11]

Although the last of the original Northwest Spiritual Band pioneers had gone to his eternal home, the effect of their work has been great. Hundreds of thousands of Christians in Xinjiang today are directly or indirectly linked to the ministry of these courageous early missionaries.

The funeral of Li Daosheng in 2017

Simon Zhao

Simon Zhao Haizhen was in his early 30s when he was appointed the leader of preaching and evangelism in the Northwest Spiritual Band. Born in 1918, Zhao grew up in Liaoning Province in northeast China. His father died when he was a young boy, and his mother was forced to raise the children alone. She was a beautiful woman, and on several occasions the village leader came to their home and tried to lure her to sleep with him. The man bought her expensive gifts but grew frustrated as she repeatedly repulsed his advances. Finally tired of her resistance, he raped her.

Many years later, Simon Zhao met God, and he found that he no longer hated or sought revenge on the man who had violated his mother. His goals in life changed, and now all he wanted to do was preach the gospel and glorify God. During a prayer meeting, the Holy Spirit first gave Simon a vision as he prayed over a map of China. The Lord focused his thoughts on Xinjiang, so he placed his hands over that part of the map and prayed with great fervency.

Wen Muling and Simon Zhao

Later, Simon met other Christians who had received the same call from God to take the gospel to Xinjiang and the regions beyond. Among them was a young woman named Wen Muling, who later became his wife. She was a fourth generation descendent of a Qing Dynasty imperial officer.

Simon Zhao led the second team of six Northwest Spiritual Band workers to Xinjiang in 1949. They traveled much of the way on foot, though in some remote areas they rode horses or camels. On the way they won many soldiers to faith in Jesus Christ, for it was a troubled time in China's history with widespread upheaval.

Eager to plant the gospel in virgin soil, in the winter of 1950 Zhao and five co-workers moved to Hotan, a remote oasis town in the far south of Xinjiang. Just two weeks after they arrived, however, the authorities ordered them to leave. They were forced to move west to Kashgar, where they arrived in the midst of a chaotic situation. Within a few days Zhao was arrested and placed in prison. His pocket Bible was confiscated, and three long decades passed before he saw another Bible.

Every member of the Northwest Spiritual Band was imprisoned and given extremely harsh sentences, and only Simon Zhao came out alive. His wife, Wen Muling, was pregnant with their first child at the time of the arrest, but she suffered a miscarriage. In 1959 she died in the women's prison, but cruelly, Simon wasn't informed about her death until 14 years later in 1973.

During the first few weeks and months in the prison labor camp, the guards tried to make Simon renounce his faith, but when that failed, they ordered him to stop praying and beat him every time they found him doing so. He never stopped praying but learned to do so in secret when nobody was watching.

After a while, the prison guards thought he must have changed because they never saw him praying, so they ordered Zhao to write an article for the prison newspaper praising the transformative power of the Communist system. When they saw what he had written, the guards flew into a rage. His article consisted of a short poem about the beauty of Jesus and a sketch of the cross.

The prison authorities tortured Simon mercilessly, slamming a heavy wooden bench on his back and kicking him all over his body. His sentence was extended for many more years, and he was sent to work in a coal mine where most prisoners died within a few months because of the filthy conditions and back-breaking work. He was required to meet a daily quota of several tons of coal—an impossible task for such a small and frail man. Not only did he have to mine the coal; he also had to carry it out in a basket tied to his back.

Year after year, the prisoners were forced to work 14 hours a day, seven days a week. The food was meager and rancid. In the summer there was sweltering heat, and the winter temperatures plummeted to well below freezing. Hundreds of prisoners, most of them physically stronger than Simon, came to the mine only to perish within a few months. Many times, "he was so exhausted that he could only crawl on the ground with his load. His body deteriorated, yet his mind remained clear."[1]

For years Simon discreetly witnessed to many of his fellow prisoners, and some believed. There were a few other Christians in the labor camp with him, but the authorities placed them in separate cells and work units, allowing Simon only fleeting contact with them.

Apart from the faithful presence of his Lord, who had promised never to leave or forsake him, Simon felt completely alone. For all the years he remained in confinement, he was not allowed to receive any visitors. Back in his home province his relatives didn't know whether he was dead or alive, and as the years of silence stretched into decades, few people thought about or prayed for him.

Simon Zhao later recalled that, during those harsh years, he would periodically look up at the stars and remember the vision

God had given him and his co-workers to take the gospel all the way back to Jerusalem. He often prayed, "Lord, I will never be able to go back to Jerusalem, but I pray you will raise up a new generation of Chinese believers to fulfill the vision."[2]

After many years of suffering in the coal mine, Simon was almost dead, so the prison authorities transferred him to a chemical factory in another part of Xinjiang. This new job was even worse, for he was exposed every day to toxic gases and poisonous chemicals. Every evening after work he was required to report to the local prison, where the beatings continued.

Despite the brutal treatment meted out to Zhao, God had not forgotten His servant. On one occasion in the midst of a severe winter storm, the guards refused to let Simon stay in the heated cell block, stripped him to his underwear, and forced him to stand outside in the snow. As they pushed him out the door they mockingly said, "You believe in your God, so why don't you pray to Him and ask Him to keep you warm!"[3]

For the first few minutes the cold wind tore into his flesh like a razor. Simon cried out to the Lord for mercy—and something amazing happened. He felt a tremendous warmth, so much so that he soon had sweat dripping from his body as if he was relaxing in a sauna! The snow around his feet began to melt from the warmth emanating from his body, and he called out to his cellmates. When they looked out the window, they could scarcely believe their eyes. Steam was rising from his body![4]

Yet such dramatic miracles were uncommon, and for most of the time Simon suffered terribly. The Uyghur prisoners were especially cruel to Simon because he was a hated Chinese "pig-eater." He later described the way the Uyghurs beat him as "the same way they surround and pounce on a goat just before they kill it."

On one occasion, Simon was beaten and kicked so severely that his skull was fractured, and he fell to the ground. While unconscious, he had a vision in which the Lord spoke lovingly to him: "My child, I am with you. I shall never leave you or forsake you." When he regained consciousness, he touched his head where his skull had been smashed and discovered that the wound had been miraculously healed.

Simon Zhao was beaten for most of the 31 years he spent in prison. It was only during the last several years—when he was an elderly man in his sixties—that he wasn't subjected to physical torture. During those long years behind bars, he wrote this poem:

> I want to experience the same pain and suffering of Jesus on
>   the cross
>   The spear in His side, the pain in His heart
> I'd rather feel the pain of shackles on my feet
>   Than ride through Egypt in Pharaoh's chariot.

One day in 1981, the prison superintendent ordered Simon to come to the main office where the official announced: "The government of the People's Republic of China has decided to have mercy on you and show you lenience for the crimes you have committed against our nation. I have been authorized to release you. You are free to go."[5]

The man of God shuffled back to his cell dazed and numb. He had never expected this day would come.

When Simon was first arrested in 1950, he had been in the prime of his life, an energetic man in his early thirties, and his beautiful young wife was expecting their first child. God had called them to take the gospel back to Jerusalem, and life was rewarding and exciting. Thirty-one years later, he had a long, white beard, and his wife and baby had died decades earlier.

Zhao walked out of the prison gates into a completely different China from the one he had known. He had missed all but the first few months of Mao Zedong's reign, including his death in 1976. He had missed the insanity of the Cultural Revolution from

1966 to 1976, when millions of people were killed by fanatical Red Guards. His body was damaged from decades of torture and back-breaking work, and his face was marked with deep lines from more than three decades in the lion's den.

Nobody was waiting for Simon Zhao outside the prison. Everyone he knew had either died or had long forgotten about him. He had nowhere to go, and nobody to see. Penniless, he couldn't even afford to catch a bus into the city. The prison labor camp had been a part of his life for so long that he decided to construct a makeshift hut just outside the entrance. As he lay in his damp, cold hut, his mind sometimes wandered back to

Simon Zhao after his release from prison

his life as a young man and the call God had once given him. He had tried to obey God, but it hadn't worked out. He hoped he would soon die, for he knew that heaven was a much better place where the pain he had experienced for so long would be removed forever.

After some time, Christians in Kashgar learned about Simon Zhao and his testimony. With deep respect they brought the old saint food and a Bible, and they helped him however they could. News spread from church to church in Xinjiang, and soon stories about Simon Zhao were carried back to other parts of China.

A new ministry

After news spread, God used Zhao to renew the mission vision of the Chinese Church. A Henan house church leader traveled to Xinjiang to meet him and persuaded him to make the long journey to Henan to share the Back to Jerusalem vision with a new generation of Christians. One senior house church leader told the author about the impact Simon Zhao had on his churches:

> When he walked out of the prison in 1981, Simon Zhao had missed an entire generation of history and was unknown to the Church in China. For years after his release he lived a reclusive life, but finally news of his existence reached our ears. We were keen for him to make the long journey from Kashgar to Henan, as we knew this saint had a message that would revolutionize our vision. This proved to be true, and he had a tremendous impact on every church he visited.
>
> I remember Simon Zhao as a most respectful older brother. He was a great soldier for Christ, one of the greatest Chinese Christians. He was a tremendous Bible teacher, able to wisely handle the Word of God. The Holy Spirit always spoke to people's hearts through his ministry. Until that time, the Back to Jerusalem vision had not been a major priority in our churches. We were busy winning people to Christ, but the Lord began to

show us that we also needed to lift up our eyes and expand our vision beyond China's borders, especially to the countries bound by Islam, Buddhism, and Hinduism.

Our church members loved Simon like their own father and were very close to him. He had been deprived of fellowship with other believers for decades, but now the Lord gave him spiritual sons and daughters who deeply respected him. Sisters in the church cooked for him, washed his clothes, and helped him however they could. They treated him as they would an angel of God.

At that time we published a magazine to encourage house church believers. Simon Zhao refused to write any articles or share his testimony, saying, "I don't want to have any attention focused on me."

His ministry was very powerful, and a fire was lit in the heart of everyone who heard him. Many tears flowed, and thousands of believers were touched and received a call to missionary work.

Simon Zhao encouraging believers in 1988

Even Simon's unique physical appearance added to his ministry. He looked like an ancient sage, with a long white beard and white hair.

For many house church leaders, the Back to Jerusalem vision became clear because of Simon Zhao's presence, and God gave us a heavy burden to see this vision fulfilled.[6]

Brother Yun, in his best-selling autobiography *The Heavenly Man*, recalled the day in 1995 when he met Simon Zhao in a house church meeting that he was leading in central China:

With tears in my eyes I sang a song I had learned from an old book about the Back to Jerusalem Movement. . . . While I was singing, I noticed an old man in the congregation who was visibly moved. He was weeping and could hardly contain himself. I had no idea who he was, and thought my preaching must have been really powerful to cause such a response! The old brother, crowned with white hair and a white beard, slowly walked to the front of the room and asked to speak. A respectful hush fell over the audience.

He said, "I am Simon Zhao, a servant of the Lord. Forty-eight years ago my co-workers and I wrote the words you just sang. All of my co-workers were martyred for the Name of Jesus. . . . I am the only one who survived."

We all wept loudly. We felt like we were standing on holy ground in the presence of the Lord. . . . That meeting was a pivotal point in my life. I felt like God passed a flaming baton from this dear old man of God to the house churches, giving us the responsibility to complete the vision.[7]

Simon Zhao finally went to be with the Lord on December 7, 2001, among Christians who loved him. He was 83 years old. He had learned that the Lord always finishes what He starts and is faithful to fulfill all of His promises.

1950s and 1960s

After the Communist government gained control over all of Xinjiang in 1949, hundreds of thousands of troops were sent to the remote region to secure it from external forces and to crush any dissent from the Muslim population. After military command was established, an influx of Han immigrants from other parts of China entered the region. Between 1950 and 1978, an estimated three million Han civilians were either forcibly relocated to Xinjiang by the national government or came willingly, lured by the promise of cheap land and economic prosperity.

Some of the Chinese families who volunteered to migrate to Xinjiang were Christians who saw the move as an opportunity to

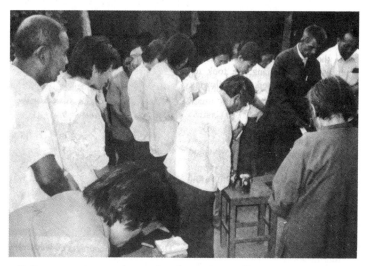

Believers praying at a house church meeting in Aksu, western Xinjiang

spread the gospel among remote, unreached peoples who were perishing without a witness. All of those families formed the basis for millions of later Han arrivals so that by the start of the twenty-first century, the Uyghurs were on the cusp of being a minority population in their homeland. Mark Chuanhang Shan, a Han Christian from Xinjiang, notes,

> Since the Han formed the dominant unit of society, politics, and the economy in Xinjiang, the growth and prosperity of the Han Chinese Church directly provided a favorable platform and stable support among Turkic nationalities. This blueprint for evangelism in Xinjiang was developed by the churches, shaping the future Christian history of Xinjiang.[1]

Although northwest China was now under the firm control of Mao Zedong's forces and news of Christianity dried up, occasional glimpses of spiritual life emerged from the region. One outstanding testimony was that of a young Uyghur man named Asimon who had grown up in the Swedish orphanage at Yarkant.

Asimon was a teenager when the revolution swept through southern Xinjiang, and he and other boys his age were taken and trained to be soldiers. Asimon was assigned to Kashgar where he remained a dedicated follower of Christ. He witnessed to his people even though he was enlisted in the Communist army. It's not known what happened to Asimon, but his brave witness was proof that the flame of the gospel was still flickering in Xinjiang.

Indigenous Chinese missions

By 1954, despite severe persecution occurring throughout China, a group of young Han Christians from the Shanghai-based Christian Workers' Mission came to Xinjiang intending to spread the fragrance of Christ throughout the region. That year, one of the young evangelists reported that "the church in Hami continues to grow and now has many members."[2]

The same preacher wrote from Aksu, 400 miles (650 km) west of Urumqi, "By God's grace the church is growing! There is no hindrance to the growth of the gospel, and we can continue our work. We have registered with the authorities."[3]

In northern Xinjiang, a key Christian leader was Paul Li who was associated with the Christian Native Evangelistic Crusade which had earlier sent postmaster Li Kaihuan and his wife to Xinjiang. For nearly a decade, Paul Li and his wife led an effective ministry. The following was said of them:

> Before the Lis were arrested in the mid-1950s, they managed to run a small theological institute. Many of the students were later arrested by the government and sent as internal exiles to remote parts of the province as factory laborers. Some managed to establish Christian communities at places where there had been no Christian presence, and eventually developed these communities into church fellowships, including at Altai on the Russian border. Paul Li spent years in jail, like most of his colleagues, and later died in the 1960s.[4]

Despite the harsh environment of militant atheism, most of the arrested Christians in Xinjiang continued to discreetly worship and serve God. One lady, a student of Paul Li, was ordered to work in a local shoe factory in Altai where she secretly spread the gospel among her fellow workers. Decades later, when conditions for Christians finally improved, she became a leader in the Altai Three-Self Church.

Another indigenous group that commenced work in Xinjiang just prior to the Communist takeover was the Chinese Christian Mission, which was based in Shanghai. They first sent workers to Xinjiang in 1947, and by the early 1950s they had about 100 missionaries scattered throughout China. The Chinese Christian Mission was unique in that they specifically focused on ministry to the Uyghurs. Alas, their influence in Xinjiang was fleeting, and they were shut down by the Communists in the early 1950s.

Before a curtain of silence descended on Xinjiang for many years, veteran British missionary Leslie Lyall summarized the state of churches in the region in this report from July 1954:

> At Hami, the son of a Chinese father and a Russian mother is eagerly engaged in witnessing to Muslims with a converted Muslim companion. The church in this center is still very active and, besides the Sunday services and Sunday school, holds a nightly cottage meeting, a weekly prayer meeting and a woman's meeting. Evangelistic work for outsiders is very difficult.
>
> At Urumqi, the Xinjiang capital, there were 19 baptisms at Easter, largely the result of meetings conducted last year by a Chinese evangelist, which were marked by deep conviction of sin and great interest in the gospel. . . .
>
> Several churches in the district which had been in a low spiritual condition have been revived, and attendance at worship has greatly increased. The witness to both Muslims and tribespeople has been continuing, and a Muslim priest and his wife have professed conversion.
>
> In southern Xinjiang, a new church was planted in 1950 composed of Chinese, Russian and Uyghur believers. The leader was born in Russia and grew up in Xinjiang, speaking all three languages. To the north, on the Russian border, one of the Chinese missionaries, supporting himself by making sweetmeats, has been ministering to a congregation of about 30 Russian and Chinese Christians. They received a consignment of Russian Bibles, New Testaments and other literature with great joy.[5]

After years of increasing persecution, all visible Christian work was gradually closed down in Xinjiang, and by the mid-1950s, all news of Christianity in the region came to an abrupt halt. A long period of silence ensued when all external props were removed from the churches, and the body of Christ was left to trust in Christ alone as they battled the forces of darkness.

In the arms of Jesus

Christians in Xinjiang suffered terribly when the full force of hatred was unleashed on them. One church leader who protested against the Communists' indiscriminate killing was promptly arrested, dragged into court, and accused of numerous "crimes against the people." The judges ordered the onlookers to march past the pastor and to

> hit him with a club until he was beaten to death. But the people refused, declaring, "He's a good man." Changing tactics, the judges promised that if he renounced Jesus he would be set free. "Which do you choose-Jesus Christ or Communism?" they demanded.
> "Jesus! Jesus! Jesus!" he shouted back.[6]

The pastor was dragged down to the river bank for execution. Along the way he sang "Jesus Loves Me" and the 23rd Psalm as a crowd of onlookers followed. When they arrived at the river, he asked permission to pray. He knelt down and prepared his spirit to meet the Lord Jesus Christ. Then as he stood up, he was shot in the back. Instead of "falling on his face to grovel in the dust as victims usually do, he fell backward, as if he was falling into the arms of Jesus. The entire community was reportedly stirred by his testimony."[7]

Unexpectedly in 1967—just months after the launch of the Cultural Revolution when all churches, mosques, and other places of worship were forced to close—the former Swedish missionaries were astonished to receive a string of letters from a Uyghur believer who used the pseudonym Rose. The missionaries recognized her as one of the girls they had raised in the Yarkant orphanage 30 years earlier.

Rose had worked as a midwife for years, using skills she learned from the missionary nurses, but in 1940 she had been arrested and imprisoned because of her faith. Because she was placed in solitary confinement and deprived of sunlight for months, she nearly became blind but gradually recovered after her release.

Rose shared how she had prayed for two years about whether she should write to the missionaries in Sweden and was aware of the potential risk to her life. In the end, she decided her old friends needed to be updated. Her letters, which continued into the early 1980s, were a healing balm to the Swedes who had poured their lives out on the sandy wastes of Xinjiang. The stories she told were the first evidence in decades that their labors had not been in vain.

One of the many Christians called to endure intense persecution in the 1950s and 1960s was Yu Jiade who was an art student when his family was arrested in 1958 during Mao's "anti-rightist movement." Yu was dispatched to Xinjiang where he was forced to attend brainwashing sessions to uproot his religious thinking. Yu stubbornly held on to his faith, and later he continued to glorify God through his gift as an artist. He ultimately became China's most loved Christian artist, and his best-known works are traditional Chinese watercolor paintings of Bible scenes in which Jesus is invariably depicted as an Asian.

The Uyghur Bible

The history of the Uyghur Bible is complicated and difficult for people outside the region to comprehend. Although the first Scripture in the Uyghur language was translated by Johannes Avetaranian in the 1890s, the New Testament was not completed until 1914. The script used for those translations fell into disuse and was obsolete, unable to be read by later generations of Uyghur people.

A new project to translate the entire Bible into Uyghur was duly completed in 1950. Missionaries John Andersson and

Anders Marthinson frequently sent parcels of the new Uyghur Bible and other books from India to Kashgar, hoping that some of the surviving Christians there would benefit from them. In 1950, a "thank offering" was unexpectedly received from the believers in Kashgar which brought great joy to those who had labored so long in the area, for it was confirmation that the body of Christ had survived.

Not long after the publication of the 1950 Bible, however, the translation proved increasingly problematic for readers because the linguists who had completed the work in India had been out of touch with the rapid changes that had taken place in Xinjiang, including a reformation of the Uyghur Arabic alphabet. As a result, later translators found the 1950 Uyghur Bible "not usable

The cover of the current Uyghur Bible, which was revised in 2005

or even suitable as a basis for revision."[8] One source decades later explained:

> The entire Bible was translated in 1950, but this version used exalted religious language modeled on the Qur'an, which was too flowery for the average Uyghur to understand. More recent translations of Bible books have wrestled with the need to respect the holiness of God's Word while communicating to the educational level of the average Uyghur.[9]

Decades passed before yet another translation of the Uyghur Bible was launched in the late 1980s. Finally in 2005, the New Testament with Genesis and Exodus was published in modern Uyghur in the script most commonly used by Uyghurs in Xinjiang today. The entire Bible was completed in 2018 and was available to be downloaded online until the Communist authorities blocked access to the website.[10]

More than 120 years after Johannes Avetaranian first translated the Scriptures into Uyghur, the number of Uyghur Bibles distributed in Xinjiang remains extremely low because of the severe risks involved with printing and distributing what the Chinese government considers an illegal publication.

1970s and 1980s

The camel herder's daughter

Although the number of Christians in Xinjiang was relatively low at the time of the Cultural Revolution from 1966 to 1976, the believers suffered terribly for their faith, and many went to an early grave as martyrs for God. One testimony of victory through adversity told of God's sustaining hand during those dark years.

In 1955, a baby girl was born in a remote part of Xinjiang, right as the political situation was changing for the worse. Her mother, who had gone to the region as a missionary after graduating from seminary, died when her daughter was just two. The girl was raised by her father, a poor camel herdsman, and only when she was 14 did she discover that her father was actually highly educated, could speak several languages fluently, and had

A house church gathering in Xinjiang

been exiled to Xinjiang because of his Christian faith. He deeply loved his precious daughter and taught her mathematics, music, English, and the Bible.

When the fanatical Red Guards swept through their area, they destroyed all of the camel herder's books except a copy of the English Bible because they didn't know what it was. He was arrested and sent to a prison labor camp, and the young girl was forced to struggle on alone with her father's final exhortation to endure suffering like a good soldier of Christ ringing in her ears.

With only the English Bible to keep her company for the next three years, the teenage girl learned to trust God, and she entered into her own rich relationship with Jesus Christ. Only then did she understand that her parents had carried their crosses as faithful servants of God, which made her heart swell in love and respect for them.

Later she entered university where despite the risks, she witnessed to her classmates, telling them that atheism is a bankrupt philosophy and that God is real and can be personally known. Most of the students treated her with contempt, but some visited her discreetly to ask further questions. One girl became her close friend and sister in Christ.

In the early 1970s, with the Cultural Revolution still raging, the camel herder's daughter was publicly invited to join the Communist Youth League—a rare opportunity for someone from a "counter-revolutionary" family. She knew there was no way she could reconcile her faith with the atheistic organization, however, so she declined the invitation, simply stating, "I am a Christian." The meeting was thrown into chaos by her confession, and the leader was enraged with fury. She recalled the events of that day as follows:

> In the din of the meeting I closed my eyes to pray: "Heavenly Father, from the time I was small you have protected me. If this

is ordained by You to test my heart, give me grace and allow me to stand up in my weakness."

When I opened my tear-filled eyes, the entire hall was as still as a mouse. Facing the whole school of more than 200 students and teachers, I poured out my sin and told of my insignificance before the cross. I told them of Christ's suffering for the world and that Christians don't harm society—they only do good to others and help them to know eternal life. . . .

When I finished what I had to say, the leader of the Workers' Propaganda team looked as if he had suddenly awakened from a dream. He immediately upbraided me for using the university as a platform from which to spread my "poison." He wanted everyone to criticize me, but they had already felt the goodness of God. . . .

At once I became the school's "person in the news." Wherever I went people pointed at me behind my back. Nevertheless, many students were sympathetic and . . . came to me privately to ask questions about salvation. . . .

Quickly I gathered around me a small group of seekers, which soon grew to include more than 30 people. We divided into two groups and assembled on Sundays and holidays. Right up to our graduation we were never discovered by the school authorities. The brothers and sisters grew in spiritual discipline, and by the time they graduated their faith was mature and they were able to stand as Christians.

At graduation we were all assigned to different places. From Altai to Karakoram, every city received the soles of our feet. I was sent to a country school to teach English, but I often requested leave to go and visit my friends who were scattered in every place.[1]

God provides both stones and fish

Throughout the 1950s, Sister Gan Huiping and her husband were used greatly by God to strengthen churches in northern Xinjiang, until the authorities imprisoned them as counter-revolutionaries.

Their son was forced to grow up alone in the family home. He survived and even managed to attend school, helped by occasional cash-filled envelopes that were anonymously dropped through a hole in the gate. He later learned that the money was given by a caring Christian.

When he was 14, Gan's parents were suddenly released from prison and returned home. They had aged markedly, and their bodies bore the marks of years of torture and stress. Compelled by the love of Christ in their hearts and despite the great personal risk, they continued to preach the gospel and were soon rearrested.

Later, when he graduated from high school, Gan was further punished for his parents' faith by being sent to a remote border area to work on a manual labor team. He recalls, "The village that 12 of us 'bad' children were assigned to was ringed by mountains. There were 70 Uyghur households in the village, and they discriminated terribly against us. The leader worked us so hard that we could hardly breathe."[2]

The group of teenage boys was ordered to work on a flood control project, which required them to gather four cubic meters (141 cubic feet) of stones each week. Once a week a supervisor dropped by to inspect their work, and if they had failed to collect the required amount of stones, no food would be issued the following week.

In their malnourished state the boys searched along the river banks. But soon all the large and medium sized stones had been used, and they had barely managed to gather one cubic meter. The exhausted boys reached a low point, and in agony of mind they wept bitterly, crying out for their mothers' warm embrace. In the depths of depression, Gan cried out, "Oh God, save us!" The other boys stared at him in amazement, for all religious expressions had been banished from China. The 17-year-old Gan then closed his eyes and prayed:

My loving Heavenly Father, I pray to You in the midst of despair. Please draw near to me now. In this world there is nothing left that would make me reluctant to leave; I only ask that You comfort me in the time that I have remaining. . . .

God, what sin have we committed to receive this kind of punishment? My parents had no sooner begun to spread the gospel than they were persecuted. In my whole life there has not been a day that I recall with pleasure. No good opportunities have ever come my way; I have even given up hope of living with my parents. I just ask that I'll be able to find stones and carry on living.[3]

After completing his prayer, Gan was so hungry and exhausted that he fell asleep on the ground. That night he had a vivid dream in which a man asked him, "Have you looked in the river?" The boys had carefully searched along the riverbanks, but it now dawned on Gan that they should also search in the water. He awoke and was so struck by the reality of the dream that he immediately gathered the other boys and told them what he had experienced.

Under the bright moonlight, the boys followed Gan down to the river, and he waded in until the current was up to his waist. He stood on a large stone, and he lifted it up and carried it to the riverbank. He then stood on another stone, and another. Soon they had enough stones to meet the quota. They would soon be able to eat again!

Together, the boys raised their hands above their heads and praised the Living God Who had answered Gan's prayer. The other boys placed their trust in Jesus Christ, and they asked Gan to baptize them. They waded into the river one by one, except for a Uyghur named Mai Jianguo, who was too weak from malnourishment and collapsed on the ground.

Gan again prayed, and the Lord Jesus told him that He would provide fish for them to eat if they would just believe. Gan tore off

his trousers and cut holes in them so that fish would swim into the holes and be trapped. He then waded back into the current and dragged his trousers back and forth in the water. A long time passed without any fish being caught, and the teenagers looked on anxiously as the first rays of sunlight appeared on the horizon.

Then suddenly a small fish swam into the "trouser net." Gan triumphantly held it aloft as he brought it to the riverbank. Soon more fish were caught, and a fire was lit. The boys thanked God from the bottom of their hearts as they ate delicious grilled fish together! Mai Jianguo recovered his strength, causing Gan to comment:

> I looked at this child of a Uyghur cadre, totally happy inside. He was the first member of a minority group that I had known to receive God's grace and become a Christian. . . . I fervently hoped he would turn into an active force for the gospel and bring forth a lot of fruit among the Uyghur people.

Elderly Christian sisters at Hancheng (Shule) in 1988

As the sun continued to rise, we started to pray, and I announced in a clear voice, "This is the first worship service of the Borderlands Gospel Fellowship."

Tears flowed from my eyes and ran into the corners of my mouth. I knew this was how my parents had prayed. . . . What tomorrow will bring we cannot know, but we will be prepared for anything, right up to being imprisoned on behalf of Jesus' Name.[4]

The ice begins to thaw

The 1980s saw a dramatic shift in the religious atmosphere in Xinjiang and throughout China. With Mao having died in 1976, religious repression was relaxed, and old church buildings that had been seized by the government in the 1950s and 1960s were returned to the Christian community. In 1985, the Xinjiang Christian Church that had been founded by the postmaster Li Kaihuan in the 1940s resumed services, and hundreds of believers crammed into the meeting hall to hear the teaching of God's Word. That year, the number of Evangelical believers in Urumqi was estimated to be at least 600.[5]

A flurry of persecuted Chinese pastors and mission leaders had their sentences overturned in the early 1980s as the government admitted that they had treated people more harshly than they deserved. Men of God such as Simon Zhao, Huo Chaoran, and Chen Xiaoqing were freed after decades behind bars.

Reports emerged that told of groups of believers scattered throughout Xinjiang. In 1981, house churches were found among the officially recognized Russian minority group "in about 20 small towns along the Sino-Russian and Sino-Afghanistan border,"[6] although no Russian or Chinese Bibles were available in any of the fellowships.

In the ancient city of Kashgar, the Christian community had survived due to the ministry of faithful saints like Mecca Zhao

Chen Xiaoqing preaching in 1988

and He Enzheng, although the local authorities refused to allow any churches in the city because they feared a backlash from the Muslim leaders.

Soldiers for Christ

To the dismay of the hardline atheist leaders of the Chinese Community Party, the Spirit began to move in the hearts of many army officers stationed in Xinjiang, and there were reports of significant numbers of soldiers and their families placing their trust in Jesus. In October 1985, the *Tianfeng* (Heavenly Wind) magazine of the Three-Self Church printed a letter from a believer in Wushi County, which is a restricted military zone along the Kyrgyzstan border in western Xinjiang. The letter said,

> The Fourth Regiment is stationed here. Although we are in such a remote area, the Spirit of the Lord is as active here as elsewhere. At one time there were few Christians in this area, but since we

began to meet together in January 1983 our numbers have risen to 40. Last year six people were baptized, and four more have been baptized so far this year. . . .

Although we are a small church with few members, we are quietly getting on with the work, expressing our love, and shining the light of the Lord. The work of teaching hymn-singing has been undertaken by 80-year-old Chen Tongsheng and 18-year-old Jiang Xiang, who has recently been baptized. . . . May the grace of the Lord be with the members of the Fourth Regiment Church, both now and in the future.[7]

British missionary Leslie Lyall, meanwhile, blessed Christian readers around the world by publishing updates on the Church in China in the early and mid-1980s. Lyall, who was now in his 80s, was expelled from China in 1951 but maintained contact with a number of Chinese believers and authored several books about the Church in China. In many cases, his reports provided the first details on the state of Christianity in three decades. In 1985, Lyall wrote this of Christianity in Xinjiang:

Thousands have believed in Xinjiang; and in Urumqi, the provincial capital, several hundred believers meet for worship in seven or eight households. In another town it is reported that 120,000 new converts meet in 330 separate venues, many having been converted through the radio.[8]

Registered Three-Self Churches emerged across most of Xinjiang in the 1980s, although they generally weren't permitted in densely populated Muslim areas because the government did not want to antagonize the Uyghurs. Tony Lambert visited a Three-Self Church in Urumqi in 1984 and filed this report:

The church met in a small courtyard down a back-alley. More than 120 Christians squeezed into a hot room, while others sat on stools listening to a loudspeaker in the narrow courtyard outside. . . .

The pastor, a tall, stately man, proceeded to administer the Communion. He admonished those present to do everything decently and in order and, in particular, not to pray simultaneously. His advice was ignored, because as soon as the Communion service began many Christians began to weep and confess their sins together. The atmosphere was charged with strong emotion, like an old-fashioned revival meeting.[9]

Interestingly, two decades later when Lambert visited the same church in Urumqi, he discovered, "3,000 people meeting on Sundays in four halls on four different stories of a large, modern church building."[10]

As the Church in Xinjiang emerged from the shadows into the light during the 1980s, many congregations consisted of a small number of believers with few Bibles, often led by members who were chosen because of their ability to read. In 1987, a young woman wrote from a typical rural house church:

I have been a Christian for three years. I preach in our little village where we have some 30 believers, about a third of the village. Some have believed through healing. The other villagers mostly worship idols and spirits. I know little of the Bible and have several questions. When I became a Christian an itinerant preacher baptized us. Now I see that several things he taught do not conform to Scripture. Does this mean our baptism is invalid? Also, I want to serve God fully, but I'm afraid I won't be able to resist the natural urge to marry. Please pray for me.[11]

A paradigm shift

As the Church in Xinjiang expanded throughout the 1980s, it became clear that almost all of the growth had taken place among the Han Chinese. Muslim groups such as the Uyghur, Kazak, Hui, and Kirgiz were still almost completely untouched by the gospel, as were other minority groups in the region.

To help rebalance the situation, Western Christians began to return to Xinjiang for the first time in more than 40 years. They were not allowed to openly serve as missionaries, but a steady trickle came as students, teachers, and researchers and by other means, but all were focused on sharing Christ with people by whatever means possible.

The major paradigm shift that came to Christianity in Xinjiang in the 1980s, however, was not the return of foreign Christians. During the decade a tremendously powerful, heaven sent revival swept through house churches in other parts of China, saving millions of people into the kingdom of God. As these transformed believers cried out to the Lord and asked Him to use their lives, a new focus for the unreached peoples of China came upon many house church believers, and the spiritual needs of Xinjiang were discussed and prayed for by Christians in faraway provinces.

The prominent house church leader Peter Xu Yongze, who founded the large Born-Again movement, told the author how his network's work in Xinjiang blossomed during the 1980s:

Muslims on their faces in prayer to Allah in Kashgar, late 1980s
IMB

Our first workers were sent to Xinjiang in 1986. Two sisters arrived first, paving the way for many more to follow, and every year additional missionaries were sent to this most remote part of China. A strong church emerged in Shihezi City, west of Urumqi. We also experienced encouraging growth in Aksu and Kashgar.

Our workers were determined to not only preach the gospel among the Han, but they also shared Jesus Christ with the Kirgiz, Kazak, and many other Muslim groups. In one location near the Kazakhstan border we were able to plant more than 50 house churches, which were attended by a mixture of Han, Hui, Uyghurs, and other minorities. Many former Muslims who believed kept their identity secret because they were afraid of what their families would do to them if they discovered they were Christians.[12]

Some Han Christians from other parts of China were so eager to take the gospel to Xinjiang that they didn't wait for the house churches to develop sending strategies. In the early 1980s, two young men were convinced that God had called them to the northwest, but in those days, it wasn't possible to move across China without proper paperwork and a good reason.

After thinking and praying about how God might send them to Xinjiang, the youngsters hatched a plan which some might consider hopelessly misguided, while others may see it as courageous—perhaps even akin to the Moravian missionaries of the 18th century who sold themselves into slavery so that they could reach slaves for Christ. The two young Chinese men knew there was one sure way to be sent to Xinjiang, so according to one report,

> They purposely committed a crime. They took a cadre leader's radio and walked down the street with it. They were immediately arrested and were sent to the frontier, where there would be no prayer cards or furloughs. People in their village have a

24-hour-a-day prayer chain for those two men. The church made a covenant with the Lord to pray for the two men around the clock until the Lord says, "You can stop now; I've taken them home." They are, the last we heard, still praying.[13]

1990s

Death and destruction

The early 1990s saw an increase in ethnic tension between the Chinese authorities and Muslims in Xinjiang because many Uyghurs felt threatened by the constant influx of hundreds of thousands of Han into the region. Violent protests broke out, and 30 people were left dead or seriously wounded after a bus explosion in Urumqi on February 5, 1991.

The following year, more than 1,000 Uyghurs protested at the Lopnur nuclear weapon testing facility. The People's Liberation Army was mobilized, and they opened fire on the protestors, and many were killed.

For the next six years trouble continued to simmer until another major explosion of violence took place at Ili in February 1997. A riot broke out with mobs of Uyghurs shouting, "Drive out the Han people and establish an Islamic kingdom!" More than 200 people were killed by both the rioters and in the subsequent crackdown by the authorities. For the rest of the decade, numerous buses and police stations were bombed by Islamic insurgents, and a gas pipeline was blown up. China responded with overwhelming force. Local reports say that in 1997 alone, 57,000 Uyghurs were arrested and 1,700 executed for "separatist activities" in Xinjiang.

In a futile effort to control the situation, the Chinese government implemented a widespread program in the 1990s designed to impose "proper Islam" on the Uyghurs. Eight state-approved Islamic schools were established in the region to train thousands of students in a blend of Communist ideology and Islam. Local Muslims frequently mocked the graduates of those schools by calling them "Red Imams."

Instead of controlling the spread of religion, the government's strategy appears to have caused many Uyghurs to take Islam more seriously and to push the practice of it underground. As a result, in later decades a more virulent form of militant Islam surfaced in Xinjiang that poses far greater challenges to Chinese rule than if they had left the Muslims alone.

An elderly sister exhorting believers in Xinjiang
RCMI

Despite the tensions, the Church in Xinjiang extended its growth during the decade. An official estimate of 150,000 adult, baptized members of Three-Self Churches in the region in 1991 were distributed in 27 different cities and counties. One report notes, "These local, mostly Han Chinese Christians, form an encouraging potential for bridging the barriers which keep the Uyghur people from the saving knowledge of Jesus Christ."[1]

Undercover missionaries

Although no foreign missionary had been officially allowed in Xinjiang since the last Swedes were escorted to the border in 1938, the 1990s saw a marked increase in the number of foreign Christians living in the region. One of them, a bold American named Patrick Klein, recalled his experiences when he first reached Xinjiang and commenced work as a teacher among the Uyghurs:

> Right from the beginning when I started working with these people, I felt a spirit of fear come over me. This fear gripped me for three weeks. During that time, I did not share the gospel at all. I knew this was not God's will, for the spirit of fear was sent from the enemy to paralyze me, but I could not seem to shake the dread that continued to hang over me.
>
> Finally, I decided I'd had enough. I told the Lord that I was going to pass out one Gospel of Mark in the Uyghur language, and the consequences were up to Him. I was very excited to go out—nervous, but excited! As I walked around the city, I kept praying and praying. I knew I had to pass out that one booklet if I was ever going to get victory over the fear.
>
> After several hours, I went into a shopping center. As I walked around, I saw a young Uyghur lady, obviously from a Muslim background. . . . I bought something from the stand where she was working, and I gave her the Gospel booklet. She seemed

genuinely excited to receive it, and I was so thankful for a victory over fear.

The next day I prayed and thought I would give away two booklets this time. Again I headed out, walked around the city, and prayed for the Lord's guidance. I had to take a bus to get where I wanted to go. When I got off the bus, right away I saw a Muslim lady and her son. I approached them, but even before I could offer her the booklet, the lady cried out, "Isa, Isa!" (this is how the Uyghurs say "Jesus"). She knew what the booklet was, even before I gave it to her, and she was thrilled to get it. Later, I gave the second book to a Muslim man. Again, I was excited to have victory over fear.

On the third day I decided to go back out again, and this time I would give away three booklets. As I did this, I found that I was met with such a warm reception to the gospel. People were eager to receive the booklets and to hear the truth of Jesus Christ. I kept doing this, and on the fifth day I finally felt the oppression break off me. I was then free to share the gospel and to minister to my students.[2]

Although his time teaching in Xinjiang came to an end, Klein never lost his burden to reach the Uyghurs. He later led a team of 17 Christians who flew to Pakistan before crossing the border into Xinjiang with 10,000 Gospels of Mark in the Uyghur language and thousands of other booklets. His experience, like that of many other foreign Christians in Xinjiang, required a victory over fear before he was able to enter into the ministry God had called him to do.

Unexpected visitors from the north

In the 1990s, many Christians around the world gained a fresh burden to pray for the salvation of the Uyghur people. The small number of Uyghurs who had turned to Christ invariably suffered severe persecution, and they were often rejected by their families and expelled from their communities. It was virtually impossible for a Uyghur Christian to get a job, so a request went out for foreign Christian businessmen to invest in Xinjiang by opening factories, orchards, or other ventures that could employ local believers.

A new and unexpected avenue of blessing came when many Uyghurs and Kazaks across the border in Kazakhstan turned to Christ in the 1990s. One report remarks,

> In the spring of 1994 an American couple came to start a business venture in a small town outside Almaty, the capital of Kazakhstan. Their first challenge was to learn the language and culture. To their great surprise, shortly after they arrived a group of 20 Uyghurs asked the American couple to baptize and disciple them. With limited language skills, the Americans baptized and discipled one of the first Uyghur churches.[3]

House church believers gladly receive Bibles in Xinjiang
VOM Canada

221

After being challenged to lift up their eyes and consider the spiritual claims of Muslims in Xinjiang, teams of local Kazak and Uyghur believers in Kazakhstan volunteered to cross the border and preach the gospel. As a result, small pockets of Turkic Christians emerged in Xinjiang. One account said,

> One Christian Uyghur woman from Kazakhstan went to visit relatives in a tiny village in Xinjiang. She shared with them the freedom she had found in Jesus and explained the way to eternal life. Leaving some Christian books and Uyghur worship tapes with them, she returned home. Months later, she received word that her brother and cousin had accepted Christ!
>
> Now that there are several Uyghur fellowships in Kazakhstan, workers are focusing on discipleship, Bible training, song-writing in the Uyghur language, and literature translation work. Several church plants in Kazakhstan and Kyrgyzstan were started by Uyghur believers in partnership with Turkish, Korean, and Western Christians. At a partnership meeting, Uyghur believers confessed their bitterness toward the Chinese and asked forgiveness in a breakthrough outpouring of the Holy Spirit.[4]

The Chinese government and Xinjiang's Islamic leaders appear to have been so focused on the threat of undercover Western missionaries that they were caught completely by surprise when the gospel entered the region from their Muslim neighbors to the north.

The Han Church advances

At the same time, bold witnessing by Chinese Christians soon attracted the attention of the authorities in Xinjiang. One story surfaced that describes how

> Han Christians who dedicated themselves to the evangelization of Xinjiang's minorities were attacked by their Muslim neighbors. Despite the persecution, several Muslims believed and

were converted. This only outraged and provoked the devout Muslims even more, resulting in them burning down the Han group's church. . . .

Some new Muslim converts to Christ experienced intense persecution, being subjected to a radical form of exorcism, where the "apostates" are tied to the ground and soapy water is poured down their throats for a period of three days in order to wash away the evil spirits. The new believers are forced to endure a week-long crash course in the Qur'an, and are ordered to turn from their faith in Christ or leave the area. To counter Christianity, local Muslim leaders launched a new program to "reclaim Muslims from the evil spirits of apostasy."[5]

Feng Jianguo, one of the founders of the China Gospel Fellowship—which boasts millions of Christians throughout China—told the author that in 1996, the Xinjiang authorities were so impressed by his church's success in reaching Uyghurs that they sent officers all the way to his home in Henan Province to meet him. Feng recalled,

> They asked, "How come your workers have been so successful in reaching so many people in Xinjiang, even Muslims? Please tell us your secrets because these Muslims will not even listen to us, but they listen to you."
>
> I could not tell these atheists anything useful for them, because our co-workers had learned the lesson that they must pray and go only in God's strength, and that all else is in vain.[6]

In 1997, a flurry of short testimonies about the advance of the gospel in Xinjiang appeared in Western mission publications indicating that the kingdom of God was spreading among Muslims in the region in ways not seen since the 1930s. Here are some of the encouraging accounts:

> A Han Christian was working one day in his field when a Muslim woman came to ask help because her husband was sick. Her husband recovered from his long illness after the Christians

prayed for him. He became a believer and shared with his friends, who also converted to Christ. Now they have joined the church and worship with their Han neighbors every week.[7]

A young Muslim man hurt his head while fighting and was taken to hospital since he was losing a lot of blood. His family was poor and could not afford the treatment, so they took him home to prepare for his funeral. Then they remembered a Christian neighbor who had once spoken about Jesus being a Savior and healer. As the neighbor prayed, the young man realized his wound had stopped bleeding. After a while he fully recovered, and he and his family became Christians.[8]

An old Muslim man was one day taken ill while visiting the mosque. He recalled hearing that Jesus was the one true God, and as he thought on this he had a vision of Jesus. After he left the mosque the man realized he had recovered.[9]

In one Muslim village in Xinjiang the Jesus film was shown. Various villagers started asking, "Who is the true God?" Later they met some Han Christians who explained the Christian faith, and the whole village turned to Christ.[10]

In another part of Xinjiang, some elderly sisters from a local church were taking care of an old Uyghur widow who lived alone. She was sufficiently touched by the loving care given to her over a long time that, with the encouragement of these Christian sisters, the widow started to attend church. Later she believed in Jesus. Hallelujah![11]

An 18-year-old Kazak had suffered terrible urinary incontinence since his youth, and no doctor had been able to help him with his bed-wetting problem. His distressed parents heard that Christians could heal by prayer, so one day they turned up at a house church and asked the believers to pray over their son, with a promise that they would offer a sheep to God and the church. The young Kazak was immediately healed of incontinence, and the youth and his parents started attending meetings in Urumqi. Through reading the Kazak Bible, they came to know Jesus.[12]

Notwithstanding the encouraging breakthroughs among Muslims, severe persecution of Christians was also evident. One especially brutal incident occurred in March 1996, when

> Five Evangelical women were arrested and detained in western Xinjiang after a raid on a house church in a predominantly Muslim region. A total of 17 church members were initially arrested, but 12 were released when the other five women accepted responsibility for the gathering. Police severely beat several of the Christians, knocking out one woman's front teeth, and poured scalding water on those who resisted orders. The five women were imprisoned.[13]

Steven—a martyr in Xinjiang

Steven was a poor, illiterate farmer from a rural area of Xinjiang who came to faith in Jesus after being diagnosed with an incurable disease when he was 46 years old. Just after the doctors told him to go home and prepare to die, Steven heard the gospel from a house church evangelist, and he believed in Christ. The evangelist laid his hands on Steven and prayed for healing, and he soon recovered.

Steven realized that he had met the true and Living God, and was eager to share the good news with as many people as possible. During the summer months he did farm work, while each winter he traveled extensively throughout the region sharing his powerful testimony. God confirmed the preaching of His Word with signs and wonders, and many people experienced miraculous healing.

By the winter of 1995, Steven had established two house churches, and two more were started the following year. Each of the four churches contained about 20 families. This development caught the attention of the authorities, and Steven was warned and fined. He refused to stop preaching, however, and was consequently sent to prison.

In the dingy cell, Steven continued to take every opportunity to share the good news of Jesus. Threats and beatings did not deter him. Two Muslim inmates had been sick for a long time, but after Steven prayed for them, they were instantly healed. This healing opened many new opportunities, and the gospel spread further. Soon, ten Muslim men had repented of their sins and placed their faith in Christ. Realizing there was nothing they could do to stop Steven, the authorities decided to release him before he converted the entire prison!

One night in January 1997, he was ordered to leave the facility. It was eleven o'clock at night, and the temperature outside was -20°C (-4°F). Without a good winter coat, Steven walked through the bitter cold for many miles until he reached the home of a Christian. When he knocked on the door, the believers inside were praying for his release.

When Steven planted two more house churches, the authorities felt provoked beyond what they could bear. They arrested both Steven and his son and held them for 45 days. Steven was bashed and kicked around the head, but when the authorities offered to release them if his family paid a fine, Steven refused. He told his son he would have to bear the cross of the Lord and that if they paid the fine, the police would keep arresting Christians to extract more money.

Back home, Steven's injuries did not heal, and great fears were held for his health. He was unable to work because of pain in his head and could not preach the gospel. He encouraged his wife and son to take his place, and they continued to travel widely, evangelizing unbelievers and strengthening Christians in God's Word. As a result, Steven's son was arrested on four different occasions over an 18-month period.

In May 1999, Steven's health deteriorated, and he died from the injuries he had sustained in prison two years earlier. He had been a Christian just five years, during which time

> He established six new churches with more than 150 believers. Steven had never learned to read or write, and had never attended a seminary, yet he gave what he had to Jesus, and God blessed him mightily. When local Christians heard that Steven had died as a martyr, many dedicated themselves to take his place as an evangelist.[14]

By the end of the 1990s, the number of Christians in Xinjiang had grown markedly, but almost all of the growth had occurred among Han people, with comparatively few strong converts from Islam. In 1999, the disparity between different ethnicities in the Xinjiang Church was lamented in this report:

> The tension between ethnic groups has led to a serious situation among the churches in Urumqi. Many of the Chinese who volunteered to settle in Xinjiang were Christians, who saw the move as an opportunity to share their faith with the minority groups there. Hatred and prejudice, however, run so hot in Xinjiang that the Han Christians have found it virtually impossible to share the gospel with the Uyghurs or the other Muslim minorities. One visitor reported: "Many Han church leaders in Xinjiang openly acknowledge, without guilt or shame, that they do not have a burden for these people. One church elder, when asked about evangelizing Uyghurs, responded by shouting, "You're crazy!"[15]

The less influential Catholic Church also continued to grow in Xinjiang throughout the 1990s. In 1994 a modest total of 6,000 Catholics was reported in the region,[16] with the number rising to 9,000 in 1997.[17]

Letters from Xinjiang

We conclude this chapter by reprinting a selection of letters that were received from Xinjiang by various Christian ministries during the 1990s. These precious communications reveal both the strengths and weaknesses of Christianity in Xinjiang and provide insights into the daily lives and personal struggles of believers as they followed God. Their experiences also offer a fascinating snapshot of the ever changing conditions experienced by the body of Christ at this time.

1993

> Greetings! I have been listening to your Uyghur broadcast for half a year. I am a Uyghur student. I listened to what you said about Christianity, and the following questions came to mind: Why did God create man? Why do we exist in this world? It is said that we are all sinners, and if we do not repent, we will suffer in hell. But if God continues to create sinners, why should the sinners be punished in hell? It seems unfair. How can I receive a book about Christianity?[18]

> Thanks to the enormous grace of the Lord who leads us, the Church in Yining has been thriving after several years of trials and tribulations. Recently, however, an evangelist from Henan Province arrived. Because he is a good preacher, quite a few people from our churches were attracted to his services. According to him, Saturday is the Pentecost of the Lord, and so observing the Sabbath on Sunday will not lead to redemption. As a result, his teaching has produced factions and severe disputes within our church. Having been a Christian only a short time, I planned to

apply to study at the seminary in order to dedicate myself to the work of God. I am now hesitant. Please help me to avoid making a mistake.[19]

1995

The church here is desolate and without a pastor. It's difficult to preach the gospel because of widespread heresies and suppression from the local authorities. Some officials even ask for bribes. We do not have money and refuse to pay, so they prevent us from gathering together. Some fellow Christians have boldly exposed false teachings, but their efforts seem ineffective. My youngest son is two years old. I would like to offer him to the service of God for the rest of his life.[20]

1996

I live in a village. Since graduating from junior high school, I have been knitting carpets at home. Not many people like this kind of monotonous work but I do, because I can listen to your broadcast, meditate on God's Word, and praise Him at the same time. Our church is made up of many home groups. As the number of believers increases, we are short of preachers. I find it very difficult to prepare sermons. Even if I have prepared thoroughly beforehand, my mind becomes blank on stage. I hope God will give me strength to overcome my shyness and transform me to become His faithful servant.[21]

1999

I am serving a youth fellowship and have pioneered Sunday school work. This work is very hard because of the constraints from our environment. We have no systematic teaching material or place to study . . . but amazingly, the work continues. Whenever I see the children memorizing Scripture or copying down hymns and worshiping together, I am filled with indescribable joy, but I am not so optimistic now about the state of the gospel here. In the early 1980s there was explosive growth, and we saw many new meeting points set up. But now, although numbers have not dropped, few believers are deeply rooted in the truth.[22]

I am a retired worker. I first heard about Jesus when I was a young child, but later I moved a long way from home for work, and without guidance from anyone I abandoned God. Today I borrowed a booklet entitled, "Knowing the True God." I was deeply touched after reading it, and now I realize how insignificant I am. I have no reason to reject such a loving Savior, and I am determined to entrust my life to Jesus and to rely on Him as my only support and help.[23]

2000s

Old hostilities carried over into the new millennium, with much blood spilled on the streets of Xinjiang. On September 8, 2000, a massive explosion occurred near Urumqi when a truck loaded with explosives rammed into more than 30 vehicles stuck in a traffic jam. The government officially claimed there were 73 deaths and 300 wounded, but locals said the number of dead was closer to 500 people.

The success of the terrorist attacks in the United States on September 11, 2001, seemed to embolden Muslim extremists in Xinjiang who felt increasingly marginalized by Chinese dominance. The 9/11 attacks gave a sense of boldness to many Muslims in Xinjiang who sensed an opportunity to throw off Chinese control.

In 2012, the US government included the "East Turkestan Islamic Movement" in its list of terrorist organizations. A total of 22 Uyghur fighters were captured by US forces in Iraq and sent to the Guantanamo Prison camp in Cuba. A short time later the United Nations also placed the East Turkestan movement on its sanctions list.

A rumor had been circulating on the internet that young Uyghur girls were being abused by Han men while working in factories in faraway Guangdong Province. Feeling overwhelmed by Chinese power in the region, on July 5, 2009, several hundred Uyghur extremists rioted in the streets of Urumqi and in the People's Square, beating and killing Han Chinese. The conflict lasted several weeks, leaving at least 200 people dead and over 2,000 injured. The violence was broadcast live into people's living rooms across China and throughout the world for the first time, causing a sharp deterioration in the Han-Uyghur relationship which has continued to be toxic to the present day.

Living martyrs

Despite the massive ethnic tension in Xinjiang, Han Chinese Christians did not give up praying and trying to establish God's kingdom among the Uyghurs and other peoples in the region. Foreign believers were startled to learn of the success one

Dedicated believers in Xinjiang meet in temperatures so cold that frozen meat was left to hang from the church ceiling
VOM Canada

Chinese ministry had encountered in their Xinjiang work. The ministry reported,

> We first began our work at the start of 2004 on a very low-key basis, discreetly visiting one home at a time. Because of the response, all the members of our church expressed a desire to be involved in the work. As a result, we have now visited 32,000 homes and started another 35 new meeting places. Please pray with us as we have a lot of follow-up work to do.[1]

Progress in Xinjiang was not without great struggle and hardship, however. Many believers were arrested and endured brutal treatment. In response, the Christian organization Asia Harvest launched a project called the Living Martyrs' Fund which continues to the present day. In a country where no government pension or medical insurance is available to "illegal" house church members or their families, the fund provides support for house church leaders who have been injured or have a long-term illness due to persecution.[2]

In the year 2000 alone, Asia Harvest received many applications from Xinjiang. The following excerpts from just a handful of applications—most from the one town of Fukang, north of Urumqi—are a small sample of the type of hardships faced by many Christians in the region:

> Brother Li is a house church pastor who has been arrested and imprisoned on several occasions, each time suffering brutal beatings and then having to endure the filthy conditions. He now has tuberculosis, and his inability to work means he is unable to get adequate medical treatment.

> Brother Luo is a Bible teacher who was arrested and forced to work in a chemical factory while in a prison labor camp. Since that time he has suffered terrible respiratory problems because of the dangerous toxins and poisons. He has no income and is destitute.

Brother Hua is a senior house church leader who has long been targeted by the authorities because of his zeal for the gospel and his wise leadership. After being imprisoned on three occasions he now suffers from gastritis, and is confined to bed.

Brother Zheng is a house church pastor who was arrested for preaching the gospel. The prison guards kicked and stomped on his chest and body, and since that time he has been ill with heart murmurs.

Brother Chen has led dozens of people to faith since he first believed in Jesus seven years ago. In that short time he has been arrested several times and suffered humiliation, torture and deprivation. Now he is suffering from anemia and malnutrition, which require long-term medication. His body has been crushed, and he needs help to live from day to day.

Brother Wu's father died as a Christian martyr during the Cultural Revolution. He grew up living with his mother and decided to remain single so he could devote himself more fully to the work of God's kingdom. The authorities consider him an enemy, and they have tried everything they can to destroy Wu and his church. He has been arrested several times and inhumanely tortured in various ways. He has never forsaken his faith, in spite of all the abuse, and his testimony has encouraged many believers. Wu now suffers from heart disease and is in need of long-term medication.

Brother Ning has served as a house church leader for 20 years. He came into the government's crosshairs and has been arrested and tortured several times because of his refusal to join the Three-self Church. He never lost his hope and faith in the Lord, and he has become a hero in the hearts of many fellow Christians. He now suffers from diabetes and is in need of long-term medication. Thank you for considering helping Brother Ning and his precious family.

At the same time that many Christians were being brutally mistreated, the gospel was being boldly proclaimed and powerful miracles occurred in many parts of Xinjiang. In one place an elderly Christian, Sister Li, had faithfully prayed for the salvation of her family members for years. When she fell gravely ill and was close to death in November 2003, Li's heart grieved to know that apart from her daughter, all other members of her family remained unbelievers. Suddenly, as the life appeared to drain from her body, the power of God came into Sister Li's home and shook her family to the core. When they gathered around her bed to mourn,

> They felt the earth vibrate and the thunder roar. They thought a huge truck was rumbling past, not realizing that signs and wonders were unfolding in quick succession. Next, a ball of bright light entered the house and swiftly enveloped the body of Sister Li. The light moved and circled the people a few times. This continued for two or three minutes as the room was lit up like a fireworks display.
>
> All the non-believers present in the room witnessed the phenomena and were dumbstruck. The believers saw nothing, however, but from the gaping expressions it was clear that they understood that miracles were taking place. All of Sister Li's relatives who had previously rejected Jesus now wanted to believe and follow Christ. Some of them subsequently became church leaders, full of fervor and commitment for the Lord. All glory to God![3]

Three-Self expansion

While the unregistered house churches experienced a boom throughout Xinjiang in the 2000s, the government-approved Three-Self Churches also expanded greatly. The British author Tony Lambert remarks: "The Church in Xinjiang has enjoyed rapid growth. There were probably only about 200 Christians in 1949. In 2004, Three-Self sources estimated 131,000. There are at least 56 registered churches and meeting points in this huge region, and many house churches. Urumqi may have 40,000 believers. In 1949 there were fewer than 100."[4]

Lambert provides details of one evangelistic initiative which reaped great results for God's kingdom in Xinjiang, especially among the Han Chinese population:

> "Love every household" aims to evangelize the whole town or village in which a church is situated. Firstly, believers with the gift of evangelism are identified in each congregation. They are then formed into small groups of two or three evangelists. Secondly, the area is divided into four districts (north, south, east and west), and the number of residential work units in each is estimated. . . . No tracts are used in evangelism as the words and lives of the Christians are seen as the best means of communicating the gospel.
>
> Each church seeks God for ways to make contact with non-Christians. For instance, one group of evangelists went from house to house selling soft drinks and collecting bottles for free, arousing the curiosity of the people. . . . An immediate consequence was a revived zeal among the churches, and greater vision and closer co-operation in practical evangelism.
>
> The aim is that all the Chinese in northern Xinjiang should hear the gospel and that 50,000 people will become Christians. Then the strategy will be taken to southern Xinjiang. When that is completed they pray that the Lord will move His churches to evangelize the Muslims.[5]

House church strategies

Each year in the new millennium saw an increase in the number of Christians in Xinjiang, much to the consternation of the Communist authorities who appeared to view Christianity as an unsettling influence in an already volatile region. With their plans for peace thwarted by violence and ethnic strife, the last thing the government wanted to see was a rising Church trying to convert Uyghurs and other Muslim minorities.

One of the largest and most effective house church networks to emerge from the massive revival in China is the Tanghe Church, named after the county in which it was established in Henan Province. In 2007, a school teacher from Tanghe moved to Xinjiang where she hoped her job would provide ample opportunities to share the gospel with Uyghur people.

After seven Uyghur students in her class accepted Jesus as Lord and Savior, the school heard about her, and they fired the teacher and expelled the students. Instead, all seven students were invited to attend the Tanghe Bible School in Beijing. For 18 months the new Uyghur Christians studied the Chinese language, the Bible, and a vocation. After completing the training, they returned to Xinjiang, and according to one source,

> After almost two years, the leaders traveled to Xinjiang to seek out the students and see how they were doing. What they found surprised them: the students had led more than 300 Muslims to the Lord in four different cities.
>
> In 2012, the Tanghe Church started another Bible school in Xinjiang, with 20 students. All of them are Uyghurs who converted from Islam. They plan to use this school as a launching base to send graduates as missionaries into Kazakhstan, Uzbekistan, Pakistan, Kyrgyzstan, Afghanistan, and the Middle East.[6]

The same source later notes, "When many of the foreigners were forced to leave Xinjiang, there were very few Uyghur Christians. It was not easy to find more than one or two. Today, in the city of Kashgar and the surrounding area there are an estimated 400 to 500 believers. This may not sound like a lot, but to have this many Muslims come to Christ in such a short time is evidence of an amazing revival among the Muslims in western China."[7]

Evidence of revival in many parts of Xinjiang emerged during the first decade of the twenty-first century. Snippets of information from field workers told of 15,000 house church believers at Xinyuan in northern Xinjiang as well as breakthroughs among various ethnic groups, including the emergence of 24 new Kirgiz Christians and "perhaps 150 Kazak believers in various places."[8]

The revival burned brightest among the Han Chinese, however. A German mission organization shared the story of a Chinese couple they met in 2001:

> Shortly after marrying in 1994, we traveled as missionaries to Xinjiang with four other couples. We discovered 20–30 small churches with a total of around 300 believers. In a span of only three years, the growth was so strong that we had almost 500 churches in four districts, with a total of about 100,000 members.
>
> The government began persecuting our movement, infiltrating the churches and labelling it a cult on local television. I was arrested, but was able to escape and now live in hiding. My wife was arrested and taken to prison, together with six other Christians, where they suffered hunger, torture, and hard labor. In her free time she preached the gospel to the other inmates. She was moved to a different cell every three months, so at least half of the prisoners heard the gospel.[9]

A torrent of persecution

With both registered and unregistered churches experiencing exponential growth throughout Xinjiang, the authorities appeared to be at a loss at how to stem the flow of people coming to Christ. Starting in 2005, an uptick in persecution of Christians was recorded in Xinjiang as the government attempted to crush the revival. Just a few of the documented cases included the following incidents.

On August 7, 2005, police officers in more than 20 vehicles descended on a house church meeting in Hejing County. Shamefully, "about 30 Christians were arrested and more than ten women were stripped and paraded in front of the others. The women who refused to take off their clothes were beaten severely. One woman attempted to commit suicide by beating her head against the wall because of this extreme humiliation."[10]

The following year, in October 2006, the police raided a house church Bible school in the suburbs of Urumqi which was hosting a Korean pastor from America. Thirty-five Christians were arrested and taken away for interrogation, including the Korean-American pastor and his interpreter. After some of the believers were beaten and fined, the group of Christians was

16-year-old Luo Lanlan, arrested for attending a children's Bible study
China Aid

released, while the visiting pastor was placed under arrest in a hotel before being expelled from China.[11]

On Christmas Eve 2006, Pastor Luo Yuanqi was taken away by the Huocheng police. He was beaten the whole night by the inmates at the detention center who were offered benefits by the guards to do their dirty work for them. Luo was released a week later, but he had been so mercilessly tortured that he wanted to commit suicide to escape the pain. He was later charged with "undermining the implementation of state law through superstition," a charge often leveled against house church leaders who refuse to register their fellowships with the corrupt Three-Self Patriotic Movement.

Two years later in May 2008, Luo Yuanqi was rearrested and accused of "inciting separatism," a charge that carries a potential death sentence in Xinjiang. The trouble extended to Luo's family. Even his 16-year-old daughter, Luo Lanlan, was detained with 11 other minors and two adults after they were caught attending a children's Bible study.[12]

Luo Yuanqi remained in prison for 12 months, during which time his health deteriorated after he contracted hepatitis B. He was very frail when he was finally released in April 2009. His wife and three children were overjoyed to welcome him home, and Luo thanked God for His goodness and for all the Christians inside China and around the world who had prayed for him.

Zhou Heng

The year 2007 saw further arrests of Christians in Xinjiang. Zhou Heng, a prominent house church leader, was detained in Shayibake District near Urumqi after he went to a bus station to collect a shipment of three tons of Bibles that had been sent from another part of China.[13]

Zhou Heng and his family in happier times
VOM Canada

Zhou managed a registered bookstore that sold Christian books. However, five officers were waiting for Zhou inside a van that was parked outside the bus station. He was seized, and in prison he was forced to lie on a concrete floor for the first month despite the freezing conditions. Wardens ordered the 14 other inmates in Zhou's call to beat him regularly in a bid to make him incriminate himself, but he steadfastly proclaimed his innocence despite the torture.

Zhou was finally charged with "illegal business operations," and his bookstore was closed by the authorities. He faced a possible 15-year prison sentence, and many Christians around the world were mobilized to pray for Zhou. In April 2008, the court in Xinjiang surprisingly threw out his case for insufficient evidence, and he returned home.

When he was told that many Christians around the world had been praying and advocating for his release, Zhou Heng broke down in tears and said, "Although I am still physically weak, my heart is filled with peace and light from the Holy Spirit. Let us, in Christ, continue to focus on our Father's kingdom and righteousness. Let us thank and worship the great, Almighty and loving God."[14]

At about the same time, a Uyghur Christian named Phillip was summoned from south China where he was living and ordered to report to the police station in his hometown of Hotan or face serious consequences. He immediately caught a train for the four-day journey, not knowing what laws he had supposedly broken. Upon arriving in Xinjiang, he was escorted to the Public Security headquarters where "the police tortured him, beating his lower back with a club and using devices to poke and twist the skin on his arms. Alligator clips wired to electrical currents were clamped on his earlobes, and he was electrocuted. This went on for 13 days."[15]

After being threatened with a lengthy prison sentence, Phillip finally learned the true reason for his ordeal: he was under arrest because he had forsaken Islam, and the Uyghur leaders were infuriated because his new faith posed a threat to their spiritual authority.

In November 2007, another Uyghur Christian, Osman Imin (known as Wusiman Yiming in Chinese) was arrested in Hotan and sentenced to two years in a prison labor camp for the crime of "divulging state secrets."

Alimjan Yimit

In January 2008, Alimjan Yimit—known as Alimujiang Yimiti in Chinese, but simply as Alim to his friends—was arrested in Kashgar on the charge of "assisting foreigners to conduct unlawful activities." Aged 35 at the time of his arrest, Yimit was imprisoned for more than 18 months before his case came to trial.

Since 2002, Yimit had worked as a project manager of the Jiaerhao Foodstuff Company, where he was responsible for the company's orchard in Hancheng. The authorities had originally accused him of "engaging in unlawful religious infiltrative activities, disseminating Christianity, spreading religious propaganda among the Uyghur masses, and raising up Christian believers."[16]

In reality, Yimit was a man who had experienced a radical transformation when he met Jesus Christ in 1995. He changed within as he abandoned the dark oppression of Islam and came into the light and liberty of God's Son. He was a highly valued employee because of his ability to speak Chinese, Uyghur, and English. Advocate Bob Fu remarked,

> Alimjan is an innocent, law-abiding citizen. He has been a peace-maker between Han Chinese and Uyghurs. He has even been sending his children intentionally to study Mandarin in school, even though they are Uyghurs, in order to encourage them to be peacemakers.[17]

Yimit's arrest became international news and caused embarrassment and anger among the Chinese authorities who refused to respond to numerous queries from overseas media outlets.

Alimjan Yimit, a Uyghur Christian who remains in prison today

In September 2008, the United Nations Working Group on Arbitrary Detention ruled that his arrest and detention was arbitrary and in violation of international law.

Finally in October 2009, Alimjan Yimit was sentenced to a "fixed term" of 15 years in prison after his charges were upgraded to "providing state secrets to people outside of China." After lodging a failed appeal against the conviction, two of Yimit's lawyers had their certificates to practice law in China revoked.

Yimit's courageous wife, Guli Nuer, and their two sons continue to do all they can to advocate for his release, but they have been stonewalled at every turn. When Guli first heard about the 15-year sentence imposed on her husband, she expressed her trust in God by declaring, "I am no longer thinking about this from a human perspective. Our Heavenly Father must have His perfect will in it."[18]

Guli Nuer and her sons continue to trust in Jesus
as they pray for their husband and father

Guli Nuer remains an active member of the body of Christ in Kashgar and spends much of her time encouraging and comforting others. In 2016, she gave a rare interview to a Western mission organization in which she revealed some of the hardships she and her sons have faced.

> We have joy, real joy. The joy in this difficult situation is real joy. It must be joy from the Lord! Otherwise, how could we endure the hardship?
>
> I have regular gatherings with brothers and sisters. I am able to share my thoughts and feelings with them, and I need their support and prayers. Without their prayers we could not endure!
>
> My elder son misses his father so much! Very often he remembers the precious moments with his dad when he was a child. The more he thinks of how his father loves him, the more he misses him. He now understands that his father is suffering for his faith. He is proud of his dad! He does not feel ashamed of his father's imprisonment.
>
> My younger son was only one-year-old when my husband was put in jail. He cannot remember anything about him but has been growing up without a father figure. . . . Praise the Lord, both my mother and mother-in-law converted several years ago. They have found Jesus to be the true God.
>
> Above all, we still put our faith in Jesus and strive to live godly lives under the hardship. My husband always asks me to live well, take good care of our sons, and teach them to love God. This is the way we witness for Him.
>
> I ask my sons to behave, to study hard, and to always tidy up our home as if my husband was coming back today. I understand my husband will come back to us in time. I wait for his return as if I wait for the second coming of Jesus. We are the Bride of Christ![19]

At the time of the writing this book, Alimjan Yimit remained behind bars on account of his Christian faith and is not due for release until 2024, by which time he will be 51 years old.

A changing tide

In the same year that the Uyghur Christian Alimjan Yimit was arrested, a campaign was launched to identify and systematically expel undercover missionaries from Xinjiang. By the end of 2008, at least 100 foreigners had been blacklisted. Many were given just a few hours to gather their belongings before being escorted to the airport and placed on flights out of China. Some of the expelled families had lived in Xinjiang for more than a decade and had put down deep roots in the community. They owned apartments and vehicles and some had children enrolled in school, so the sudden upheaval caused much grief to those families.

The final year of the decade had scarcely begun when 51 Christians were arrested in the Shayibake District near Urumqi on January 2, 2009. The net of persecution was cast even wider. Church leaders and missionaries were not enough, so even Christian schoolchildren were targeted by the authorities. Chen Le, a second-grade student at the Huashan Middle School,

Chen Le
China Aid

was expelled after he signed a document confirming he was a Christian. Although the expulsion threatened to deprive him of future educational and vocational opportunities, the courageous young disciple of Christ said, "I would rather be forced out of school than deny my faith."[20]

Letters from Xinjiang

2000

The young sisters in Christ here are facing a trial: the issue of marriage. Because there are generally few Christian brothers in China, some of the sisters are considering marrying non-believers. It's not easy for these sisters to stand firm on the Word of God and be faithful to Him, because they have to face the misunderstanding of their family members, mockery from society, and Satan's temptations. Please pray the young sisters in Xinjiang and throughout China may have a wonderful testimony even in these trying circumstances.[21]

2001

We live in a mountainous area controlled by the army. Christianity is virtually outlawed; even two or three people are forbidden to meet together. Brothers and sisters have to meet secretly to worship. I happened to obtain a recording which gave an overview of the books of the Old Testament. This has been a great help, so I have copied it for others, as we have very few opportunities to read Christian books. We are under close surveillance here, so I had to mail this letter from Urumqi.[22]

I received Jesus as Lord after suffering from heart disease in 1991. The following year I met a man who had a Bible and who claimed to preach the truth. I purchased the Bible from him and even though I carried it with me, I didn't even know the characters that represent the Name of Jesus. I relied on listening to your programs to learn about God's Word.

When he learned that I listened to gospel radio broadcasts and intended to write to you, the preacher ordered that no one in the congregation was allowed to listen to the radio or study any spiritual books. He said only listening to his teaching could save us. He preaches a "spiritual baptism," but your radio station preaches only water baptism, so I am confused.

Afterwards, I brought my radio with me when I worked in the field every day. My fellow workers said I was addicted to your programs. The preacher heard about this and confronted me, asking if I was still listening to the radio. "Yes," I admitted, "I'm a lonely old man who is eager to learn the truth." He called me a traitor, and one Sunday he cast me out of the church fellowship.[23]

2002

In Xinjiang, members of the "Wilderness" cult dare not openly attend churches to proclaim their beliefs. However, they often sneak into Christians' homes to confuse them. They declare that the Lord is returning soon, and teach people not to enjoy life, but to confine themselves to eating no more than three ounces of food each day and by living in the wilderness without any shelter. Moreover, they teach people not to farm or do other work, but just to proclaim their beliefs everywhere. Some believers sold their properties and gave the money to the leaders of this cult. Much farmland has been abandoned and left desolate.[24]

In Xinjiang half of the churches in both urban and rural areas have fallen under the control of the Eastern Lightning cult. Members of the cult use despicable methods to steal God's flock. For instance, they hold training sessions to attract church leaders and then they kidnap them. While they detain the leaders they send workers to the churches to deceive the believers. Those who refuse to submit to them fall prey to their cruelty. Two sisters were led into the woods and died after being bitten by poisonous snakes.[25]

Sister K. has lived in a Muslim area of Xinjiang for years. She was visited by an old Kazak lady who was dying of cancer, and she prayed for her. The lady recovered completely and later summoned her entire family to hear Sister K. All received Christ, and several other families also came under the influence of the gospel.[26]

I am a newborn Christian living in Xinjiang. In March I followed my mother to church and have since begun to glorify and worship God. Over the last few months I have listened to your Bible broadcasts through the internet. I have faithfully attended church, hoping that through worshiping God my mother will find peace and blessings in her old age. She is now over 50 but has lost her zest for life. We pray the Lord Jesus Christ will save us.[27]

2003

Words cannot express our appreciation for the Bibles you have provided for our fellowships over the last few years. We strongly encourage you to focus on providing God's Word because we are so grateful that our Lord and Savior Jesus Christ died for our sins and gave us new life! We are also thankful that He has blessed us with brothers and sisters abroad who care about us and have shared the sacred Scriptures with us. We pray God's richest blessing will be on you.[28]

2004

In the past, our church was attacked by members of the Eastern Lightning cult. We resisted them and lifted up no other name but Jesus Christ. However, some of our members chose to follow the cult. When we discovered this, it was already too late to bring them back. Those deceived former believers have been harassing churches everywhere, proclaiming, "Forget about Jesus! Forget about the Bible!" Such rebellious words against God hurt us deeply.[29]

2005

We began our work at the start of 2001 in a very low-key manner, visiting villages that had never heard the gospel. We have planted eight house churches now, but there was no way to obtain Bibles within 500 miles (810 km) of where we live. Then, when we received your loving gift of two boxes of Bibles we wept before the Lord, as He has truly answered our prayers. We will need more soon, so please remember us next time. Thank you.[30]

2006

One time I felt so weak and hopeless that I wanted to kill myself by overdosing on sleeping pills. Thanks to Jesus, I heard a gospel radio program and heard a story about a paralyzed man who walked again and gave glory to Jesus. I was inspired, because I realized I was just like that paralyzed man. I believed in the risen Savior Jesus, and my life has turned around 180 degrees. The greatest richness in my life is to know Jesus Christ. He chose me and set me free from the powers of darkness, sin, and death. I became a new creation, and now I am eager to spread the gospel.[31]

2007

When I became a Christian my relative, who is the imam of a mosque, told me to renounce Christ because my ancestors were all Muslims, and I should remember my heritage. I told him that Jesus Christ is the only true Living God.[32]

My wife and I were tricked by the government to move to northwest China 39 years ago. We were true believers in Communism and thought Mao could do no wrong. We were told that we would be part of the glorious development of Xinjiang, and that the government would even pay us to be part of the worthy project. After we arrived, not only did the government not pay us as promised, they even took away the little money we had to ensure we could not return to our home province.

When we lost faith in our government we felt devastated, and our lives were miserable for many years. We developed very poor health and practiced qigong to try to get better. Our sons became so involved in qigong that they began acting very strangely. Then, one day my oldest son was given a Bible by one of his former classmates. He began to read it just so he could explain to his friends how wrong it was. That was the spark that led to our entire family believing in Jesus Christ. How happy our last two years have been! Thank you for providing our son's classmate with the Bible that changed our lives![33]

A young girl in our area was possessed by a demon. She became incredibly strong, and she looked horrific, staring at people with a terrifying expression. After some time Christians prayed and shared the good news with her. The girl was completely restored and she now loves the Lord. I realized that if demons are real, then God must also be real, and my heart began to open up to Him. One day, while alone in the house, I knelt beside my bed and prayed, "O God, if you really exist, let me have a personal encounter with you." . . .

It is now more than five years since I received Jesus as my Savior. I want to know His love, which will mature me as a believer.[34]

2008

I and the other single women in my church feel hopeless and lost about the marriage issue. The Bible teaches us not to marry unbelievers, yet there are just too few brothers in our church. Most of the men are already married. Some sisters in their 30s feel pain as their non-Christian families try to force them to get married. Some who chose to marry unbelievers have suffered persecution at their hands. They are worse off than if they had remained single. Please pray earnestly for our single sisters. May the Lord preserve our hearts and help us to trust in Him.[35]

The Modern
Back to Jerusalem Movement

*Original Back to Jerusalem pioneers in the 21st century:
Top row, left to right: He Enzheng, Zhou Enying, Mark
Ma; Bottom row: Ruth Lu De, Li Daosheng*

254

Transferring the baton

In the early 1940s, God gave a clear call to a small group of Chinese Christians to preach the gospel in Xinjiang and the border regions and ultimately to go all the way through the Islamic world back to Jerusalem. As outlined in previous chapters of this book, many dedicated believers such as Mecca Zhao, Simon Zhao, and Wen Muling traveled to Xinjiang and paid a dear price for their calling, and some spent decades in prison labor camps before they died.

The end of an era was reached on March 6, 2018, when Zhou Enying, the last surviving member of the original Back to Jerusalem Band, died at the age of 105. A native of Henan Province, Zhou was adopted by an American female missionary and raised as a Christian. She later attended university in the United States before returning to China and becoming a missionary in 1944. In 1959, when Communist persecution of the Church was at its high-water mark, Zhou was arrested and falsely charged with spying for America. She was imprisoned for ten years, and after being acquitted she spent many years teaching English and serving God's people in Gansu Province. Zhou Enying never married, but she raised three adopted children.

One year earlier, in 2017, Zhang Moxi (Moses Zhang) died at the age of 93. Seven decades earlier, a then 22-year-old Moses Zhang and his wife, Zhang Huixi, joined four other students from the Northwest Bible Institute as they traveled to Xinjiang to preach the gospel. They were the second group of workers from the Back to Jerusalem Evangelistic Band. As a young man, Zhang's heart had been stirred as he read the Bible, and he declared: "I determined to work in the toughest place for God and would not hesitate to lay down my life. I would be faithful unto death and not give up halfway. I offered my entire life to God."[1]

The new government in China brought Zhang's mission to an end in 1949, and he was compelled to return to his home province of Henan where he became a farm laborer. Later during the Cultural Revolution, the authorities learned he had been a missionary in Xinjiang. He was accused of being a spy and sentenced to a prison labor camp where he endured a fiery trial for his faith in Jesus Christ. Zhang never lost his zeal to serve the Lord, however, and even at the age of 85, he was actively shepherding God's flock. When he died, many Christians were grief-stricken, including the children and grandchildren he and his wife had raised to follow Christ.

At the memorial service for Moses Zhang, the great love and respect people had for him was shown as his body was carried to its final resting place at a cemetery that required a perilous uphill journey in temperatures below freezing. Believers were determined to show their respect for this man of God, and although even teenagers were struggling to make it up the slippery hill, many elderly church members crawled on their hands and knees to reach the gravesite. Their determination was symbolic of the

The funeral service for Moses Zhang in 2017

kind of life Moses Zhang had led. He never gave up, and he refused to let any obstacles stand in his way.

The last two Back to Jerusalem pioneers went to their eternal reward, and the baton was handed to the current generation of Chinese believers. They would now be called upon to kindle the flame and take the light of the gospel through the unreached nations surrounding China, and ultimately all the way back to Jerusalem.

Teething problems

After the 2003 publication of the book *Back to Jerusalem*,[2] which shared the missionary vision of the Chinese Church, many Christians around the world realized for the first time that China held the potential to send thousands of cross-cultural mission-aries into some of the hardest places on earth that were without the gospel. While there was much enthusiasm for the initiative, the reality of the difficulties the Chinese Church faced in seeing the vision become a reality soon became obvious.

For all their strengths and zeal, the house church Christians in China often have weaknesses which need to be addressed before cross-cultural missions will be effective. For example in March 2000, a team of 39 Back to Jerusalem missionaries from two Chinese house church networks combined to visit Myanmar (formerly Burma). Full of excitement at the prospect of serving God outside their homeland, the workers agreed to meet at a guesthouse on the Chinese side of the border before crossing together. One of the house church groups customarily liked to pray early in the morning, while the other preferred to hold meetings late at night. This difference resulted in a heated disagreement which attracted the attention of the local people. The authorities came to investigate the commotion, and after learning that a Christian group was intending to enter Myanmar for religious purposes, the 39 prospective missionaries were not permitted to cross the border and were ordered to return to their home provinces.

In June 2005, a similar incident took place at Kashgar in Xinjiang when 34 Chinese missionaries, all of whom were holding valid passports and Pakistan visas, were arrested after one of the team members foolishly revealed that they were Christian missionaries. Most were released after 15 days in confinement and were ordered to return home. Fearing further repercussions, all 34 went into hiding—their missionary careers in disarray due to the loose lips of one of their colleagues.

Fast learners

Because most of China's house church Christians were from impoverished rural areas, the task of enabling them to become effective missionaries in other nations posed significant challenges. Few candidates spoke English, let alone Arabic or other languages in target areas, and few of the initial candidates knew how to apply for visas or to conduct themselves in another country where they would be cut off from their families and communities. Within a few years it became apparent that, generally speaking, Chinese believers from urban areas were likely to be more fruitful and adaptable as cross-cultural missionaries than those from a rural farming background.

This realization led to a joining of the mission vision between rural and urban churches in China. Many rural church leaders— who had experienced decades of suffering and affliction in the midst of white-hot revival—began to train the more sophisticated city believers. Between the know-how of the urban Christians and the spiritual fervor of their rural brothers and sisters, many effective workers were ultimately trained and sent from China.

By the late 2000s, teams of undercover Chinese missionaries were already serving in far-flung corners of the globe including East Africa, Yemen, Iraq, and other parts of the Middle East, and Central Asia.

Other expressions of the Back to Jerusalem vision emerged. Hundreds of Chinese Christians crossed into neighboring countries like Vietnam, Laos, Myanmar, Nepal, Kazakhstan, and North Korea where they engaged in a host of activities to spread the gospel. Many went as businessmen or traders which gave them legitimate reasons for being in those countries. Often because of visa restrictions, workers traveled back and forth from China, spending six months at home followed by six months of service in their target nation.

Over time, a clear division emerged in the mission world between enthusiastic promoters of Back to Jerusalem. While some people offered constructive criticism, others seemed eager to openly mock the mission vision of the Chinese Church. They were quick to point out the movement's failings, usually without being willing to raise a finger to help the Chinese missionaries succeed in their noble task.

Some observers rushed to report the most ludicrous situations they had heard about, including one missionary who claimed to have encountered a group of Back to Jerusalem workers in Iraq. To his surprise, "they had no knowledge of Iraq and certainly none of Arabic. Furthermore, they were pig farmers, not the best profession for gaining acceptance in the Muslim world!"[3]

As the years progressed, the Chinese Church gradually matured and learned from their early mistakes, and an increasingly effective group of missionaries emerged. The vision was also aided by unexpected developments. For example, the Chinese found that missionaries from South Korea were already established in many places along the Silk Road. Where possible, they agreed to work together with the Koreans, learning from them and adapting their methods.

At the same time, training resources were developed in China, and many good mission books and videos were translated into Chinese to help new missionaries gain an understanding of the challenges they would face without compromising their great zeal and boldness for God.

Hijacked

By the late 2000s, many observers of the Chinese Church had become strong critics of the modern Back to Jerusalem Movement, or at least the part that some claim had been "hijacked" by a small group of Westerners, complete with website, newsletters, and public meetings.

Ironically, the very first newsletter of the newly formed, US-based Back to Jerusalem entity, published in June 2004, contained an article entitled, "Who 'Owns' Back to Jerusalem?" The article was very clear in its answer:

> It is essential to understand that Back to Jerusalem is a vision, not an organization. There is nowhere that people have to sign up or become a member. Back to Jerusalem was given to the whole Body of Christ in China more than 70 years ago. . . .
>
> All involved should be careful not to claim any exclusive right to the vision. . . . This newsletter itself is merely a mouthpiece for some house church leaders to share their views and prayer requests, and should not be taken as the authoritative voice on matters related to Back to Jerusalem. . . .
>
> Who, then, is the true "owner" of Back to Jerusalem? Let us be clear, the owner is none other than the Lord of the Harvest, God Almighty. Back to Jerusalem is His idea, His vision, His passion. May we never forget this fact.[4]

Despite these claims, a group of Western Christians had done exactly what the above warned against. They registered a non-profit organization in the United States and elsewhere and held meetings around the world at which they were implicitly portrayed as the authorized voice for the Back to Jerusalem vision.

Waves of criticism

Unsurprisingly, it did not take long before strong pushback arrived from concerned Christians both inside and outside of China who rejected the foreign-run Back to Jerusalem entity and its claims. Respected researcher Kim-Kwong Chan, the executive secretary of the Hong Kong Christian Council, went as far as describing the movement as a "hoax."[5]

One of the earliest criticisms leveled at the movement came from people who didn't understand the vision at all. Many were hung up over the name "Back to Jerusalem," assuming it was an end-times, Zionist dream rather than simply an outlet to facilitate overseas mission work by the Chinese Church. To this day, many people still seem unable to grasp that the goal is the evangelization of the unreached parts of the world and not Jerusalem itself.

One person concerned about the contemporary Back to Jerusalem initiative lamented, "Among those who have gone to the nations beyond the borders of China, a high attrition rate of up to 90 percent has been recorded. Some of the returned missionaries were interviewed and reported their sad missionary experience as the so-called 'cannon fodder.' They suffered from severe burnout, depression, and shame."[6]

Probably the main criticism of the US-based Back to Jerusalem organization was the claim by several house church leaders that their goal was to train and send 100,000 Chinese missionaries to fulfill the vision. To some scholars in the Western world this was a preposterous and delusional claim. The Chinese leaders, however, had simply shared their aspirations, which is clearly explained in the Back to Jerusalem book:

> We have noticed that many Westerners tend to be very excited and motivated by numbers, but we are not. Our goal is not to send 100,000 missionaries out of China. Our goal is nothing less than the completion of the Great Commission, so that the Lord Jesus Christ will return for his bride. . . . That is our goal and purpose! We are willing to do whatever it takes to fulfil this vision and be obedient to the calling.[7]

In 2013, Kim-Kwong Chan again chimed in with this sober analysis of the modern Back to Jerusalem Movement:

> The severe lack of qualified pastoral workers within China due to the rapid growth of Christianity in the past 20 years, compounded with the strong governmental control on normal development of the Church, also hinders the availability of recruiting qualified Back to Jerusalem candidates. . . . It appears that the current Movement is founded more on enthusiastic desires of Western mission groups, nationalistic aspirations of the Chinese, opportunistic mission leaders, the threat from the global expanding Islamic influence, and the mythologized Christian community in China. It will require a lot more serious missiological and spiritual groundwork before it can become a credible and sustainable mission movement bearing impact on global Christianity.[8]

In subsequent years, while some sought to marginalize the Back to Jerusalem vision and even mock reports of progress, one servant of the Church in China wrote the following in 2013: "For a while, it was unclear to many Western observers just to what degree the vision had been adopted by the Chinese Church at large, but it is now evident that the vision for a missionary China has become almost universal among the house church networks."[9]

In 2018—although it was clear that the figure of 100,000 missionaries had been aspirational and was far from becoming a reality—Ai Hua, an expert on the Chinese Church, demonstrated that such a figure is not unreasonable:

> If there is one missionary out of every 1,000 believers, then China would send out 50,000 to 130,000 missionaries. If China is to be the largest Christian nation with 160 million believers by 2025 and 257 million by 2032, according to Yang Fenggang of Purdue University, then it shall become the largest missionary force in the world.[10]

As a result of all the controversy, a sad dichotomy emerged around the term "Back to Jerusalem." There appeared to be two "Back to Jerusalems" in existence—a Chinese one and a foreign-led one that received all the attention and publicity. The two did not always overlap, as evidenced by the large number of Chinese Christians who denounced the US-based entity and rejected any claims that it had the authority to speak on behalf of the Church in China. Today, few Chinese churches still use "Back to Jerusalem" as the term to describe their foreign missionary efforts.[11]

Because of the discontent and controversy surrounding the "Back to Jerusalem" label, other initiatives emerged to fill the void and to facilitate the mission burden that still burns in the hearts of multitudes of Chinese Christians. One of the plans that seeks to serve and nurture the Chinese Church in its missionary vision is called Mission China 2030. More than 900 Chinese church leaders attended its launch in Hong Kong in 2015 where the attendees expressed a desire to mobilize at least 20,000 Chinese missionaries by the year 2030.

The Xi'an to Jerusalem road trip

In November 2006, Gao Quanfu, a house church leader from the ancient Chinese capital city of Xi'an, was praying at three o'clock in the morning when he said the Holy Spirit powerfully told him, "I want you to gather a team of people who will drive from Xi'an to Zion. I have already chosen those who will take part."[12]

The Chinese are generally a people who need to personally visit a place to gain a vision in their hearts, so when this news spread around the churches, thousands of people applied to join the team. After much prayer and discussion, a group of 15 men and women were chosen to make the long trip in four, four-wheel drive vehicles. After several delays, on September 8, 2008, the team finally set out on their journey through Xinjiang and on to Pakistan, Iran, Turkey, Syria, Jordan, and finally Israel. More than one million Christians in China had committed to pray for the expedition.

As they made their way through Xinjiang on the first stage of the journey, Gao and the team members met with some of the surviving Back to Jerusalem pioneers, including the wife of Zhang Guquan, the founder of the Northwest Spiritual Band who had laid down his life for the vision more than half a century earlier in a lonely Xinjiang prison cell. She wept as she prayed for the team. It seemed as if the spiritual baton had finally been passed on to the next generation of believers, and she died in peace a short time later.

The team also met with Brother Tian, another of the early pioneers. He prayed a blessing over the team members before he passed into the presence of God just a few days later. It was as though the Heavenly Father had perfectly completed the circle and allowed His servant to see the next generation of believers who would carry the baton forward.

When the travelers met with Grace He Enzheng, who was 92 at the time, she turned her eyes toward heaven and called out the name of her husband, Mecca Zhao, who had gone to heaven the year before. "Mecca, can you see? The Chinese Church is finally going out!" she exclaimed.

The first stage of the journey was the most difficult because the 15 leaders soon discovered there were many significant theological divisions among them. Hao Xin, one of the women on the team, prophesied that if they didn't work out their differences, then God would not allow them to leave the country. After taking Communion and asking forgiveness of one another, the trip proceeded.

As well as the spiritual challenges, a lack of understanding of practical requirements also plagued the team. Although all of them had secured the required visas in their passports to enter each country, they didn't realize that they also needed permits for their vehicles to cross international borders. The trip was delayed by weeks as they secured the required documents. They finally crossed into Pakistan on a new highway recently built by the Chinese government, and they whizzed along through the same stunning terrain that missionaries had once spent weeks traversing by foot and on the backs of mules.

After crossing Iran, Turkey, Syria, and Jordan, they finally reached Jerusalem, and realized it had been exactly 40 days since they had left China. An Israeli television network wanted to interview the travelers, and a spokesman for the team told the reporter that they represented 100 million Chinese Christians who loved Israel and were praying for peace in the region. The reporter was moved to tears on camera.

The epic trip had concluded, and a spark had been set alight in the hearts of the 15 Chinese church leaders. They returned home with renewed vision and many stories to tell, accompanied by video footage to share with their congregations. Most of all, they now realized the task of reaching the nations between China and Jerusalem was an extremely difficult one that would require many years of prayer and careful planning and would cost the lives of many participants.

The leaders also returned to China with a sense of shame, for during their journey they had visited approximately 100 Chinese missionaries who had been sent to the field in the preceding years. Many of the workers they spoke with reported that they had not received the financial support the churches had promised, and some had nearly starved as they tried to find work to make ends meet. Many of these missionaries had also experienced

> grave loneliness and much frustration at what they perceived as a lack of fruit, which was not helped by the pressure of similar expectations back home to win new converts. People were simply not getting saved at the rate they were all accustomed to seeing in China. To make matters worse, many of the missionaries felt as though they had been abandoned in the field . . . which led them to think they had failed. As far as they were concerned, they had lost face.[13]

One of the Chinese team members, a mechanic named Ruth, was involved in one of the "many, many miracles" that took place on the journey:

> One of the vehicles was involved in an accident on one of the many rugged hillside roads in Pakistan, leaving the axle bent and the left wheel twisted outwards. It was the middle of nowhere, which made it impossible to call a tow truck or a garage. As an experienced mechanic, Ruth knew that the extent of the damage sustained rendered the vehicle not worth fixing anyway; it would be better to scrap it. In that moment, she heard the Lord say, "Trust Me." She radioed the rest of the convoy and told them to continue on. She and her passengers were unharmed and would catch up with them.[14]

After laying her hands on the hood of the vehicle and praying, Ruth decided to keep driving. Amazing, she was able to continue the rest of the journey without further mechanical problems, even though locals along the way often shouted and pointed at the front of the vehicle as it drove by.

Ruth drove a further 2,160 miles (3,500 km), all the way to Jerusalem, before shipping the vehicle back to China where an astonished car repairman didn't believe it had been driven all that way apart from a divine miracle of God. He said an angel must have been lifting up that side of the car as they made their way across the Middle East.

The Belt and Road Initiative

In 2013, the hardline Chinese President Xi Jinping launched his new Belt and Road Initiative. When details of the plan were announced, many Chinese Christians who were aware of the Back to Jerusalem vision quietly smiled to themselves.

The plan that was intended to spread Chinese economic and cultural influence throughout the world lined up almost perfectly with the vision the Holy Spirit had given the Chinese Church in the 1940s. The world had changed dramatically in the decades

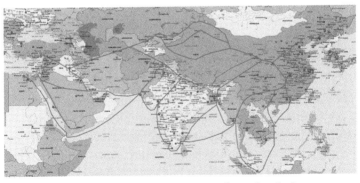

The ancient land and maritime Silk Roads, which closely reflect both the Back to Jerusalem vision and the Chinese government's Belt and Road initiative

since the Second World War. Whereas Western Christians had previously spearheaded mission efforts around the globe, they were now unable to gain entrance into many countries. Chinese people, on the other hand, are generally welcome in all countries.

Now aided by new roads, tunnels, bridges, airports, and high-speed trains—and with tens of thousands of Chinese laborers working in the most unreached areas of the world—Christians realized that the timing of Xi's initiative was more than coincidental. Plans were stepped up to train more cross-cultural Chinese missionaries, even though persecution of believers in China was the worst it had been for decades.

Although details of most of the activities of Chinese missionaries cannot be published due to security concerns, snippets of information occasionally emerge which provide a glimpse into the movement. In 2012, a report told how a Chinese couple in their fifties obeyed God's call to take the gospel to Laos. The Lord led them to open a restaurant, even though they had no culinary training. The wife said,

> I had never been a chef before. I cooked only home-style food. Whatever customers asked me to cook I would do it, or else I would just guess and kind of throw it all together. But I prayed often. Whenever I was cooking I would pray, "Lord help this to taste good." I would also pray that customers would receive God's blessing. . . . Restaurant work allows for many opportunities to interact with people and to share the gospel with them.[15]

The same article also told of a Chinese missionary who started a pig farm and a Bible school in Cambodia and of a married couple who moved to Pakistan to construct simple homes for people whose communities had been devastated by floods. They noted, "After we help them build their new homes we continue to interact with them, arranging regular times to go see them and share the good news of the gospel."[16]

The first of the modern martyrs

The Church in China understands that the countries in the Back to Jerusalem vision contain many of the most fanatical Muslim people groups on earth, and those who venture into the dark realms beyond China will risk their lives to establish God's kingdom. This reality was seen in June 2017, when 24-year-old Chinese Christian Li Xinheng and 26-year-old Meng Lisi were murdered by ISIS militants in northern Pakistan. Li and Meng had traveled there to teach Chinese to Pakistani children and were paid US $280 per month for their work. They were also learning Urdu which they hoped would later enable them to share Christ with the people of Pakistan.

Li and Meng were kidnapped off the streets of Quetta and held in a cave before being brutally slain a few weeks later. News of the deaths of these two young Chinese Christians was widely broadcast throughout China, and many people admired them for their courage and faith. The atheistic Chinese government, however, appeared embarrassed by the revelation that the duo were dedicated Christian missionaries who were seeking to spread the gospel.

Eager to protect their $57 billion investment in Pakistan and the more than $1 trillion commitment to the entire Belt and

Li Xinheng and Meng Lisi, martyrs for Christ

269

Road project, the Chinese government warned citizens not to engage in religious activity beyond their borders, and a tougher screening process was implemented for those who wished to work overseas. Eleven other Chinese citizens who taught at the same institution in Pakistan were immediately ordered to return to China where the government launched an investigation into their activities.

Overall, it remains to be seen how much the Chinese Church will take advantage of the massive Belt and Road plan to spread the gospel of Jesus Christ in the world's most unreached nations. The initiative is the largest project in human history, covering around 70 countries which contain 65 percent of the world's population. Just as the expansion of the Roman Empire ushered in new opportunities and ease of movement two millennia ago, it is hoped that the plans of the Chinese Communist Party will end up aiding the Back to Jerusalem vision and speeding its implementation.

Getting on with the job

Over the years, supporters of the modern Back to Jerusalem mission movement have continued their work undeterred by the years of bruising they had experienced at the hands of many Christian critics. They have largely chosen to ignore the commotion surrounding the vision and have simply got on with the job.

Eugene Bach, a former US Marine sniper who emerged as a main communicator of the Back to Jerusalem vision to the Western Church, provided the first statistics about the size and scope of the Back to Jerusalem missionary movement. Citing information gathered in 2015 from house church leaders from seven large networks, Bach enumerated a total of 1,288 Chinese missionaries at the time serving in 37 different countries.[17] Of those workers, 798 came from three house church networks based in Henan Province; 395 missionaries were from Anhui Province; and an additional 95 were from various church groups in Shandong and Guangdong provinces.

The countries with the largest number of Back to Jerusalem missionaries in 2015 were Myanmar (Burma) with 176; Pakistan (173); Egypt (87); Cambodia (77); Thailand (73); Indonesia (69); Vietnam (61); United Arab Emirates (60); Uzbekistan (58); and India (50).

Bach further qualified his statistics by explaining that they are a very conservative sample of the overall missionary sending force of the Chinese Church. Security considerations mean that no more recent figures have been released since 2015, and other parts of the body of Christ, such as the large church groups from Wenzhou in Zhejiang Province, were not counted in this report. Bach remarked,

> It can safely be assumed that the total number of Back to Jerusalem missionaries is five to ten times higher. House church network leaders do not keep detailed lists of missionaries, and because of the fluid situation in China, many network leaders are not aware of all the missionaries they have sent out.
>
> Finally, there are many organizations working with Back to Jerusalem missionaries that are not connected to any of the seven main networks represented in this study. Groups like Youth with a Mission, the International Mission Board, and several agencies from South Korea, Singapore and Hong Kong have programs focused on helping Chinese missionaries that are not included in these numbers.
>
> The Back to Jerusalem vision is to send out at least 100,000 missionaries. The Church sent out their first Back to Jerusalem missionaries in 2000. Fifteen years later, it can be best estimated they have sent out anywhere from 5,000 to 10,000 missionaries.
>
> For a country to go from zero to 5,000 to 10,000 missionaries in only 15 years is a massive accomplishment for the Body of

271

Christ. The achievement is even greater when one considers the countries they have sent the workers to.[18]

Despite encountering some severe turbulence along the way—especially from believers who prefer to mock the Chinese mission effort rather than attempting to win the lost and dying world themselves—the Back to Jerusalem vision of the Chinese Church remains very much alive. They have also displayed an ability to quickly adapt and learn from their mistakes. This God-given vision, birthed almost 80 years ago, continues to have the potential to play a key role in God's plans for global evangelization.

2010s

The situation for Christians in Xinjiang continued to be tense at the start of the 2010s. However there were few indications of the massive jolt that would shake the region later in the decade—a jolt so severe that not only the Church, but Xinjiang society as a whole was fundamentally and permanently altered, and the region would feature in news broadcasts around the world.

Some extraordinary claims of miracles in Xinjiang were made at the start of the new decade. On July 6, 2010, a team of Chinese intercessors traveled to the desert near Aksu, 250 miles (405 km) northeast of Kashgar. Aksu is one of the more strongly Islamic areas in Xinjiang, and Uyghurs make up around 80 percent of the population.

Elderly believers at a Xinjiang house church
RCMI

The intercessors had been deeply troubled by the intense hatred between the Han Chinese and Muslim minorities in Xinjiang. So they went to Aksu to ask God's forgiveness and to pray for His release of love and power to dissolve the racial barriers that separate people and block the progress of the gospel throughout the region. While they in the desert near Aksu, praying for God's blessing to quench the people of Xinjiang, the intercessors reported that "water started to bubble up from hundreds of little openings in the ground. Before long, water was gushing out everywhere, transforming the whole desert area around them into a huge lake of water!"[1]

Fire and blood

The 2010s brought hope that the long awaited breakthroughs among Islamic groups in Xinjiang would occur. Encouraging reports from throughout the region hinted at a wider acceptance of the gospel among Muslims than previously thought.

The Christian organization Asia Harvest supports many Chinese and ethnic minority evangelists throughout China through their Asian Workers' Fund.[2] At the start of the decade, the evangelists they were working with in Xinjiang included a female doctor who met Christ in 1998. She subsequently led 25 Uyghur families to the faith, and Bible teachers were sent to help establish these new Christians in the Word of God. Other local Christians being supported by Asia Harvest included a Kirgiz believer who had become a Christian at the age of 22. He was so deeply touched by the love of Jesus that he gave his life unreservedly to God and traveled extensively throughout Xinjiang to encourage and teach Muslim-background believers.

A Kazak Christian was saved by Christ in 2000, and after three years attending a Bible school in central China, he returned to Xinjiang to do evangelism and discipleship among his own people. At the time he was overseeing a group of 50 believers, most of whom were Kazaks.

Going hand-in-hand with the encouraging stories of breakthroughs and salvations, the Christians in Xinjiang continued to experience sporadic persecution in the first half of the 2010s, with many arrests of house church leaders taking place as the gospel continued to be advance. The decade began with the arrest of 14 house church Christians in Aksu. One of the leaders of the meeting, Yang Tianlu, had previously been arrested in 2007 along with 30 other believers during a meeting with four American missionaries.

In April 2010, a Christian woman named Feng Yongji was arrested while attending the opening ceremony of Expo 2010 in Shanghai. She was sent back to her hometown of Shihezi in Xinjiang where "four or five officers beat her so severely that she passed out, and she was in dire need of medical attention."[3]

Not for the first time, the Xinjiang authorities chose the festive season to vent their fury on Christians. A gathering of 31 Han and Uyghur believers was broken up in Yarkant as they celebrated the birth of Jesus Christ at the end of 2010.

Mass arrests and beatings continued in subsequent years. More than 30 Christians were seized during a Bible study meeting at Wusu, near the Kazakhstan border, on February 16, 2012. The believers were interrogated and fined 5,000 Yuan (US $795) each. The officers also confiscated their Bibles, books, laptop computers, phones, and other items.[4] The following month in Aksu, the authorities raided a house church that had been established nearly two decades earlier. Ten agents burst into the room, and more than 70 Christians were arrested and taken away for questioning.[5]

Other harassment included believers having their electricity and water cut off, Christian children who were discriminated against at school and found their pathway to higher education blocked, and lawyers who had represented Christians in court being beaten and intimidated to ensure they would not represent believers in future cases.

The most high profile arrest of a lawyer was that of Gao Zhisheng who credited his faith in God for giving him strength during the years of imprisonment and torture that ensued. In 2006 Gao was convicted of subversion. He was released several times only to be rearrested, including a period he described as "hellish" in a Xinjiang prison from 2011 to 2014. Gao appears to have been particularly hated by the Communist authorities because he was a former People's Liberation Army soldier. He secretly penned a book entitled *Unwavering Convictions* which was smuggled out of China and published in English in 2017.[6] His heart-breaking testimony laid out the satanic nature of his Communist tormentors and described experiences that are difficult to read, including one occasion when toothpicks were inserted into his private parts to torture him.

At the present time, Gao remains incarcerated in China at an undisclosed location, despite years of untiring efforts by many international advocates. These include his own family who fled to the United States in 2009 after their 17-year-old daughter Grace tried to take her life several times due to bullying at school because of her father's work. They have bravely fought for Gao's release, and he has twice been nominated for the Nobel Peace Prize.

Gao Zhisheng

New Bibles for Xinjiang

As churches among the majority Muslim people groups of Xinjiang began to take root, the new believers longed to have the Scriptures in their own language. The available Uyghur translations were problematic for many Uyghurs themselves, let alone for Kazak, Kirgiz, and people from other ethnicities.

Responding to the need, missionaries began working with local believers to produce a Bible translation for the Kazaks of Xinjiang. A Kazak Bible already existed across the border in Kazakhstan, but it was done in the Cyrillic script, making it completely unusable to the 1.8 million Kazaks in China. The

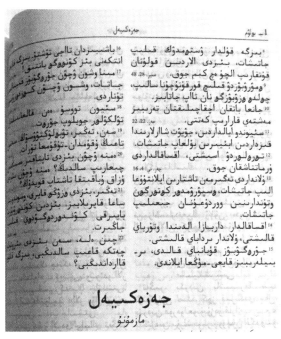

A page from the 2011 Kirgiz New Testament, which can be read by the 230,000 Kirgiz people in Xinjiang

translation of the New Testament for Xinjiang's Kazak people used a modified Arabic script and was completed in 2008. Three years later the entire Bible was published, bringing great joy to the growing number of Kazak Christians in Xinjiang as well as serving as a vital evangelistic tool to reach Muslim Kazaks.

At a mixed-ethnic church meeting in Xinjiang in 2009, a French missionary saw how happy the Kazak believers were to have their own New Testament, but the small number of Kirgiz Christians in the room looked downcast. When asked what the problem was, they replied, "We don't understand the Kazak Bible. When is God going to bless us with His Word in Kirgiz so we can be full of joy too?" Up to that time, Christian meetings were usually conducted using the Kazak or Uyghur vernaculars, and the Kirgiz were forced to huddle in a corner as messages were translated for them.

Two years later, broad smiles covered the faces of Kirgiz believers as the first copies of their New Testament—also using the modified Arabic script—rolled off the printing press.

The last "normal" year

In many ways, 2016 proved to be the last "normal" year for Christians in Xinjiang, perhaps for a very long time. The usual pattern of salvations and arrests continued throughout the year, but it was apparent to believers that pressure was ramping up little by little, like a slow-simmering pot coming to the boil.

Unfortunately, trouble for believers in Xinjiang was exacerbated by the unwise actions of some foreign mission organizations which led to mass arrests of church leaders. For example, one church group in South Korea had invested substantial funds to promote gospel work in Xinjiang, so the Korean leaders traveled to the region to meet some of those who had been helped by their generous giving. Later, in a bid to provide accountability and reports to their supporters in South Korea, the church held a special service where photos of Xinjiang church leaders were displayed on a notice board. A Chinese agent living in South Korea discreetly took photos of the images, and a short time later all of those church leaders were arrested in Xinjiang.

At times, the level of force used by the authorities against Christians was overwhelmingly disproportionate. For example on March 5, 2016, more than 200 armed officers raided a house church meeting in Changji City where a group of 40 house church believers was holding a Bible study. Just five church leaders were arrested and charged, and a week later a female believer, Liu Yan, was also arrested because she had driven several Christians to the meeting.[7]

More house churches were raided in Hotan in July 2016.[8] Two Christian women, Zhou Yanhua and Gao Ming, were arrested in Yining and incarcerated simply because they were planning to drive a group of children to a summer Christian camp. They were charged with "indoctrinating minors with religious and superstitious belief."[9]

A female Christian named Ma Huichao was sentenced to three years in prison for hosting a Bible study for just three believers at her home in Huocheng.[10] A Christian couple, Dai and Li, were arrested in Yining simply for displaying a cross on the wall of their home, and the authorities also detained a woman who was visiting the couple at the time.[11]

The most heavy handed punishment of a Christian occurred in September 2016 when Zhang Haitao was sentenced to 19 years in prison and fined 120,000 Yuan (US $18,000) for posts he made on social media which drew attention to the lack of religious freedom in Xinjiang. Zhang was charged with "inciting subversion of state power" for his posts on Twitter and the Chinese social media platform WeChat.

*Li Aijie, beaten for refusing to divorce her husband (left), and
after fleeing to the United States with her son (right)*
China Aid

Zhang's wife, Li Aijie, who was three months' pregnant at the time of his arrest, was beaten by her own family for refusing to divorce her imprisoned husband. She had been strongly advocating for his release since the arrest which enraged the authorities and caused them to intimidate other family members. They even interrogated Li's 80-year-old mother. When Li Aijie refused to divorce her Christian husband, her siblings brutally beat her, "giving her a black eye, headaches and nausea, and a suspected brain injury."[12]

In December 2017, Li Aijie and her little son, Li Mutian, were able to escape from China and relocate to the United States where Christian friends help them live in safety. They have struggled to adjust to their new lives knowing that Zhang is facing unmentionable hardships in a Xinjiang prison. He isn't due to be released until 2035, at which time the son he has never met will be 19 years old.

However, all of the abuses inflicted by the Communist authorities throughout Xinjiang in 2016 were to pale into relative insignificance compared to the tidal wave of oppression that was about to be unleashed on the people which prompted house church leaders to say that the level of persecution they were experiencing was even worse than during Mao's Cultural Revolution.

2017—The Year Everything Changed in Xinjiang

"Nets above and snares below"

The renowned Chinese evangelist and mission leader Andrew Gih (Chinese name Ji Zhiwen) was an insightful man who saw the threat and nature of Communism from its earliest times in China. In 1961, he wrote the following words which help to explain what has unfolded in Xinjiang since 2017:

> The standing army of Communist China is three million with ten million reservists, and the people's militia would constitute tens of millions too. The standing army is not productive. It consumes, but the army is necessary for two purposes—internally for suppression and externally for aggression. . . .

A concentration camp at Turpan—one of dozens built to detain up to three million Muslims in Xinjiang

Since they have to maintain large standing armies, concentration camps are a necessity—politically to silence the opposition by taking people away after midnight, sending them to concentration camps, and their families do not hear from them. They arrest so many that they instill fear into the minds of the people, so there is no opposition or rebellion.

Communist countries are not for commerce or trade. Their aim is always political. . . . Communism is against human nature. It cannot stay in power except by brute force. So, in Communist countries the people not only have no freedom, but constantly live in fear.[1]

As detailed in the earlier chapters of this book, tensions have existed in Xinjiang between the Han Chinese and Muslim peoples, especially the Uyghurs, for centuries. However the situation broke into full-scale death and destruction in 2017 when conventional arrests were discarded in favor of mass detainment of every person the Communist Party considered to be a potential threat.

Although to the outside world the dramatic actions in Xinjiang seemed haphazard and rushed, they were carefully formulated and systematically implemented by the government. According to one reporter, during a late 2014 meeting,

Xi called for a focus on fighting terrorism, mobilizing civilians to support policing and setting up "nets above and snares below." In the same month, China kicked off a year-long crackdown on terrorism in Xinjiang and beyond. But the attacks and clashes went on. By 2016 there was a sense that whatever was being tried had not worked and something new was needed.[2]

In 2016, President Xi Jinping decided that the Communist head of Xinjiang, Zhang Chunxian, was too weak to implement his brutal policies, and he was replaced by hardliner Chen Quanguo. The unprecedented crackdown resulted in up to three million people being interned in concentration camps throughout the region. There they were subjected to brainwashing and "re-education" programs that the Communist authorities cynically described as "vocational retraining centers."

Although life for most Han people in Xinjiang continued without much direct dislocation, life for the Muslim ethnic minority peoples was shattered and would never be the same again. Tragically, the fledgling churches that had only recently emerged among these groups were also decimated as believers found themselves caught up in the chaos. Many Uyghur, Kirgiz, Kazak, and Hui Christians were lost in the violence that engulfed the region.

The Kunming trigger point

The Chinese government had long sought ways to subjugate Xinjiang's Muslims. However a major tipping point which led to this overwhelming action did not take place in Xinjiang but in the leafy city of Kunming in faraway southwest China at about nine o'clock in the evening of March 1, 2014.

On that fateful day, a group of eight Uyghurs (six men and two women), dressed in black and wielding long knives, ran through the crowds of people inside the Kunming train station, slashing men, women, and children at random. Police shot dead four of the assailants and subdued the others, but not before a stream of blood covered the floors. By the end of the night, it emerged that 31 people had been slashed to death and another 143 injured, many with life-threatening conditions.

The incident in Kunming understandably shocked the nation, and questions were asked as to how such a brazen attack could have been planned and carried out without the knowledge of the authorities. For a time, the ability of the Communist Party to protect its own citizens was brought into question, and the nation's leaders—including President Xi Jinping who had assumed office just 15 months earlier—appeared shocked that the violence which had long plagued Xinjiang had now spread far outside the region's borders.

It emerged that the terrorists hailed from the Hotan area in southwest Xinjiang. They had been incensed by the closure of a mosque and the arrest of its imam the previous year which resulted in riots in Hotan and saw 15 people killed and more than 50 others injured.

The threat to Xi's vision

A cornerstone of Xi Jinping's ascent to the presidency of China at the end of 2012 was his comprehensive plan to make China the greatest military and economic power in the world. The centerpiece of his plan was the "Belt and Road Initiative" which was designed to link China to the rest of the world and spur trillions of dollars in trade. Of all the places in China that are key to the implementation of this ambitious plan, none is more vital than Xinjiang which serves as China's gateway to South Asia, Central Asia, the Middle East, Russia, and ultimately Europe.

The timing of the Muslim insurgency in Xinjiang, therefore, could not have been at a worse time for Xi's plans. The increase in violence occurred right as the initiative was being launched and billions of dollars of investment were flowing into surrounding countries. Facing a possible threat to the entire Belt and Road program and to China's subsequent plans for prosperity and world dominion, it is not surprising that the Chinese Communist Party launched such a massive crackdown against the Uyghurs and other Muslims of Xinjiang.

The trends had been disturbing to the Communist hierarchy in Beijing. At the same time the government sent businessmen into the Middle East to open new regions for commerce, hundreds of Muslim men had traveled for jihad to Syria and other nations where they joined the Islamic State. President Xi was determined that his country would not fall prey to Islamic terrorism. He would do whatever was necessary to stop its spread, even if China's actions would place it offside with the rest of the world.

Another, lesser known reason for why China came down so hard on the people of Xinjiang is the rampant drug trade that flowed through the region, primarily opium smuggled across the border from Afghanistan and Pakistan. As many as 70 to 80 percent of men in some areas of southern Xinjiang are believed by some to have been involved in the drug trade which was destroying millions of lives throughout China.

For many years, China had spent considerable resources trying to stem the flow of narcotics, and tens of thousands of Uyghurs and other suspected drug smugglers had been executed. Despite their efforts, the drug trade kept growing, so the Chinese government may have seen their brutal crackdown as an opportunity to end the flow of narcotics once and for all.

Overwhelming force

After an initial crackdown across Xinjiang in response to the Kunming massacre, during which thousands of Muslims are believed to have been killed, the government appeared to pause as Xi formulated a long-term plan of action. A new iron-clad determination to "permanently fix the Uyghur problem" emerged and was supported by most Chinese people who felt traumatized by the events in Kunming.

The authorities realized that their decades-long efforts to bring peace to Xinjiang had totally failed. For a generation, they had used a "velvet glove" strategy of trying to appease the Muslims of Xinjiang through investment and by building schools, hospitals, and other infrastructure. This strategy was abandoned, and the glove was removed to reveal a clenched fist of steel. A new hardline approach was implemented which shocked the world by its severity and scope.

To start, new laws were introduced in Xinjiang which caused even more anti-Han sentiment among Muslims. One of the new rules prohibited parents and guardians from "organizing, luring or forcing minors into attending religious activities or forcing them to wear religious dress or symbols."[3] Citizens were encouraged to spy on their neighbors and to report parents whom they suspected of raising their children in a religious faith.

The police and military were given new wide-ranging powers in Xinjiang, aided by hundreds of thousands of facial recognition cameras that processed everything that went on in the region. Police were granted authority to stop and search anyone on the street and could demand to see their phones or other electronic devices. If any questionable emails, texts, or websites the person had visited were found, he or she could be immediately taken into custody.

Next, every person in Xinjiang who had a passport was ordered to hand it over to the police and to apply for permission if they wanted to leave the country. This policy aimed at cutting off Muslims' ability to connect with extremists in neighboring countries like Afghanistan and Tajikistan and caused great inconvenience to hundreds of thousands of genuine travelers, including the many businessmen who ply their trade across borders.

In 2017, the government further infuriated Muslims in Xinjiang by issuing a list of 29 Islamic names that people were no longer permitted to call their children. The list included "Mohammed," "Islam," "Imam," and "Hajj."[4]

Prominent Uyghurs sent to the camps included professional footballers, the president of Xinjiang University and several professors, and the director of the Xinjiang Medical Institute. All of these people were arrested for showing insufficient loyalty to the Communist Party and for exhibiting "nationalistic tendencies."

Locals in Xinjiang identified 48 "evil bans" which the government used as reasons for arresting people and sending them for "re-education." The list included "traveling abroad, knowing someone who has traveled abroad, watching foreign videos or movies, fasting, praying, attending religious seminars, downloading foreign software, not submitting voice recordings to the government, and speaking in a native language in public."[5]

By the end of 2017, a glimpse into the scale of China's plans emerged with news that in addition to implementing a national facial recognition database, the government created a DNA database of every adult in Xinjiang. Human Rights Watch reported the following:

> Chinese authorities in Xinjiang are collecting DNA samples, fingerprints, iris scans, and blood types of all residents in the region between the ages of 12 and 65. . . . Authorities state that the Population Registration Program is meant for "scientific decision-making" that promotes poverty alleviation, better management, and social stability. . . . Compelled DNA sampling of an entire region or population for purposes of security maintenance is a serious human rights violation in that it cannot be justified as necessary or proportionate.[6]

"Adem Yoq"

Throughout 2017, awareness of the scale of the crackdown in Xinjiang gradually dawned on the rest of the world. Visitors to many cities and towns reported how entire Muslim neighborhoods had been boarded up and were largely devoid of people, while grandmothers were left to take care of children whose parents had been suddenly taken away. Satellite images appeared on Western news websites showing how dozens of massive secure facilities, surrounded by barbwire and high walls, had quickly been constructed throughout the region. Many camps were so large that they were able to house tens of thousands of detainees.

As the world struggled to come to terms with developments in Xinjiang, the estimates of the number of people incarcerated in the camps increased markedly. In May 2018, the US Department of Defense stated the number was "at least a million but likely closer to three million citizens."[7]

If the Muslim population of Xinjiang thought the preceding years were as bad as things could get, 2018 commenced with the Chinese constitution being altered to appoint Xi Jinping "President for life," and the concentration camps were filled to overflowing. The government also built hundreds of "orphanages" throughout the region to house the children of parents who had been taken away. According to local media reports, just one county near Kashgar built 18 new orphanages in 2017.

The Chinese Communist Party did not limit their suppression to adults. Under direct command from Beijing, hospitals in Xinjiang were ordered to perform late-term abortions on minority babies, and in many cases newborn babies were killed as soon as they were delivered. A hospital worker, Hasiyet Abdulla, described the carnage:

> They wouldn't give the baby to the parents—they kill the babies when they're born. It's an order that's been given from above. It's an order that's been printed and distributed in official documents. Hospitals get fined if they don't comply, so of course, they carry this out. . . . There were babies born at nine months who we killed after inducing labor. They did that in the maternity wards because those were the orders. Babies born alive were taken from their parents, killed, and then discarded like trash.[8]

Dr. Joanna Smith Finley of Britain's Newcastle University comments, "It's not an immediate, shocking, mass-killing-on-the-spot-type genocide, but it's a slow, painful, creeping genocide. . . . A direct means of genetically reducing the Uyghur population."[9] So devastating were the effects of the changes to society that the Turkic phrase *adem yoq* (everybody's gone) was commonly heard throughout the villages and towns of Xinjiang. When asked how a person's family was doing, the answer was often, "adem yoq."

The number of news reports on the dire situation in Xinjiang could fill several books, but we will try to cover a few of the main developments in this brief section with sources provided in the notes for those who desire to read more. Punitive new actions designed to strip Muslims of all that is precious to them were also implemented, including a ban on people studying the Qur'an or the Arabic language. Families were visited in their homes and forced to sign a document that said, "Today, I pledge to report what I know to the government. I understand there is a legal liability for hiding the truth. I swear that no one in my household is studying the Qur'an or Arabic."[10]

Uyghurs were ordered to bring all knives to their nearest police station to have them registered. In May 2018, Muslims in Xinjiang were strictly forbidden to celebrate Ramadan, and Muslim-owned restaurants and shops were forced to remain open and serve food during the month normally reserved for fasting in the Islamic world.

Traditional Muslim marriages were outlawed. In June 2018, as part of the plan to transform Uyghurs into patriotic Chinese citizens, 40 Uyghurs from Kashgar, Aksu, and Hotan were arrested and tortured in concentration camps after they refused to participate in a Chinese Dragon Boat Festival. An additional 100 families

> were fined for refusing to eat zongzi, or leaf-wrapped rice dumplings common during the festival . . . and they were required to write a letter of guarantee promising that they would never participate in any illegal religious activities and would celebrate the Dragon Boat Festival from now on.[11]

Muslim men were banned from growing long beards; women could not wear veils in public; and homeschooling was outlawed. China also officially banned all Chinese citizens from going on pilgrimage to Mecca—a journey seen as the pinnacle of the faith for Muslims throughout the world.

Arbitrary arrests of people with no connection to terrorism at all continued to occur across the region. For example in December 2017, a Kazak man, Jierebaike Yelimaisi, was sent to a concentration camp simply because he had traveled abroad for heart surgery.[12]

Genocide

The Chinese government's determination to crush all possibility of Islamic separatism spread beyond its borders. Hi-tech electronic pigeons with GPS tracking and listening devices have been discovered inside neighboring countries. Russia, meanwhile, "stopped importing steam irons, cell phones, and phone charges from China after Chinese listening devices were discovered in the exports."[1]

In 2018, advertisements appeared in neighboring Kazakhstan that encouraged people with dual citizenship to return to China by a certain date to update their passports or risk losing them.

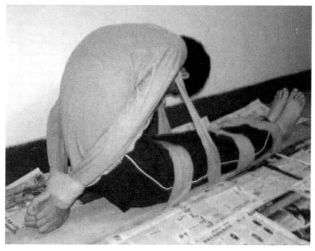

*Inmates were tortured in poses like this for weeks
in the Xinjiang concentration camps*
China Aid

Thousands of trusting Kazaks made the journey across the border only to be arrested and be put into the concentration camp system. There detainees were forced to only speak Mandarin, which is a language unknown to most Kazaks. Prisoners were even required to pass written examinations in Chinese or face severe beatings and deprivation. Many Kazaks committed suicide after realizing they had been tricked and would never see their families again.

Many citizens of Kazakhstan who did not hold Chinese passports were also detained after visiting relatives in Xinjiang. The government of Kazakhstan, which relies on China for its economic wellbeing, lodged a few weak protests on behalf of their people, but Kazak leaders were not willing to risk offending their giant neighbor. The Chinese government was not troubled about who they arrested. Even a famous Kazak singer, Otanbek Ensekhan, was seized from the stage as soon as he finished his performance at a concert in Urumqi, although he appears to have been released a short time later.

While the Chinese government continued to deny even the existence of the camps they had filled to the brim, some of the foreign detainees who were able to return to Kazakhstan reported that people were "being forcibly medicated and injected with unknown substances. Those released suffered from loss of memory or even loss of reproductive ability."[2]

Finally, after mass protests on the streets of Turkey in February 2019, the Turkish government broke its silence and spoke out against the treatment of their Uyghur cousins in Xinjiang. One official described the concentration camps as "a great embarrassment for humanity."[3] However the Turkish authorities were cautious in their denunciation, worried about the possible loss of hundreds of billions of dollars of Chinese investment. Turkey is a key ally in Xi Jinping's "Belt and Road Initiative" and a strategically placed nation to help China gain access to the European markets.

Over time some foreign news agencies led by the BBC, CNN, and Reuters managed to document many of the camps in Xinjiang. Some were even allowed to film inside the facilities where stage-managed smiling Uyghurs nervously proclaimed the glories of the Chinese Communist Party.

One Kazak man, Omir Belaki, said people in the camps were mercilessly tortured in multiple ways, while Muslims were forced by their captors to eat pork and drink alcohol.[4]

Electronic surveillance has turned Xinjiang into a totalitarian police state, and an atmosphere of fear permeates every part of society. Many towns and neighborhoods are emptied of people, and Omer Kanat of the World Uyghur Congress says,

> Every household, every family has had three or four people taken away. In some villages you can't see men on the streets anymore—only women and children. All the men have been sent to the camps. . . .
>
> People supposedly prone to influences of Islamic extremism undergo a "brainwashing" process inside the detention camps—often housed in converted schools or government buildings. Detainees are required to praise the ruling Communist Party, sing revolutionary songs, learn to speak Mandarin, study the thoughts of Chinese leader Xi Jinping, and confess perceived transgressions such as praying at a mosque or traveling abroad.[5]

At first, the BBC estimated that at least one million people were being incarcerated throughout Xinjiang as the world's media drew comparisons to Hitler's death camps. Bizarrely, when Chinese officials were challenged on the existence of the camps that had already been visited and filmed, they denied that the facilities existed before later saying they were "vocational training centers" where people were willingly and happily learning new skills that would enable them to have better lives in the future.

There were no limits to their efforts. Uyghurs as far afield as Australia, Turkey, Scandinavia, Malaysia, and the United States have been harassed and threatened by Chinese agents. Economic pressure made it hard for governments to resist. *Financial Times* reported that, "Chinese officials have been sending notices to overseas Uyghur students demanding their immediate return—often after detaining their parents in China—and about 150 Uyghur students at Al-Azhat University in Cairo, Egypt, have been detained by local authorities, with at least 22 being deported."[6] Uyghurs living overseas also soon learned it was best not to contact their relatives in China because all calls and emails are monitored and could bring trouble to the recipients.

By late 2018, a few Muslims who had managed to survive the camps emerged in the West where they testified before the US Congress, the United Nations, and other bodies. Their experiences were shocking, but foreign governments seemed powerless to intervene because the Chinese authorities set their faces like flint and rejected all international pressure and condemnation. A 29-year-old Uyghur woman, Mihrigul Tursun, told the National Press Club in Washington DC the following:

> I thought that I would die rather than go through this torture and begged them to kill me. The authorities put a helmet-like thing on my head, and each time I was electrocuted, my whole body would shake violently, and I would feel the pain in my veins. I don't remember the rest. White foam came out of my mouth, and I began to lose consciousness. The last word I heard them saying is that being a Uyghur is a crime.[7]

In 2019, Adrian Zenz, a world expert on mass incarcerations, reviewed official documents and estimated that the Chinese government had constructed at least 1,000 detainment camps in Xinjiang capable of holding 1.5 million people. He estimated one in six Muslim adults in the region were being held and subject to brainwashing.[8]

Belatedly in December 2019, the US Congress voted 407 to one to pass the "Uighur Act of 2019" which censured China for their actions and issued sanctions against those involved. Republican Congressman Chris Smith called China's actions in Xinjiang "audaciously repressive," involving "mass internment of millions on a scale not seen since the Holocaust."⁹ The Chinese authorities reacted angrily after President Donald Trump signed the act into law. They said their policies were working, and there had not been a single terrorist incident in the region in three years.

News also filtered through that thousands of Han cadres and officials in the region had resigned or sought early retirement because of the stress they felt having to implement Xi's goals against their own citizens. One official complained,

> The Han people are deeply dissatisfied; Life is harsh [in Xinjiang] even for cadres. Officials are exhausted as nobody is allowed days off [even after working for weeks]. . . . China has set up what is called a "sent-down system" in the region that requires cadres to live in the homes of Uyghurs as part of surveillance programmes.
>
> The cadres sent down must bring gifts and pay out of their own pocket and anyone refusing to go is sacked right on the spot. Measures like these have triggered widespread resentment . . . Xinjiang authorities regularly advertise jobs with lucrative packages, but it is hard to retain people and requests for early retirement have been rejected in the past year.¹⁰

Survivors begin to speak

As the rest of the world began to acknowledge the scale of atrocities being committed against the ethnic people of Xinjiang, a small number of escapees managed to give interviews. Horrific stories of brainwashing, killings, and systematic rape emerged.

In October 2019, a Uyghur woman named Sayragul Sauytbay described how she was forced to work as a language teacher in one camp, teaching Chinese to Uyghur and Kazak prisoners. She revealed that the "curriculum" of the camps consisted of systematic brainwashing that targeted the prisoners' ethnic identity, religious beliefs, and humanity. Language lessons consisted of rote memorization and recitation of propaganda such as "I love China," "I am Chinese," and "Thank you for the Communist Party."

The living nightmare for the prisoners caused Sauytbay to speak out once she had a chance. She shared the following:

> One elderly woman was imprisoned for making an international phone call with a cell phone—but this woman was from a tribe so remote that she did not even know how to use a phone. When she denied making the call, she was taken to a torture room. I saw her when she returned. She was covered with blood, she had no fingernails and her skin was flayed.
>
> Rape of both men and women was routine in the camps. Prisoners live in densely packed cells with a single bucket to relieve themselves, and they survive on watery soup, with only one serving of meat per week. That meat is pork. All of these prisoners are Muslims, and eating pork violates their religious convictions. Camp guards forced them, week in and week out, to eat the pork, breaking down even their privately held beliefs about God. . . .
>
> The afternoons are spent confessing all manner of "sins" against the Communist regime—and if prisoners do not have enough to confess, they are punished. Some of those sins included showing emotion at the sight of another prisoner's punishment. In one horrifying incident, prison guards publicly gang-raped a woman, all the while watching to see if any prisoner registered shock, horror, pity, or even tried to look away from the terrible scene. All those who did "were taken away, and we never saw them again."[11]

A senator's analysis

Many foreign governments are reluctant to criticize the Chinese authorities for their draconian actions in Xinjiang. But Arkansas

Senator Tom Cotton's press statement in December 2019 shows a clear understanding of the nature of the atrocities being perpetrated on the people of Xinjiang:

> This reign of terror began in 2014, after a string of terror attacks in Xinjiang. But instead of bringing those terrorists to justice, the Chinese Communist Party used the attacks as an opportunity to eradicate all dissent, all wrong thinking—if you will—from a province with 25 million residents. It would be as if you tried to turn the state of Texas into a concentration camp.
>
> These secret documents [obtained by the *New York Times*] revealed a stunning order from General Secretary Xi Jinping. He said, "We must be as harsh as them and show them absolutely no mercy."
>
> So to beat these terrorists, Beijing chose to adopt the tactics of terror. Every Uyghur and dissenter in the province is suffering as a result. . . .
>
> They've turned the province into a garrison state with ruthless and pitiless competence. . . .
>
> Uyghurs, young and old, were loaded onto buses and taken to camps with thick concrete walls and razor-sharp barbed wire. The police informed anxious relatives that these were schools. Their loved ones were being "re-educated." And no, they were not free to leave the school, nor would there be any recess or field trips. . . .
>
> Beijing now holds—let me say again—more than one million people in these reeducation camps—supposedly for reasons of national security, but the truth is a lot more chilling.
>
> The Chinese Communists, like all totalitarians, are paranoid about their own survival—and rightly so, as a conspiracy of greedy, power-mad princelings with no democratic legitimacy whatsoever.
>
> And like all totalitarian rulers, the Chinese Communist Party is also a very jealous master. Every attachment, every conviction, every loyalty—whether to one's family, one's culture, even one's Creator—must be sacrificed on the altar of the Party.

According to the Chinese Communist Party, every knee must bow before it, and every tongue must profess the slogans of Xi and Mao. . . .

A paranoid communist power won't limit itself to one province or people, nor will it ultimately limit itself to its own land. It will extend its tyrannical reach to every corner that it views as its own, creeping ever outward until it commands the deference of all the world. Until it "deals with" the rebellious billions who haven't yet learned to love the Chinese Big Brother.

The Chinese Communist Party is running concentration camps today, but make no mistake: its appetite for expansion is far greater, its methods of control applicable to anyone, anywhere. The Free World must confront this threat in plain view, and act now to avert such a dark and chilling future.[12]

After strenuously denying the existence of the camps for years, in 2020 the Chinese authorities finally admitted that on average, they provided "vocational training" to 1.3 million Xinjiang residents each year between 2013 and 2019.[13]

Finally, on the last day of the Trump administration in Washington DC, the US Secretary of State, Mike Pompeo, officially accused the Chinese government of genocide for their treatment of the Uyghur people.[14] Chinese officials responded angrily, describing the accusations as "outrageous lies" by people who hold "prejudice and hatred against China." They included Pompeo on a sanction list of 28 American officials, and these individuals and their family members have been banned from ever visiting China or doing business with Chinese companies.

If the Chinese government thought the change of US administration would bring relief, their hopes were short lived. The incoming President Joe Biden's pick for Secretary of State, Antony Blinken, agreed with his predecessor's finding.

A Christian Lament for the Uyghurs

Since April 2021, the British parliament also officially designated China's actions in Xinjiang as genocide. But by this stage the Chinese Communist Party no longer cares what governments say. President Xi's power in China has grown so great that "Xi Jinping thought" is now enshrined in the country's constitution, and all citizens are ordered to study his speeches—actions that elevate Xi to the same level as Mao Zedong.

The Chinese government has gone on the attack. Any foreign power who criticized its actions in Xinjiang is mercilessly attacked for their own actions. For example the United States was denounced for their past treatment of black people and Native Americans, and the British are slammed for their ghastly practice of deliberately getting millions of Chinese addicted to opium in the nineteenth century. When Australia spoke out, China stopped buying tens of billions of dollars of its goods, and tourism from China almost dried up overnight.

Two young Uyghur boys praying on the streets of Kashgar
IMB

Because of the Communist Party's hatred of religion and their complete inability to make a distinction between Islam, Christianity, or other religions, many Christians throughout Xinjiang have been swept up in the genocidal madness. Tragically, after more than a century of struggle and persecution, the gospel had finally begun to take root among sections of Uyghur, Kazak, and Kirgiz people in Xinjiang, with small remnants of vibrant believers emerging from each group.

The earth-shattering events have severely damaged the advance of the kingdom of God among these people groups. Reports from the field suggest that all house church leaders from minority backgrounds have been arrested and sent to the concentration camps. An article in February 2018 estimated that at least 100 Christians had been sent to camps throughout Xinjiang. One woman said,

> I don't know where my husband is right now, but I believe that God still uses him in prison. Sometimes I am worried that he doesn't have enough clothes to keep warm. . . . I am afraid it will affect my children too. The teacher in the school is paying special attention to my children after the authorities told the school about my husband.[1]

One of the key house church figures in Xinjiang was a highly respected Uyghur woman. In 2016 she visited a hotel in Urumqi and was asked to insert her national ID card into a machine at the entrance. The moment she did so, according to witnesses, security officers appeared and took her into custody. She has not been heard from since.

In Xinjiang, a small but steady trickle of Kazaks had been turning to Christ, but the brutal crackdown saw the fledgling Kazak Church suffer an egregious blow right at the moment when it seemed poised for a breakthrough. At the time of the Chinese crackdown there were a few hundred known Kazak

Christians in China, but what has become of the Kazak Church remains to be seen.

While the ethnic minority churches in Xinjiang have been plunged into disarray, Han Chinese Christians also face increased pressure as the authorities followed instructions from Beijing and unleashed their fury on all believers. On March 7, 2017, a series of raids took place across Xinjiang, resulting in the arrest of at least 80 house church Christians.[2] In the following month, five Christians from Changji were jailed for between three to five years each. They were convicted of "illegal assembly and gathering a crowd to disturb public order" after they organized a Bible study attended by about 50 believers.[3]

In January 2018, more than 100 members of the Qingshuihe house church in Yining were surprised to find the doors of their rented church building locked and a government warning poster attached to the door stating that their church was an illegal gathering. The pastor, Luo Yuanqi, had already been beaten and imprisoned in the past.

Many other arrests took place in Xinjiang, most of which were never reported because of the tight restrictions and the threats of arrest if anyone shares information from the region. Countless believers have vanished and have not been heard from again. Even a number of elderly believers in their seventies are known to have been arrested and sent to the dreaded "re-education" centers.

By 2019, it became clear that the Church in Xinjiang was being decimated. Few house church leaders were still free to minister, especially among the non-Han ethnicities. One report listed the names of six Uyghur Christians who had been given harsh prison sentences. All of them were charged with

> Illegal preaching, gathering, and spreading of "harmful" books. Mehmet Abdulla has been sentenced to seven years in prison, and Huji Abdurehim received a five-year sentence. Maimaiti Yimingjiang is also imprisoned for five years, as is a man only

identified as Brother Adil. A Christian doctor, whose last name is Rakhman, is also serving a five-year prison term, and Adil Jan has received a seven-year verdict. Many of these Christians are recent converts, and all are from the largely Muslim Uyghur people group.[4]

Summing up how many Han Christians feel about the events that have unfolded in Xinjiang, a Han Christian wrote an open letter of lament in 2019 that is addressed to the Uyghur people. Here is much of the heart-felt letter which sheds a new light on the tragic circumstances that have befallen his Muslim neighbors:

I have long wanted to write you this letter, but never knew where to start. Today I finally plucked up my courage to start writing this letter that perhaps you might never get a chance to read. I am a Han Chinese, but, like you, both of us were born and bred in Xinjiang. I remember playing with you when I was young, catching crickets together, swimming together, and racing in the Gobi sands together.

Every Chinese New Year you would come to visit our home. We would eat, drink, and make a general racket together. During your Eid al-Adha, we would visit your homes. We would also eat, drink, and make a general racket together. There was no suspicion between us, no barrier of race or religion. You are a great-hearted, authentic people who love to sing and dance freely, with no falsehood.

I do not remember when it happened, but Xinjiang changed suddenly, and became unrecognizable to me. I started praying and pleading with God to give me wisdom to see what was actually happening. Slowly, I began to see more clearly that the powers of evil were using hate to begin their slaughter. This terrifying reality is now happening! I can hear my heart crying, I really can. . . .

I have many beautiful memories of Xinjiang that cannot be forgotten. My love for you is contained in my prayers. Because I feel so helpless, I pray that the Jesus who is most precious to me will help you.

I suppose the only thing I can really do for you is to introduce you to my most precious Jesus. . . . I don't want to talk too much about the religion, history, land, and peoples of Xinjiang, because I know it's a trap that would be an endless debate. . . .

Even if the entire world has abandoned you, I think Jesus would not abandon you and me. . . . Let us walk away from this mindless hate, bravely facing and crushing the hate that has been woven from lies and fears.

I sincerely ask you to bravely hold out your hand, to open your wounded heart, and to lay down the hate that comes from the Evil One. Let us walk away from this world of lies. I know that you are unable to do this, but I believe that Jesus is able. Give Jesus a chance, and He will give you freedom.

Xinjiang has suffered too much! It has gone down too many crooked paths in history! I am tired, and you are tired as well! I want this all to change! I no longer want to see history's hatred resurface in this dry and parched land. Let us wash it all away with the sacrificial love of Jesus! Let Xinjiang once again become a blessed land flowing with milk and honey! Let us boldly forget what lies behind and press on toward the goal of peace.

Come! See what Jesus might bring us. Let us pray for Jesus to watch over our futures, Xinjiang's future. Give him a chance, and I believe that he will give us the surprise of a thousand years.[5]

Meanwhile, the Church in Xinjiang faces major adjustments because of the region-wide, severe crackdown against Uyghurs. While fellowships among ethnic minority groups are largely shut down because of the turmoil, hundreds of thousands of Han believers continue to meet with comparative freedom.

Probably the greatest challenge Han believers have is the increasingly invasive use of technology by the government. In 2020, a text message about a home meeting was sent to a pastor in Kashgar from an unregistered phone. Less than ten minutes later the police were knocking at the pastor's door demanding to know his activities and where the text had come from.

Meanwhile, the number of Chinese evangelists in the Uyghur stronghold of Kashgar who are connected to the Back to Jerusalem vision increased rapidly in 2020 from a handful at the start of the year to 30 by the end. In the midst of their dire trial, many Muslims are more open to the gospel than ever before. The number of conversions to Christ has been increasing, and a small number of Uyghur Bible study groups meet discreetly throughout the city.

The path for the gospel in Xinjiang has been tumultuous over the centuries, but it appears that God has set apart a remnant. Regardless of what may happen in the region in the future, the flame of the gospel is likely to be carried forth.

The Future of the Church in Xinjiang

At the start of this book, we quoted a 1930s missionary who described Xinjiang as "a land where rivers run into the ground, and then break forth again in oases and springs tens of miles from the places where they disappeared."[1] In much the same way, the Church in Xinjiang has also appeared to vanish at times, only to re-emerge from beneath the sands, giving life and light to the people in this dark region.

In 2020, news began to filter out of China from some of the Uyghurs who survived Xi's death camps. Many who gained release were forcibly relocated to work in other parts of China in the continuing effort to integrate them into Chinese society and strip them of their ethnic identity. The children of many of the prisoners are being "take care of" by the state in a bid to reprogram their minds and hearts away from their Uyghur upbringing and from Islam and to force them to embrace the "glories of atheism and the Chinese Communist Party."

Encouragingly, some accounts have emerged that tell of visions that Uyghur people have had of Jesus during their dark ordeals in the camps. Some became Christians as a result, while others sought more information on the Christian faith. Even in their darkest moment in history, God has not forgotten the Uyghur people. He continues to lovingly pursue them with His plan of salvation.

Xinjiang's neighbors also face a difficult future as the Chinese Communist Party extends their ever increasing ambitions across borders. In 2020, Chinese media reported that all of Kyrgyzstan historically belonged to China until it was annexed by the Soviet

Union, and claims have been made that Kazakhstan is "eager to return to China."[2]

The Chinese government appears to have cornered Kazakhstan in a thick web from which they will struggle to break free. The large oil- and gas-rich nation is a crucial part of Xi Jinping's "Belt and Road Initiative," and a succession of Kazakhstan leaders have accumulated such massive debt that the country is now beholden to China for their economic survival. As a result, Kazakhstan's leaders are reluctant to criticize their giant southern neighbor for the atrocities committed against their own citizens.

As we reach the end of our look at the great things God has done in China's wild northwest, there is much for which to thank the Lord Jesus Christ. We learned about how the first Christian witness in Xinjiang occurred over 1,000 years ago when Nestorian missionaries arrived in northwest China, and many thousands of people from various ethnic groups converted to Christ.

Centuries of cruelty followed, marked by constant clashes between the Han Chinese and Uyghurs as various kingdoms and dynasties wrestled for control over the strategic land. In the eighteenth and nineteenth centuries, many Chinese Christians were exiled to this "realm of the barbarians" where they laid down their lives after moistening the sands of Xinjiang with their blood and tears.

The 1890s saw the arrival of the first Evangelical Christians, with Nils Fredrik Höijer and Johannes Avetaranian breaking the ground for dozens of Swedish missionaries to serve in a fruitful mission in southern Xinjiang. In the same era, the unique personalities George Hunter and Percy Mather dominated work in northern Xinjiang for many years before they passed on to their eternal reward.

The high-water mark of missionary work in Xinjiang was reached in the early 1930s before progress was stopped dead in its tracks by brutal Muslim persecution, which saw many Uyghur and Kirgiz Christians slaughtered. For a time Christianity in Xinjiang disappeared from view, only to later resurface as a clear, life-giving oasis.

The 1940s was a pivotal time in the history of Christianity in the region as Han Chinese missionaries arrived in obedience to God's call for them to take the gospel back to Jerusalem. These early Chinese pioneers suffered greatly. Many were called to lay down their lives for Jesus, while others like Simon Zhao spent decades in prison before God supernaturally granted them a voice to a new generation of dedicated believers. The Chinese Church took up the baton and remain determined to impact both Xinjiang and the unreached world for Christ before His return.

Astonishingly, because of the massive influx of Han immigrants, the tables in the following pages indicate that the Church in Xinjiang today is made up of approximately 900,000 believers, a dramatic increase since 1949 when just 200 Christians were estimated to live in Xinjiang.

While the world has been shocked to learn of the atrocities committed by the Chinese government against the Uyghur people in the last five years, genocide has been a common practice in Xinjiang for more than 3,000 years—long before the founding of Islam. Beginning with the Scythians, Wusun, Hun, and Tocharian civilizations before the time of Christ, ethnic groups that have conquered Xinjiang have customarily slaughtered hundreds of thousands of their enemies. The current situation, though diabolical, is far from unique in Xinjiang which has long been a land of death of destruction.

The Chinese Communist Party appear to be somewhat surprised by the level of worldwide fury against their actions in Xinjiang. In 2020 even the Disney movie *Mulan*, which cost the media giant $200 million to produce, was caught up in the storm. The film was boycotted by most Western media outlets because parts of it were filmed in Xinjiang, and the end credits thank the provincial authorities, including the Public Security Bureau, for their assistance. Stung by the tide of criticism, the Chinese government banned the movie in China as well, possibly to prevent their citizens finding out why it has caused such an uproar around the world.

This incident highlights one of the problems related to Xinjiang today. Most Chinese citizens have no idea that their government has imprisoned and tortured millions of their fellow citizens in Xinjiang. They cannot read this information online or via any other forum, and all criticism from overseas is cleverly redefined by the Communist Party to be racist attacks on the Chinese people and culture. Today, many Christians in China remain blissfully unaware that many Uyghur, Kazak, and other believers have been killed or tortured by the government. Others, however, are deeply concerned. They realize that the experiment of reprogramming millions of people in the Xinjiang concentration camps is now being implemented in Tibetan areas and can easily be expanded to eliminate Christians if God doesn't intervene to thwart the plans of the Communist Party.

What will become of the Xinjiang Church remains to be seen, but the body of Christ has proven to be extremely resilient. Wicked people in the past have found it impossible to destroy a faith that lives in the hearts and minds of redeemed men and women.

Let us pray that God will cause the Uyghur people to emerge from this period of intense suffering as broken vessels who are disillusioned with the empty religion their forefathers have followed for centuries. May this humbling cause them to seek Jesus with all their hearts, resulting in a great turning to Christ.

The final word on the future hopes for Christianity in Xinjiang should be left to local Christian Mark Chuanhang Shan who has lived through both the good times and bad as the gospel has struggled to gain a foothold in Xinjiang. Shan writes the following:

> The hatred and mistrust between Han and Uyghurs in Xinjiang . . . including bombings, race conflicts and riots, spread all over Xinjiang, but in my personal experience, Uyghur Christians and Han Christians have maintained and deepened their relationships during these sensitive periods. They show concern as usual, and help and pray for each other.
>
> History will prove that Christian faith, the freedom to spread Christianity and the broad voluntary acceptance of it, is the only feasible solution for peace in Xinjiang. Only the gospel can produce in this troubled region a lasting peace, stability, and the development of a multi-cultural society where social justice and mutual love are displayed among various nationalities.[3]

Appendix

Table 1. Evangelical Christians in Xinjiang (1888–2020)
(both Three-Self and house churches)

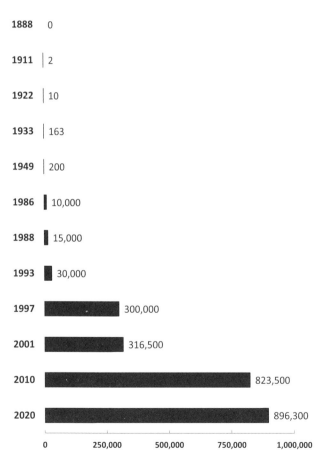

Year	Count
1888	0
1911	2
1922	10
1933	163
1949	200
1986	10,000
1988	15,000
1993	30,000
1997	300,000
2001	316,500
2010	823,500
2020	896,300

Appendix

Sources for Table 1:

0	(1888)
2	(1911 – *The Missionary Review of the World,* March 1913)
10	(1922 – Stauffer, *The Christian Occupation of China*)
163	(1933 – "Intercessors for China" prayer calendar)
200	(1949 – *Pray for China*, October 1995)
10,000	(1986 – *Bridge*, October–November 1988)*
15,000	(1988 – *Bridge*, October–November 1988)*
30,000	(1993 – Amity News Service, February 1993)*
30,000	(1994 – Amity News Service, November–December 2004)*
300,000	(1997 – Hosanna Ministries, "Report on the Xinjiang House churches")
316,500	(2001 – Johnstone and Mandryk, *Operation World*)
131,000	(2004 – Amity News Service, November–December 2004)*
823,500	(2010 – Mandryk, *Operation World*)
896,300	(2020 – Hattaway, *The China Chronicles*)

* These sources may only refer to registered church estimates. TSPM figures typically only count adult baptized members.

Map of All Christians in Xinjiang

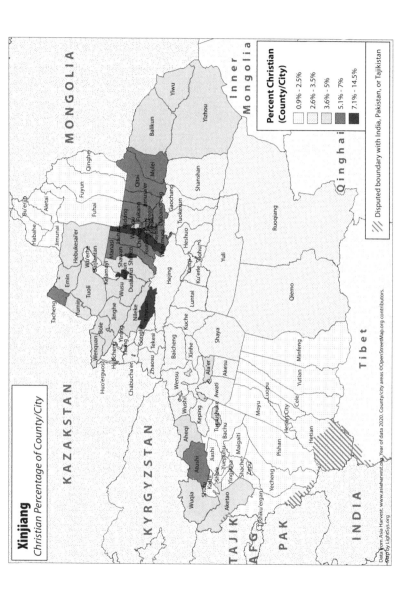

Xinjiang
Christian Percentage of County/City

Percent Christian (County/City)
- 0.9% - 2.5%
- 2.6% - 3.5%
- 3.6% - 5%
- 5.1% - 7%
- 7.1% - 14.5%

Disputed boundary with India, Pakistan, or Tajikistan

Data from Asia Harvest, www.asiaharvest.org. Year of data 2020. County/city areas ©OpenStreetMap.org contributors. Map by LightSys.org

Table 2. All Christians in Xinjiang

Xinjiang 新疆	POPULATION					CHRISTIANS							
						Evangelicals			Catholics			Total Christians	
Location	Census 2000	Census 2010	Growth	Growth (percent)	Estimate 2020	TSPM	House church	TOTAL Evangelicals	CPA	House church	TOTAL Catholics	TOTAL	Percent of 2020 population
Akesu (Aksu) Prefecture 阿克苏地区													
Akesu (Aksu) City 阿克苏市	561,822	535,657	-26,165	-4.66%	509,492	3,057	9,171	12,228	357	535	892	13,119	2.58%
Awati (Awat) County 阿瓦提县	209,654	237,562	27,908	13.31%	265,470	1,593	4,778	6,371	186	279	465	6,836	2.58%
Baicheng (Bay) County 拜城县	203,665	229,252	25,587	12.56%	254,839	1,529	4,587	6,116	178	268	446	6,562	2.58%
Keping (Kalpin) County 柯坪县	38,584	44,261	5,677	14.71%	49,938	300	899	1,199	35	52	87	1,286	2.58%
Kucha (Kuqa) County 库车县	388,593	462,588	73,995	19.04%	536,583	3,219	9,658	12,878	376	563	939	13,817	2.58%
Shaya (Xayar) County 沙雅县	202,992	257,502	54,510	26.85%	312,012	1,872	5,616	7,488	218	328	546	8,034	2.58%
Wensu County 温宿县	219,219	233,933	14,714	6.71%	248,647	1,492	4,476	5,968	174	261	435	6,403	2.58%
Wushi (Uqturpan) County 乌什县	177,410	197,990	20,580	11.60%	218,570	1,311	3,934	5,246	153	229	382	5,628	2.58%
Xinhe (Toksu) County 新和县	139,806	172,064	32,258	23.07%	204,322	1,226	3,678	4,904	143	215	358	5,261	2.58%
	2,141,745	2,370,809	229,064	10.70%	2,599,873	15,599	46,798	62,397	1,820	2,730	4,550	66,947	2.58%
Aletai (Altai) Prefecture 阿勒泰地区													
Aletai (Altai) City 阿勒泰市	178,510	190,064	11,554	6.47%	201,618	1,028	3,085	4,113	141	212	353	4,466	2.22%
Bu'erjin (Burqin) County 布尔津县	61,633	66,758	5,125	8.32%	71,883	367	1,100	1,466	60	75	126	1,592	2.22%
Fuhai County 福海县	77,830	81,845	4,015	5.16%	85,860	438	1,314	1,752	60	90	150	1,902	2.22%
Fuyun County 富蕴县	80,986	87,886	6,900	8.52%	94,786	483	1,450	1,934	66	100	166	2,100	2.22%
Habahe County 哈巴河县	73,403	82,507	9,104	12.40%	91,611	467	1,402	1,869	64	96	160	2,029	2.22%
Jimunai (Jeminay) County 吉木乃县	35,462	35,365	-97	-0.27%	35,268	180	540	719	25	37	62	781	2.22%
Qinghe (Qinggil) County 青河县	53,843	58,858	5,015	9.31%	63,873	326	977	1,303	45	67	112	1,415	2.22%
	561,667	603,283	41,616	7.41%	644,899	3,289	9,867	13,156	451	677	1,129	14,285	2.22%
Bayinguoleng (Bayingolin) Prefecture 巴音郭楞蒙古自治州													
Bohu (Bagrax) County 博湖县	53,528	54,788	1,260	2.35%	56,048	448	1,345	1,794	39	59	98	1,892	3.38%
Hejing County 和静县	161,157	160,804	-353	-0.22%	160,451	1,284	3,851	5,134	112	168	281	5,415	3.38%
Heshuo (Hoxud) County 和硕县	62,970	72,556	9,586	15.22%	82,142	657	1,971	2,629	57	86	144	2,772	3.38%
Ku'erle (Korla) City 库尔勒市	381,943	549,324	167,381	43.82%	716,705	5,734	17,201	22,935	502	753	1,254	24,189	3.38%
Luntai (Bugur) County 轮台县	91,986	116,166	24,180	26.29%	140,346	1,123	3,368	4,491	98	147	246	4,737	3.38%
Qiemo (Qarqan) County 且末县	55,540	65,572	10,032	18.06%	75,604	605	1,814	2,419	53	79	132	2,552	3.38%
Ruoqiang (Qakilik) County 若羌县	28,636	35,580	6,944	24.25%	42,524	340	1,021	1,361	30	45	74	1,435	3.38%
Yanqi (Karashar) County 焉耆回族自治县	117,529	127,628	10,099	8.59%	137,727	1,102	3,305	4,407	96	145	241	4,648	3.38%
Yuli (Lopnur) County 尉犁县	103,681	96,068	-7,613	-7.34%	88,455	708	2,123	2,831	62	93	155	2,985	3.38%
	1,056,970	1,278,486	221,516	20.96%	1,500,002	12,000	36,000	48,000	1,050	1,575	2,625	50,625	3.38%
Bo'ertala (Bortala) Prefecture 博尔塔拉蒙古自治州													
Bole (Bortala) City 博乐市	224,869	235,585	10,716	4.77%	246,301	2,463	7,389	9,852	172	259	431	10,283	4.18%

314

Table of All Christians in Xinjiang

| 新疆 Xinjiang | | POPULATION | | | | | CHRISTIANS | | | | | | | |
| | | | | | | | Evangelicals | | | Catholics | | | Total Christians | |
	Location	Census 2000	Census 2010	Growth	Growth (percent)	Estimate 2020	TSPM	House church	TOTAL Evangelicals	CPA	House church	TOTAL Catholics	TOTAL	Percent of 2020 population
精河县	Jinghe County	133,530	141,593	8,063	6.04%	149,656	1,497	4,490	5,986	105	157	262	6,248	4.18%
温泉县	Wenquan (Arixang) County	65,641	66,502	861	1.31%	67,363	674	2,021	2,695	47	71	118	2,812	4.18%
昌吉回族自治州	Changji Prefecture	424,040	443,680	19,640	4.63%	463,320	4,633	13,900	18,533	324	486	811	19,344	4.18%
昌吉市	Changji City	387,169	426,253	39,084	10.09%	465,337	10,237	30,712	40,950	698	1,047	1,745	42,695	9.18%
阜康市	Fukang City	152,965	165,006	12,041	7.87%	177,047	2,656	7,967	10,623	266	398	664	11,287	6.38%
呼图壁县	Hutubi County	210,643	210,201	-442	-0.21%	209,759	3,146	9,439	12,586	315	472	787	13,372	6.38%
吉木萨尔县	Jimusa er (Jimsar) County	117,867	113,284	-4,583	-3.89%	108,701	1,631	4,892	6,522	163	245	408	6,930	6.38%
玛纳斯县	Manasi (Manas) County	170,533	237,558	67,025	39.30%	304,583	4,569	13,706	18,275	457	685	1,142	19,417	6.38%
木垒哈萨克自治县	Mulei (Mori) County	78,172	65,719	-12,453	-15.93%	53,266	799	2,397	3,196	80	120	200	3,396	6.38%
奇台县	Qitai County	204,796	210,566	5,770	2.82%	216,336	3,245	9,735	12,980	541	811	1,352	14,332	6.63%
哈密市	Hami (Kumul) Prefecture	1,322,145	1,428,587	106,442	8.05%	1,535,029	26,283	78,848	105,131	2,519	3,778	6,297	111,428	7.26%
巴里坤哈萨克自治县	Balikun (Barkol) County	85,964	75,442	-10,522	-12.24%	64,920	584	1,753	2,337	32	49	81	2,418	3.73%
伊吾县	Yiwu (Araturuk) County	17,418	24,783	7,365	42.28%	32,148	289	868	1,157	16	24	40	1,198	3.73%
伊州区	Yizhou District (inc. Hami City)	388,714	472,175	83,461	21.47%	555,636	5,001	15,002	20,003	278	417	695	20,697	3.73%
和田地区	Hetian (Hotan) Prefecture	492,096	572,400	80,304	16.32%	652,704	5,874	17,623	23,497	326	490	816	24,313	3.73%
策勒县	Cele (Qira) County	132,139	147,050	14,911	11.28%	161,961	972	2,915	3,887	81	121	202	4,090	2.53%
和田市	Hetian (Hotan) City	186,127	322,300	136,173	73.16%	458,473	2,751	8,253	11,003	229	344	573	11,576	2.53%
和田县	Hetian (Hotan) County	261,498	269,941	8,443	3.23%	278,384	1,670	5,011	6,681	139	209	348	7,029	2.53%
洛浦县	Luopu (Lop) County	235,716	232,916	-2,800	-1.19%	230,116	1,381	4,142	5,523	115	173	288	5,810	2.53%
民丰县	Minfeng County	32,111	33,932	1,821	5.67%	35,753	215	644	858	18	27	45	903	2.53%
墨玉县	Moyu (Karakax) County	405,634	500,114	94,480	23.29%	594,594	3,568	10,703	14,270	297	446	743	15,013	2.53%
皮山县	Pishan County	216,024	258,210	42,186	19.53%	300,396	1,802	5,407	7,210	150	225	375	7,585	2.53%
于田县	Yutian (Keriya) County	212,061	249,899	37,838	17.84%	287,737	1,726	5,179	6,906	144	216	360	7,265	2.53%
喀什地区	Kashi (Kashgar) Prefecture	1,681,310	2,014,362	333,052	19.81%	2,347,414	14,084	42,253	56,338	1,174	1,761	2,934	59,272	2.53%
巴楚县	Bachu (Maralbexi) County	375,883	336,274	-39,609	-10.54%	296,665	1,187	3,560	4,747	148	222	371	5,117	1.73%
伽师县	Jiashi (Peyziwat) County	311,733	381,767	70,034	22.47%	451,801	1,807	5,422	7,229	226	339	565	7,794	1.73%
喀什市	Kashi (Kashgar) City	340,640	506,640	166,000	48.73%	672,640	2,691	8,072	10,762	336	504	841	11,603	1.73%
麦盖提县	Maigaiti (Makit) County	201,810	258,978	57,168	28.33%	316,146	1,265	3,794	5,058	158	237	395	5,454	1.73%
莎车县	Shache (Yarkant) County	620,329	762,385	142,056	22.90%	904,441	3,618	10,853	14,471	452	678	1,131	15,602	1.73%
疏附县	Shufu County	345,282	311,960	-33,322	-9.65%	278,638	1,115	3,344	4,458	139	209	348	4,807	1.73%

Appendix

Xinjiang 新疆		POPULATION					CHRISTIANS							
							Evangelicals			Catholics			Total Christians	
Location		Census 2000	Census 2010	Growth	Growth (percent)	Estimate 2020	TSPM	House church	TOTAL Evangelicals	CPA	House church	TOTAL Catholics	TOTAL	Percent of 2020 population
Shule (Hancheng) County	疏勒县	284,853	312,455	27,602	9.69%	340,057	1,360	4,081	5,441	170	255	425	5,866	1.73%
Tashiku'ergan (Tashkurgan) County	塔什库尔干塔吉克自治县	30,454	37,843	7,389	24.26%	45,232	90	271	362	23	34	57	418	0.93%
Yecheng (Kargilik) County	叶城县	370,229	454,328	84,099	22.72%	538,427	2,154	6,461	8,615	269	404	673	9,288	1.73%
Yingjisha (Yengisar) County	英吉沙县	213,338	262,067	48,729	22.84%	310,796	1,243	3,730	4,973	155	233	388	5,361	1.73%
Yuepuhu (Yopurga) County	岳普湖县	129,441	147,688	18,247	14.10%	165,935	664	1,991	2,655	83	124	207	2,862	1.73%
Zepu (Poskam) County	泽普县	181,721	206,936	25,215	13.88%	232,151	929	2,786	3,714	116	174	290	4,005	1.73%
		3,405,713	3,979,321	573,608	16.84%	4,552,929	18,121	54,364	72,485	2,276	3,415	5,691	78,176	1.72%
Kelamayi (Karamay) Prefecture	克拉玛依市													
Baijiantan District	白碱滩区	64,297	50,422	-13,875	-21.58%	36,547	256	767	1,023	18	27	46	1,069	2.93%
Dushanzi District	独山子区	50,732	69,361	18,629	36.72%	87,990	616	1,848	2,464	44	66	110	2,574	2.93%
Kelamayi (Karamay) District	克拉玛依区	145,452	261,445	115,993	79.75%	377,438	2,642	7,926	10,568	189	283	472	11,040	2.93%
Wu'erhe (Urho) District	乌尔禾区	9,751	9,780	29	0.30%	9,809	69	206	275	5	7	12	287	2.93%
		270,232	391,008	120,776	44.69%	511,784	3,582	10,747	14,330	256	384	640	14,970	2.93%
Kezilesu (Kizilsu) Prefecture	克孜勒苏柯尔克孜自治州													
Aheqi (Akqi) County	阿合奇县	34,317	38,876	4,559	13.28%	43,435	521	1,564	2,085	22	33	54	2,139	4.93%
Aketao (Akto) County	阿克陶县	163,024	199,065	36,041	22.11%	235,106	2,821	8,464	11,285	118	176	294	11,579	4.93%
Atushi (Artux) City	阿图什市	200,345	240,368	40,023	19.98%	280,391	3,925	11,776	15,702	140	210	350	16,052	5.73%
Wuqia (Uluqqat) County	乌恰县	42,002	47,261	5,259	12.52%	52,520	630	1,891	2,521	26	39	66	2,587	4.93%
		439,688	525,570	85,882	19.53%	611,452	7,898	23,695	31,593	306	459	764	32,357	5.29%
Tacheng Prefecture	塔城地区													
Emin (Dorbiljin) County	额敏县	178,309	187,112	8,803	4.94%	195,915	2,253	6,759	9,012	98	147	245	9,257	4.73%
Hebukesai'er (Hoboksar) Mongol Autonomous County	和布克赛尔蒙古自治县	57,775	62,100	4,325	7.49%	66,425	664	1,993	2,657	33	50	83	2,740	4.13%
Shawan County	沙湾县	188,715	365,196	176,481	93.52%	541,677	6,229	18,688	24,917	271	406	677	25,594	4.73%
Tacheng City	塔城市	149,210	161,037	11,827	7.93%	172,864	2,420	7,260	9,680	52	78	130	9,810	5.67%
Tuoli (Toli) County	托里县	79,882	93,098	13,216	16.54%	106,314	1,223	3,668	4,890	53	80	133	5,023	4.73%
Wusu City	乌苏市	190,359	298,907	108,548	57.02%	407,455	4,075	12,224	16,298	204	306	509	16,808	4.12%
Yumin County	裕民县	48,147	51,919	3,772	7.83%	55,691	640	1,921	2,562	28	42	70	2,631	4.73%
		892,397	1,219,369	326,972	36.64%	1,546,341	17,504	52,513	70,017	739	1,108	1,846	71,864	4.65%
Tulufan (Turpan) Prefecture	吐鲁番市													
Gaochang District	高昌区	251,652	273,385	21,733	8.64%	295,118	2,361	7,083	9,444	148	221	369	9,813	3.33%

Table of All Christians in Xinjiang

Xinjiang 新疆 Location	POPULATION					CHRISTIANS							
						Evangelicals			Catholics			Total Christians	
	Census 2000	Census 2010	Growth	Growth (percent)	Estimate 2020	TSPM	House church	TOTAL Evangelicals	CPA	House church	TOTAL Catholics	TOTAL	Percent of 2020 population
Shanshan (Piqan) County 鄯善县	196,929	231,297	34,368	17.45%	265,665	2,125	6,376	8,501	133	199	332	8,833	3.33%
Tuokexun (Toksun) County 托克逊县	102,150	118,221	16,071	15.73%	134,292	1,074	3,223	4,297	67	101	168	4,465	3.33%
	550,731	622,903	72,172	13.10%	695,075	5,561	16,682	22,242	348	521	869	23,111	3.33%
Wulumuqi (Urumqi) Prefecture 乌鲁木齐市													
Dabancheng District 达坂城区	8,815	40,657	31,842	361.23%	72,499	942	2,827	3,770	51	76	127	3,897	5.38%
Midong District 米东区	281,748	333,676	51,928	18.43%	385,604	5,013	15,039	20,051	270	405	675	20,726	5.38%
Shayibake (Saybagh) District 沙依巴克区	482,235	664,716	182,481	37.84%	847,197	11,014	33,041	44,054	593	890	1,483	45,537	5.38%
Shuimogou District 水磨沟区	180,654	390,943	210,289	116.40%	601,232	7,816	23,448	31,264	421	631	1,052	32,316	5.38%
Tianshan District 天山区	471,432	696,277	224,845	47.69%	921,122	11,975	35,924	47,898	645	967	1,612	49,510	5.38%
Toutunhe District 头屯河区	130,146	172,796	42,650	32.77%	215,446	2,801	8,402	11,203	151	226	377	11,580	5.38%
Wulumuqi (Urumqi) County 乌鲁木齐县	328,536	83,187	-245,349	-74.68%	83,187	1,081	3,244	4,326	58	87	146	4,471	5.38%
Xinshi District 新市区	379,220	730,307	351,087	92.58%	1,081,394	14,058	42,174	56,232	757	1,135	1,892	58,125	5.38%
	2,262,786	3,112,559	849,773	37.55%	4,207,681	54,700	164,100	218,799	2,945	4,418	7,363	226,163	5.38%
Yili (Ili) Prefecture 伊犁哈萨克自治州													
Chabucha'er (Qapqal) County 察布查尔锡伯自治县	161,834	179,744	17,910	11.07%	197,654	1,482	4,447	5,930	138	208	346	6,276	3.18%
Gongliu (Tokkuztara) County 巩留县	153,100	164,860	11,760	7.68%	176,620	1,325	3,974	5,299	124	185	309	5,608	3.18%
Huocheng County 霍城县	307,492	236,878	-70,614	-22.96%	166,264	1,247	3,741	4,988	116	175	291	5,279	3.18%
Huo'erguosi (Korgas) City 霍尔果斯市	25,521	25,811	290	1.14%	26,101	196	587	783	18	27	46	829	3.18%
Kuitun (Kuytun) City 奎屯市	285,299	166,261	-119,038	-41.72%	47,223	2,715	4,073	6,788	33	50	83	6,871	14.55%
Nileke (Nilka) County 尼勒克县	142,513	157,743	15,230	10.69%	172,973	1,297	3,892	5,189	432	649	1,081	6,270	3.63%
Tekesi (Tekes) County 特克斯县	133,900	142,718	8,818	6.59%	151,536	1,137	3,410	4,546	106	159	265	4,811	3.18%
Xinyuan (Kunes) County 新源县	269,842	282,718	12,876	4.77%	295,594	5,173	18,105	23,278	591	887	1,478	24,756	8.38%
Yining (Gulja) City 伊宁市	357,519	515,082	157,563	44.07%	672,645	5,045	15,135	20,179	471	706	1,177	21,356	3.18%
Yining County 伊宁县	385,829	372,590	-13,239	-3.43%	359,351	2,695	8,085	10,781	539	809	1,348	12,128	3.38%
Zhaosu County 昭苏县	145,027	148,187	3,160	2.18%	151,347	1,135	3,405	4,540	106	159	265	4,805	3.18%
	2,367,876	2,392,592	24,716	1.04%	2,417,308	23,447	68,854	92,301	2,675	4,013	6,688	98,989	4.10%
Cities directly administered by Xinjiang 自治区直辖县级行政区划													
Ala'er (Aral) City 阿拉尔市	158,593	158,593	0	0.00%	158,593	1,427	4,282	5,709	111	167	278	5,987	3.78%
Shihezi City 石河子市	380,130	380,130	0	0.00%	380,130	8,363	25,089	33,451	1,140	1,711	2,851	36,302	9.55%
Tumushuke (Tumxuk) City 图木舒克市	135,727	135,727	0	0.00%	135,727	1,222	3,665	4,886	95	143	238	5,124	3.78%
Wujiaqu City 五家渠市	96,436	96,436	0	0.00%	96,436	868	2,604	3,472	68	101	169	3,640	3.78%
	590,115	770,886	770,886	0.00%	770,886	11,880	35,639	47,519	1,414	2,121	3,535	51,053	6.62%
Totals	18,459,511	21,725,815	3,266,304	17.69%	24,992,119	224,456	671,882	896,339	18,623	27,935	46,558	942,897	3.77%

317

Table 3. Ethnic Minority Groups in Xinjiang

People Group	Official Nationality	Primary Language	Primary Religion	Population (all of China) 2020	All Christians		Evangelicals	
Ainu	Uyghur	Ainu	Islam	7,600	0	0.0%	0	0.0%
Akto Turkmen	Kirgiz	Uyghur	Islam	2,900	0	0.0%	0	0.0%
Daur, Western	Daur	Daur	Animism	7,400	0	0.0%	0	0.0%
Kazak	Kazak	Kazak	Islam	1,855,000	186	0.0%	186	0.0%
Keriya	Uyghur	Uyghur	Islam	800	0	0.0%	0	0.0%
Kirgiz	Kirgiz	Kirgiz	Islam	237,000	474	0.2%	427	0.2%
Nubra	Uyghur	Ladakhi	Islam	700	0	0.0%	0	0.0%
Ongktor	Ewenki	Ewenki	Animism	30	0	0.0%	0	0.0%
Russian	Russian	Russian	Christianity	23,000	12,650	55.0%	115	0.5%
Tajik, Sarikoli	Tajik	Sarikoli	Islam	44,000	4	0.0%	4	0.0%
Tatar	Tatar	Tatar	Islam	8,100	0	0.0%	0	0.0%
Teleut	Kazak	Altai, Northern	Animism	76	0	0.0%	0	0.0%
Torgut	Mongol	Kalmyk-Oirat	Buddhism	192,000	0	0.0%	0	0.0%
Tuerke	Uzbek	Ili Turki	Islam	300	0	0.0%	0	0.0%
Tuva	Mongol	Tuvan	Buddhism	4,300	0	0.0%	0	0.0%
Uyghur	Uyghur	Uyghur	Islam	11,723,000	1,172	0.0%	1,172	0.0%
Uyghur, Lopnur	Uyghur	Uyghur	Islam	44,000	0	0.0%	0	0.0%
Uyghur, Taklamakan	Uyghur	Uyghur	Islam	300	0	0.0%	0	0.0%
Uyghur, Yutian	Uyghur	Uyghur	Islam	70,000	0	0.0%	0	0.0%
Uzbek	Uzbek	Uzbek	Islam	22,000	110	0.5%	64	0.3%
Wakhi	Tajik	Wakhi	Islam	14,000	0	0.0%	0	0.0%
Xibe, Western	Xibe	Xibe	Animism	56,000	280	0.5%	263	0.5%
Totals				14,312,506	14,876	0.1%	2,231	0.0%

Groups primarily located in Xinjiang. Latest stats from www.joshuaproject.net

Researching Christians in China

For centuries people have been curious to know how many Christians live in China. When Marco Polo made his famous journey to the Orient 750 years ago, he documented the existence of Nestorian churches and monasteries in various places, to the fascination of people in Europe.

Since I started traveling to China in the 1980s, I have found that believers around the world are eager to know how many Christians there are in China. Many people are aware that God has done a remarkable work in the world's most populous country, but little research has been done to put a figure on this phenomenon. In recent decades, wildly divergent estimates have been published ranging from 20 million to 230 million.

Methodology

In this appendix, in Table 2, I provide estimates of the number of Christians in Xinjiang. Full tables of the other provinces of China can be found at the Asia Harvest website. See "Christians in China Stats" link under the Resources tab at www.asiaharvest.org. My survey provides figures for Christians of every description arranged in four main categories: the Three-Self Patriotic Movement, the Evangelical house churches, the Catholic Patriotic Association, and the Catholic house churches. I have supplied statistics for all 2,800 cities and counties within every province, municipality, and autonomous region of China.

This information was gathered from a wide variety of sources. More than 2,000 published sources are noted in the tables published online including a multitude of books, journals, magazine articles, and reports that I spent years meticulously accumulating.

I have also conducted hundreds of hours of interviews with key house church leaders from many different networks who are responsible for God's work throughout China.

Before entering data into the tables, I began with this assumption: in any given place in the country, there are no Christians at all until I have a figure from a documented source or can make an intelligent estimate based on information gathered from Christian leaders in China. In other words, I wanted to put aside all pre-conceptions and expectations, input all the information I had, and see what the totals came to.

A note about security

None of the information provided in these tables is new to the Chinese government. Beijing has clearly already thoroughly researched the spread of Christianity throughout the country, as shown by the Director of the Religious Affairs Bureau Ye Xiaowen's 2006 announcement that there were then 130 million Christians in China.[1] In December 2009, the national newspaper *China Daily* interviewed scholar Liu Peng who had spent years researching religion for the Chinese Academy of Social Sciences. Liu claimed the "house churches have at least 50 million followers nationwide."[2] His figure at the time was consistent with my research.

After consulting various house church leaders in China, I found that all of them were content that this information should be published as long as the survey focuses on statistics and avoids specific information such as the names and locations of Christian leaders, as it does.

The Chinese Church in perspective

All discussion of how many Christians there are in China should be tempered by the realization that more than 90 percent of China's present population face a Christ-less eternity. Hundreds of millions of individuals have yet to hear the gospel. House church leaders in China have told me how ashamed and burdened they feel that so many of their countrymen and women do not yet know Jesus Christ. This burden motivates them to do whatever it takes to preach the gospel among every ethnic group and in every city, town, and village—to every individual—in China and to do whatever necessary to see Christ exalted throughout the land.

May we humbly give thanks to the Living God for the great things He has done in China. We are privileged to live in a remarkable time in human history, like in the days prophesied by the prophet Habakkuk:

> *Look at the nations and watch—*
> *and be utterly amazed.*
> *For I am going to do something in your days*
> *that you would not believe,*
> > *even if you were told.* —Habakkuk 1:5

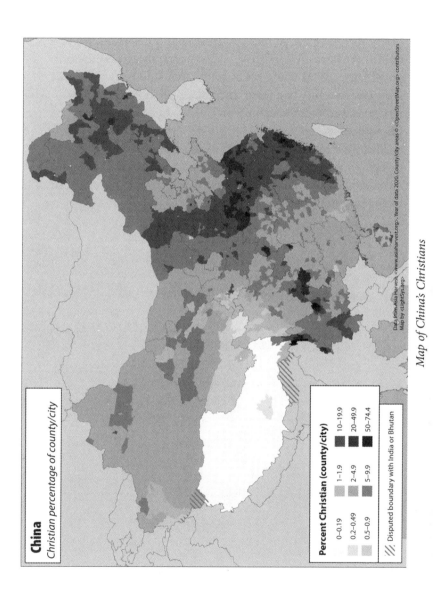

Map of China's Christians

Notes

Note: *after first mention, short titles are used for the sources.*

The China Chronicles overview

1 Griffith John quoted in R. Wardlaw Thompson, *Griffith John: The Story of Fifty Years in China* (London: Religious Tract Society, 1908), p. 65.

Introduction

1 Clarence C. Crisler, *China's Borderlands and Beyond* (Takoma Park, MD: Review and Herald, 1937), p. 319.

2 Ajiya, "The Taklimakan Desert," *China Tourism* (no. 70, n.d.), p. 55.

3 In 2011, the government of Tajikistan voted to cede over 386 sq. miles (1,000 sq. km) of land in the Pamirs to China. The terms or reasons for the deal were never made public. See "Tajikistan cedes Land to China," *BBC News* (January 13, 2011).

4 Marco Polo, *The Travels of Marco Polo: The Complete Yule-Cordier Edition*, Vol. 1 (New York: Dover, 1903), pp. 171–72.

5 Polo, *Travels of Marco Polo*, pp. 181–82.

6 Polo, *Travels of Marco Polo*, p. 187. Goiter has been a common affliction in the Yarkant area to the present day. When the Swedish explorer Sven Hedin visited Yarkant in 1899, he reported "three-fourths of the population of Yarkant are suffering from goiter, [due to the] bad quality of the water, which is kept in large basins, used indifferently for bathing, washing, or draining." (Polo, *Travels of Marco Polo*, p. 188). The Jacobites were Syrian Orthodox Christians. A large Jacobite community still exists in south India.

7 Polo, *Travels of Marco Polo*, p. 191.

8 Polo, *Travels of Marco Polo*, pp. 194, 197.

9 Polo, *Travels of Marco Polo*, p. 210.

10 H. V. Noyes, "Mohammedanism in China," *Chinese Recorder* (February 1889), p. 68.

11 Mark Chuanhang Shan, *The History of Christianity in Xinjiang, China: with a General History Background* (Boston: self-published, 2011), pp. 146–47. Note: this book—which is available in both English and Chinese—is

divided into several sections, and the page numbers re-start at the beginning of each section.

12 J. Edkins, "Mohammedanism," *Chinese Recorder* (August 1891), p. 378.

13 In this book we are using "Kazak" and "Kirgiz" as the common spellings for people from these two ethnic groups, whereas the country names are rendered "Kazakhstan" and "Kyrgyzstan."

14 Paul Hattaway, *Operation China: Introducing all the Peoples of China* (Carlisle, UK: Piquant, 2000), p. 530.

Secrets from Beneath the Sand

1 J. P. Mallory and Victor H. Mair, *The Tarim Mummies: Ancient China and the Mystery of the Earliest Peoples from the West* (New York: Thames & Hudson, 2000), p. 14.

2 Victor H. Mair, "Mummies of the Tarim Basin," *Archaeology* (March–April 1995), p. 30.

3 Ji Xianlin quoted in Clifford Coonan, "A Meeting of Civilizations: The Mystery of China's Celtic Mummies," *The Independent* (August 28, 2006).

4 Rene Grosset, *The Empire of the Steppes: A History of Central Asia* (New Brunswick, NJ: Rutgers University Press, 1970), p. 21.

5 Samuel Hugh Moffett, *A History of Christianity in Asia, Volume 1: Beginnings to 1500* (Maryknoll, NY: Orbis, 1998), p. 14.

6 C. D. Bruce, *Chinese Turkestan* (Berkeley, CA: University of California Libraries, 1907), p. 9.

7 Moffett, *History of Christianity in Asia, Volume 1*, p. 16.

8 Shan, *History of Christianity in Xinjiang*, p. 9.

9 "Uyghur" has become the most commonly accepted form of English spelling for this people group in recent years and is used throughout this book. Other variants have included Uygur, Uigher, Uighuir, Uighur, Uiguir, Uigur, and Uygher, while the Chinese pinyin transliteration of the name is Weiwuer. The name "Uyghur" as it is commonly used today only came into being after a meeting of Turkic leaders in Tashkent, Uzbekistan in 1921. The name, which means "unity" or "alliance," was chosen as the mark of their identity. Before that time, Turkic groups in Xinjiang often identified themselves by the name of the oasis near where they lived. Some scholars insist that the Uyghurs are still a collection of distinct smaller groups, and that the label "Uyghur" applied to all of them is an artificial one.

10 See Peter C. Perdue, *China Marches West: The Qing Conquest of Central Eurasia* (Cambridge, MA: Harvard University Press, 2005), p. 285.

11 John Powers and David Templeman, *Historical Dictionary of Tibet* (Lanham, MD: Scarecrow, 2012), p. 537.

12 Shan, *History of Christianity in Xinjiang*, p. 5.
13 Michael Buckley, et al., *China: A Travel Survival Kit*, 4th ed. (Hawthorn, Australia: Lonely Planet, 1994), p. 983.

Nestorians in Xinjiang

1 Shan, *History of Christianity in Xinjiang*, p. 25.
2 Malech quoted in John M. L. Young, *By Foot to China: Mission of the Church of the East* (Tokyo: Radio Press, 1984).
3 Young, *By Foot to China*.
4 John Stewart, *Nestorian Missionary Enterprise: The Story of a Church on Fire* (Edinburgh: T & T Clark, 1928), p. 144.
5 John Holzmann (ed.), *The Church of the East: An Edited and Condensed Version of Nestorian Missionary Enterprise* (Littleton, CO: Sonlight Curriculum, 2001), p. 47.
6 Zan Ning quoted in Samuel N. C. Lieu and J. C. B. Mohr, *Manichaeism in the Later Roman Empire and Medieval China* (Tubingen, Germany: Paul Siebeck, 1992), p. 265.
7 Bar Hebraeus, c. 1286, quoted in Moffett, *History of Christianity in Asia, Volume 1*, p. 421.
8 Polo, *Travels of Marco Polo*, pp. 181–82.
9 The term "Rabban" means "Master" and equates to the Hebrew "Rabbi."
10 A. C. Moule, *Christians in China Before the Year 1550* (London: SPCK, 1930), p. 98.
11 Moule, *Christians in China*, p. 98.
12 Moule, *Christians in China*, p. 98.
13 Moule, *Christians in China*, p. 99.
14 Moule, *Christians in China*, p. 100.
15 Moule, *Christians in China*, p. 100.
16 Stewart, *Nestorian Missionary Enterprise*, p. 162.
17 Moule, *Christians in China*, pp. 107–8.
18 Moffett, *History of Christianity in Asia, Volume 1*, pp. 434–35.
19 William of Rubruck quoted in Moffett, *History of Christianity in Asia, Volume 1*, p. 412.
20 James Legge quoted in John Foster, *Church of the T'ang Dynasty* (London: Society for Promoting Christian Knowledge, 1939), p. 112.
21 Later Catholic critics accused the Nestorians of heresy in regard to the person and deity of Christ. But in 1539, the German reformer Martin Luther wrote that the charges against the Nestorians were not clear, and he suspected the accusations had been fabricated by the jealous Catholics. Luther wrote, "For a while I could not understand just what Nestorius'

error was; in any event, I thought that Nestorius had denied the divinity of Christ and had regarded Christ as no more than a mere man, as the papal decretals and all papal writers say. But their own words, when I really looked at them, made me change my mind. . . . Their writing is so confused they still do not know today how and why they condemned Nestorius. . . . For it appears that the Pope and his followers put the words into Nestorius' mouth that he viewed Christ as a mere man and not also God, and that he took Christ to be two persons or two Christs. This appears (I say) not only from their histories, but also from the very words and documents of the popes and their writers." Martin Luther quoted in Stewart, *Nestorian Missionary Enterprise*, p. 148.

22 A recent Chinese academic, Li Jinxin, has studied Nestorian Christianity in Xinjiang and notes the key features in which it differed from Roman Catholicism: "They did not believe Mary to be the 'Mother of God' and did not worship her; They did not use images in worship but kept the cross; They did not believe in purgatory after death but allowed Christians to honor their ancestors; They opposed transubstantiation but acknowledged that Christ was truly present in the Lord's Supper. . . . Christians must keep their beards, shave their heads, not own slaves, not seek material wealth, and aid the poor." Li Jinxin, *Xinjiang Zongjiao Yenbian Shi* (Urumqi, China: Xinjiang Renmin Chubanshe, 2003), p. 182.

23 Li Jinxin, *Xinjiang Zongjiao Yenbian Shi*, p. 182.

24 Bruce L. Shelley, *Church History in Plain Language* (Nashville, TN: Thomas Nelson, 1995), p. 113.

Catholics in Xinjiang

1 L'Abbé Huc, *Christianity in China, Tartary, and Thibet* (2 vols.) (London: Brown, Green, Longmans & Roberts, 1857), p. 409.

2 Huc, *Christianity in China, Tartary, and Thibet*, pp. 409–10.

3 Pascal de Vittoria quoted in Huc, *Christianity in China, Tartary, and Thibet*, pp. 412–13.

4 Huc, *Christianity in China, Tartary, and Thibet*, p. 415.

5 Huc, *Christianity in China, Tartary, and Thibet*, p. 415.

6 Hugh P. Kemp, *Steppe By Step: Mongolia's Christians: From Ancient Roots to Vibrant Young Church* (London: Monarch Books, 2000), p. 249.

7 Huc, *Christianity in China, Tartary, and Thibet*, p. 192.

8 C. Wessels, *Early Jesuit Travelers in Central Asia, 1603–1721* (The Hague, Netherlands: Martinus Nijhoff, 1924), p. 25.

9 Vincent Cronin, *The Wise Man from the West* (New York: Image Books, 1955), p. 246.

10   Huc, *Christianity in China, Tartary, and Thibet*, p. 195.
11   Wessels, *Early Jesuit Travelers in Central Asia*, p. 35.
12   Huc, *Christianity in China, Tartary, and Thibet*, p. 199.
13   Joanna Waley-Cohen, *Exile in Mid-Qing China: Banishment to Xinjiang 1758–1820* (New Haven, CT: Yale University Press, 1991), p. 97.
14   Henry Lansdell, *Chinese Central Asia: A Ride to Little Tibet, Vol. 1* (London: Sampson Low, Marston, 1893), p. 193.
15   Bertram Wolferstan, *The Catholic Church in China* (St. Louis, MO: Sands, 1909), p. 450. These two churches were both in Ili, near the Russian border, and were the fruit of workers with the Scheut Foreign Mission Society.
16   Milton T. Stauffer (ed.), *The Christian Occupation of China* (Shanghai: China Continuation Committee, 1922), p. lxvii.
17   A. Thomas Planchet, *Les Missions de Chine et du Japon* (Pekin: Impremerie des Lazaristes, 1927), p. 15.
18   Ralph Covell, *The Liberating Gospel in China: The Christian Faith Among China's Minority Peoples* (Grand Rapids, MI: Baker Books, 1995), p. 161.
19   *UCA Dispatch* (November 23, 1994). "UCA" likely referred to Union Catholic Asia.
20   In 13 churches spread across 11 towns. Jean Charbonnier, *Guide to the Catholic Church in China* (Singapore: China Catholic Communication, 1997), p. 211.
21   Jason Mandryk, *Operation World: The Definitive Prayer Guide to Every Nation* (Colorado Springs, CO: Biblica, 2010), p. 248.

1890s

1   There is some confusion regarding the year of their travels in Xinjiang, and some sources say they traveled in 1876. However, a careful examination of Lansdell's travel books suggests that the confusion comes from the fact that he visited Yining in northwest Xinjiang much earlier as part of a journey through Russian Central Asia, but he returned and joined Parker on their later expedition through Xinjiang in 1888. Interestingly, Lansdell makes just one brief mention of Parker in his two 500-page accounts of the journey. See Henry Lansdell, *Chinese Central Asia: A Ride to Little Tibet* (2 Vols.) (London: Sampson Low, Marston, 1893). Lansdell's expedition was partially financed by the Royal Geographic Society, which may not have wanted to publicize his missionary activities.
2   Ann-Charlotte Fritzon, *Passion for the Impossible: The Life of the Pioneer Nils Fredrik Höijer* (Solna, Sweden: Swedish Slavic Mission, 1998), p. 8.
3   Fritzon, *Passion for the Impossible*, p. 110.
4   Fritzon, *Passion for the Impossible*, pp. 110–11.

5 Fritzon, *Passion for the Impossible*, p. 114.
6 The Swedish Slavic Mission is now called Ljus I Öster, or Light for the Peoples.
7 Johannes Avetaranian, *A Muslim who Became a Christian: The Story of John Avetaranian, 1861–1919* (Hertford, UK: Authors Online, 2002), p. 28.
8 Avetaranian, *Muslim who Became a Christian*, pp. 40–41.
9 Avetaranian, *Muslim who Became a Christian*, p. 77.
10 Avetaranian, *Muslim who Became a Christian*, p. 87.
11 Avetaranian, *Muslim who Became a Christian*, p. 89.
12 Avetaranian, *Muslim who Became a Christian*, p. 92.
13 Avetaranian, *Muslim who Became a Christian*, p. 92.
14 Avetaranian, *Muslim who Became a Christian*, p. 192.
15 Covell, *Liberating Gospel in China*, p. 169.

1900s and 1910s

1 George Hunter, "Missionary Work in the New Province," *Chinese Recorder* (August 1908), p. 467.
2 *The Missionary Review of the World* (March 1913), p. 230. Many quotes in this section come from snippets in news reports in the magazine quoted.
3 G. W. Hunter, "Travelling in Chinese Turkestan," *China's Millions* (January 1910), pp. 12–13.
4 *Chinese Recorder* (August 1910), p. 511.
5 Marshall Broomhall, *The Jubilee Story of the China Inland Mission* (London: China Inland Mission, 1915), p. 288.
6 *Chinese Recorder* (August 1910), pp. 511–12.
7 *Chinese Recorder* (August 1910), p. 513.
8 *Chinese Recorder* (August 1910), p. 512.
9 *Chinese Recorder* (August 1910), p. 514.
10 *Chinese Recorder* (August 1910), pp. 514–15.
11 G. W. Hunter, "Another Journey in Sinkiang," *China's Millions* (November 1908), p. 170.
12 SCM Annual Report, 1919, p. 17, quoted in John Hultvall, *Mission and Change in Eastern Turkestan: An Authorized Translation of the Original Swedish Text* (Erskine, UK: Heart of Asia Ministries, 1987), p. 5.
13 Hultvall, *Mission and Change in Eastern Turkestan*, p. 5.
14 G. W. Hunter, "Travelling Among the Quasaqs," *China's Millions* (February 1918), p. 17.
15 *China's Millions* (January 1917), p. 11.
16 Some sources label the translation Hunter completed not as Kazak, but the Altai dialect of the Kirgiz.

George Hunter

1 David Bentley-Taylor, "An Apostle of Turkestan," *China's Millions* (November-December 1945), p. 42.

2 *Global Prayer Digest* (January 1, 2006).

3 Covell, *Liberating Gospel in China*, p. 162.

4 Leslie T. Lyall, *A Passion for the Impossible: The China Inland Mission 1865–1965* (London: Hodder & Stoughton, 1964), p. 73.

5 Mildred Cable and Francesca French, *George Hunter: Apostle of Turkestan* (London: China Inland Mission, 1948), p. 40.

6 Cable and French, *George Hunter*, pp. 38, 54.

7 Cable and French, *George Hunter*, p. 86.

8 Cable and French, *George Hunter*, p. 8.

9 Bentley-Taylor, "Apostle of Turkestan," p. 42.

10 Kemp, *Steppe By Step*, p. 381.

11 In 2013, linguistic ministries reported a translation of the Xibe New Testament, but it was done by transcribing the Western Xibe language into Pinyin words, which are not read by the people today. One Xibe Christian from Xinjiang was baffled when shown the translation and couldn't understand why it hadn't been done using the Manchu script. When he was shown a copy of a few pages from the 1835 Manchu New Testament, he had no problem understanding it. Recently, a Manchu Old Testament translation from 1790 was discovered in the Cambridge University library in England. It appears the translation was never published.

12 Mildred Cable and Francesca French, *Why Not for the World?* (London: British and Foreign Bible Society, 1952), pp. 33–34.

13 G. W. Hunter, "The New Province," *China's Millions* (September 1907), p. 146.

14 Kemp, *Steppe By Step*, p. 383.

15 G. W. Hunter, "News from the Field: Tihwafu, Sinkiang," *Friends of Moslems* (October 1931), p. 8.

16 Percy Mather quoted in Mildred Cable and Francesca French, *The Making of a Pioneer: Percy Mather of Central Asia* (London: Hodder & Stoughton, 1935), p. 47.

17 Kemp, *Steppe By Step*, p. 383.

18 Cable and French, *George Hunter*, p. 87.

19 George W. Hunter, "In Outward Regions of Inland China," *China's Millions* (June 1921), p. 92.

20 Cable and French, *George Hunter*, pp. 9–10.

21 Cable and French, *George Hunter*, p. 10.

22 "Hunter of Sinkiang: A Tribute," *China's Millions* (March-April 1947), p. 14.

23 Mildred Cable, "Rev. George W. Hunter, M.B.E.," *Journal of the Royal Central Asian Society* (vol. 34, no. 2, 1947), p. 118.

Percy Mather

1 Kemp, *Steppe By Step*, p. 381.
2 Percy Mather quoted in Cable and French, *Making of a Pioneer*, p. 96.
3 Cable and French, *George Hunter*, p. 77.
4 Cable and French, *Making of a Pioneer*, p. 70.
5 Covell, *Liberating Gospel in China*, p. 165.
6 Cable and French, *Making of a Pioneer*, p. 233.
7 *China's Millions* (June 1931), p. 109.
8 Percy Mather quoted in Cable and French, *Making of a Pioneer*, p. 59.
9 Percy C. Mather, "Itinerating in Sinkiang," *China's Millions* (September 1929), p. 137.
10 G. W. Hunter, "Among the Qazaqs," *China's Millions* (February 1920), p. 21.
11 Percy Mather, "In Far Sinkiang," *China's Millions* (February 1932), p. 24.
12 Covell, *Liberating Gospel in China*, p. 165.
13 Cable and French, *Making of a Pioneer*, p. 126.
14 "News from Sinkiang," *China's Millions* (August 1933), p. 144.
15 "News from Sinkiang," *China's Millions* (August 1933), p. 144.

1920s

1 Stauffer, *Christian Occupation of China*, p. 275.
2 Stauffer, *Christian Occupation of China*, p. 276.
3 Stauffer, *Christian Occupation of China*, p. lxvii.
4 Planchet, *Les Missions de Chine et du Japon*, p. 15.
5 Rikard Nyström quoted in Hultvall, *Mission and Change in Eastern Turkestan*, p. 4.
6 Covell, *Liberating Gospel in China*, p. 170.
7 *The Mission Church* (June 30, 1921).
8 John Törnquist quoted in Hultvall, *Mission and Change in Eastern Turkestan*, p. 11.
9 Kenneth Scott Latourette, *A History of Christian Missions in China* (New York: Macmillian, 1929), p. 817.
10 Hultvall, *Mission and Change in Eastern Turkestan*, p. 4.
11 John Törnquist quoted in Hultvall, *Mission and Change in Eastern Turkestan*, p. 7.
12 Hultvall, *Mission and Change in Eastern Turkestan*, p. 42, note 44.

13 John Törnquist, *Från Kaschgar till Jerusalem* (Stockholm: Svenska Missionsförbundets, 1928).

14 Hans Döring quoted in Marshall Broomhall, *The Bible in China* (London: China Inland Mission, 1934), pp. 164–65.

15 Gustaf Ahlbert, *Bakhta Han, or Lucky Child: A Story of a Girl from Xinjiang* (Malmo, Sweden: Pathways, 2013), p. 53.

16 Gustaf Ahlbert, *Bakhta Han, or Lucky Child*, p. 72.

17 "From Various Centres," *China's Millions* (September 1927), p. 140.

18 H. French Ridley, "Enduring Hardness," *China's Millions* (February 1930), p. 22.

19 Ridley, "Enduring Hardness," pp. 22–23.

20 H. F. Ridley, "News from the Field: Tuhua (Urumtsi), Sinkiang," *Friends of Moslems* (October 1929), pp. 7–9.

21 Hultvall, *Mission and Change in Eastern Turkestan*, p. 4.

22 Gottfrid Palmberg quoted in Stauffer, *Christian Occupation of China*, p. 276.

The Trio

1 A more detailed description of the Trio's lives and ministries will be given in the Gansu volume of The China Chronicles.

2 Valerie Griffiths, *Not Less than Everything: The Courageous Women Who Carried the Christian Gospel to China* (Oxford: Monarch, 2004), p. 219.

3 Linda K. Benson, *Across China's Gobi: The Lives of Evangeline French, Mildred Cable, and Francesca French of the China Inland Mission* (Manchester: Eastbridge Books, 2008), pp. 117–18.

4 Linda K. Benson, *Across China's Gobi*, p. 121.

5 Griffiths, *Not Less than Everything*, p. 220.

6 Eva French, Francesca French, and Mildred Cable, "A Dispatch from Turkestan," *China's Millions* (February 1927), p. 22.

7 Eva French, Francesca French, and Mildred Cable, "From Tunhwang to Tihwa," *China's Millions* (October 1932), p. 190.

8 Percy Mather quoted in Cable and French, *George Hunter*, p. 86.

9 Eva French, Francesca French, and Mildred Cable quoted in Benson, *Across China's Gobi*, p. 156.

10 French, French, and Cable, "From Tunhuang to Tihwa," p. 188.

11 Benson, *Across China's Gobi*, p. 159.

1930s

1 Paul French, "The Last King of Xinjiang: How Bertram Sheldrake went

from Condiment Heir to Muslim Monarch," *South China Morning Post* (4 March 2019).

2   Benson, *Across China's Gobi*, p. 191.

3   Emil Fischbacher quoted in Fuya Ba, "Emil Fischbacher," https://bdcconline.net/en/stories/fischbacher-emil.

4   Emil Fischbacher quoted in Fuya Ba, "Emil Fischbacher."

5   Emil Fischbacher quoted in Fuya Ba, "Emil Fischbacher."

6   Leslie Lyall, *God Reigns in China* (London: Hodder & Stoughton, 1985), p. 19.

7   Kuwo is an unknown place and may be a metaphor for another town in Xinjiang. Still, there is no reason to doubt the story itself, which is consistent with other accounts from Xinjiang at this time.

8   Webb of Swindon quoted in Mathew Backholer, *Global Revival: Worldwide Outpourings* (self-published: By Faith Media, 2010), p. 106.

9   Webb of Swindon quoted in Backholer, *Global Revival*, p. 105.

10   Gustaf Ahlbert, "Kashgar, Sinkiang," *Friends of Moslems* (July 1932), p. 45.

11   Hultvall, *Mission and Change in Eastern Turkestan*, pp. 11–12.

12   Interview with Vendla Gustafsson, September 1972, cited in Hultvall, *Mission and Change in Eastern Turkestan*, p. 12.

13   Shan, *History of Christianity in Xinjiang*, p. 37.

Slaughter in the Desert

1   Raymond Joyce, "News from the Field: Tuhua, Sinkiang," *Friends of Moslems* (January 1934), p. 11.

2   An excellent reference documenting the end of the Swedish Mission in Xinjiang is Andrew D. W. Forbes, *Warlords and Muslims in Chinese Central Asia: A Political History of Republican Sinkiang 1911–1949* (London: Cambridge University Press, 1986).

3   R. O. Wingate, *The Steep Ascent: The Story of the Christian Church in Turkestan* (London: British and Foreign Bible Society, 1950), p. 16.

4   Wingate, *Steep Ascent*, p. 19.

5   Gustaf Ahlbert, *Habil: A Christian Martyr in Xinjiang* (Kindle edition, 2008). Translated from the 1934 Swedish edition.

6   Ahlbert, *Habil*.

7   Wingate, *Steep Ascent*, p. 24.

8   Wingate, *Steep Ascent*, pp. 24–25.

9   In some publications his name is given as Heli Ahun.

10   Wingate, *Steep Ascent*, p. 10.

11   Gottfrid Palmberg, "Heli Ahun," p. 2 of the English translation of an extract of pp. 245–52 of *I Egna Händer—Infödda medarbetare p—Svenska*

Missionsfält [In Our Hands—Native Co-workers on Swedish Mission Fields] (Uppsala, Sweden: J. A. Lindblads, 1945).

12 Wingate, *Steep Ascent*, p. 12.

13 Yusuf Khan was also known as Yusuf (Joseph) Ryekhan.

14 Hultvall, *Mission and Change in Eastern Turkestan*, p. 18.

15 Yusuf Khan quoted in Hultvall, *Mission and Change in Eastern Turkestan*, p. 12.

16 Shan, *History of Christianity in Xinjiang*, p. 41.

17 Wingate, *Steep Ascent*, p. 16.

18 Wingate, *Steep Ascent*, p. 18.

19 Ahlbert, *Habil* (Kindle edn, 2008).

20 Wingate, *Steep Ascent*, p. 24.

21 A wonderful treasure trove of old footage from Xinjiang, including some of early Swedish missionaries and local Christians, can be found online at https://archive.org/details/swedish-mission-project.

1940s

1 Covell, *Liberating Gospel in China*, p. 161.

2 Raymond H. Joyce, "The Bible in Sinkiang," *Friends of Moslems* (April 1940), p. 19.

3 China Inland Mission, *The Obstinate Horse and Other Stories* (London: China Inland Mission, 1955), p. 8.

4 China Inland Mission, *Obstinate Horse*, p. 8.

5 China Inland Mission, *Obstinate Horse*, p. 9.

6 China Inland Mission, *Obstinate Horse*, pp. 9–10.

7 C. Persson, "Christianity in the Tarim Basin," *Friends of Moslems* (April 1940), pp. 20–21.

8 Yusuf Khan's life had many tragic twists and turns. He married while in Xinjiang, but his wife left him and their children a few years later under pressure from the local imams. After escaping to India, he remarried, and for many years he ministered to Muslim refugees in Bombay. His second wife, a British missionary, disappeared and was found dead. In the mid-1940s, Khan left India and settled in Cyprus before moving to England where he died in 1975.

9 Hultvall, *Mission and Change in Eastern Turkestan*, p. 38.

10 Hultvall, *Mission and Change in Eastern Turkestan*, p. 23. Many of the Xinjiang escapees ended up in refugee camps in large Indian cities like Bombay (now Mumbai) and Delhi, as well as Karachi and Lahore in the present-day Pakistan. Others remained in the Kashmir region and integrated into local communities. Some later returned to Xinjiang to visit

their relatives, but in recent years those attempting to return to Xinjiang have been caught up in the anti-Uyghur persecution by the Chinese government.

11 Hultvall, *Mission and Change in Eastern Turkestan*, p. 29.
12 Hultvall, *Mission and Change in Eastern Turkestan*, p. 40.
13 Lyall, *Passion for the Impossible*, p. 146.

Back to Jerusalem Evangelistic Band

1 Before their deaths, several of the original pioneers were interviewed, and they said they had no idea that the name of their missionary vision was known as "Back to Jerusalem" in the Western world, "much less that the current Back to Jerusalem Movement claimed to be a continuation of the vision of this Band!" Kim-Kwong Chan, "The Back to Jerusalem Movement: Mission Movement of the Christian Community in Mainland China," in Wonsuk Ma and Kenneth R. Ross (eds.), *Mission Spirituality and Authentic Discipleship* (Oxford: Regnum Books, 2013), pp. 172–92.
2 Taken from a little known, 16-page, privately published booklet entitled *The Chinese Back-To-Jerusalem Evangelistic Band: A Prayer Call to Christian Friends of the Chinese Church* (1947).
3 *Back to Jerusalem*, pp. 3–4. A small prayer booklet with no author, publisher, or date listed (probably 1947).
4 *The Chinese Back-To-Jerusalem Evangelistic Band*, np.
5 Alice Hayes Taylor, *Back to Jerusalem Evangelistic Band* (unpublished report, 1948), p. 2.
6 Shan, *History of Christianity in Xinjiang*, p. 17.
7 J. Oswald Sanders, *Seen and Heard in China* (Melbourne, Australia: China Inland Mission, 1948), pp. 38–39.
8 Quoted in Sanders, *Seen and Heard in China*, pp. 39–40.
9 *Back to Jerusalem*, p. 6.
10 *The Chinese Back-To-Jerusalem Evangelistic Band*, p. 14.
11 *Back to Jerusalem*, p. 10.
12 "Back to Jerusalem: The Testimony of Mecca Zhao," *China Insight* (November-December 2003).
13 Frank Houghton quoted in *Back to Jerusalem*, p. 1.
14 Mecca Zhao cited in *Back to Jerusalem*, p. 14.
15 Mecca Zhao quoted in Sanders, *Seen and Heard in China*, p. 39.
16 Taylor, *Back to Jerusalem Evangelistic Band*, p. 4.
17 Shan, *History of Christianity in Xinjiang*, p. 21.
18 Mecca Zhao quoted in Shan, *History of Christianity in Xinjiang*, p. 22.

19 Paul Golf with Pastor Lee, *The Coming Chinese Church: How Rising Faith in China is Spilling Over Its Boundaries* (Oxford: Monarch, 2013), pp. 125–26.

The Northwest Spiritual Band

1 Prayer letter of Phyllis Thompson (March 3, 1949), quoted in Tony Lambert, "Back to Jerusalem: Origins of a Missionary Vision (Part II)," *China Insight* (March-April 2003).

2 Chan, "Back to Jerusalem Movement," p. 69. This page number refers to the draft article I received. The article was subsequently included as a chapter in *Mission Spirituality and Authentic Discipleship* by Ma and Ross.

3 Guang, "God's Messengers in Xinjiang," *Bridge* (October-November 1988), p. 16.

4 Quoted in Paul Hattaway, *Back to Jerusalem: God's Call to the Chinese Church to Complete the Great Commission* (Carlisle, UK: Piquant, 2003), p. 49.

5 Guang, "God's Messengers in Xinjiang," p. 18.

6 Shan, *History of Christianity in Xinjiang*, p. 10.

7 Hultvall, *Mission and Change in Eastern Turkestan*, p. 27.

8 Shan, *History of Christianity in Xinjiang*, p. 12.

9 H. R. Thompson, *Chinese Back to Jerusalem Band News Letter* (April 1950), p. 7.

10 "Xinjiang Testimonies Part V: A Driver's Story," *China and the Church Today* (February 1985), p. 8.

11 Ruth Wang, "Last Member of the Northwest Spiritual Band Dies at 94," *China Christian Daily* (July 28, 2017). Note this author is not the same person as the one mentioned in the first note 1 on p. 339 below.

Simon Zhao

1 "Uncle Simon," *Bridge* (October-November 1988), p. 12.

2 Hattaway, *Back to Jerusalem: God's Call to the Chinese Church to Complete the Great Commission* (Carlisle, UK: Piquant, 2003), p. 45.

3 Hattaway, *Back to Jerusalem*, p. 45.

4 "Uncle Simon," p. 12.

5 Hattaway, *Back to Jerusalem*, p. 47.

6 Personal interview with Peter Xu Yongze (October 2003).

7 Brother Yun with Paul Hattaway, *The Heavenly Man: The Remarkable True Story of Chinese Christian Brother Yun* (London: Monarch, 2002), pp. 280–84.

1950s and 1960s

1 Shan, *History of Christianity in Xinjiang*, p. 58.
2 Hultvall, *Mission and Change in Eastern Turkestan*, p. 32.
3 Hultvall, *Mission and Change in Eastern Turkestan*, p. 32.
4 Chan, "Back to Jerusalem Movement," p. 70.
5 Leslie Lyall, *Come Wind, Come Weather: The Present Experience of the Church in China* (London: Hodder & Stoughton, 1961), p. 67.
6 James and Marti Hefley, *By Their Blood* (Milford, MA: Mott Media, 1979), p. 74.
7 Hefley, *By Their Blood*, p. 74.
8 Email from a Wycliffe linguist in 2015.
9 Caleb Project, *The Uyghurs of Central Asia* (Littleton, CO: Caleb Project, 2003), p. 29.
10 The Uyghur Bible can be downloaded from http://www.mukeddeskalam.com/. A revision of the 1950 version is also underway and can be accessed at http://www.dunyaningnuri.com/.

1970s and 1980s

1 Quoted in Jonathan Chao, *Wise as Serpents, Harmless as Doves* (Pasadena, CA: William Carey Library, 1988), pp. 229–31.
2 Gan quoted in Chao, *Wise as Serpents*, p. 234.
3 Gan quoted in Chao, *Wise as Serpents*, pp. 241–42.
4 Gan quoted in Chao, *Wise as Serpents*, p. 248.
5 Shan, *History of Christianity in Xinjiang*, p. 49.
6 "Faith Grows in House Churches," *China Prayer Letter and Ministry Report* (October 1981).
7 *Tianfeng* (October 1985), np. A missionary magazine.
8 Lyall, *God Reigns in China*, pp. 173–74.
9 Tony Lambert, *The Resurrection of the Chinese Church* (Wheaton, IL: Harold Shaw, 1994), pp. 117–18.
10 Tony Lambert, *China's Christian Millions* (Oxford: Monarch, 2006), p. 20.
11 Letter to Far East Broadcasting (February 1987).
12 Personal interview with Peter Xu Yongze (October 2003).
13 Carl Lawrence with David Wang, *The Coming Influence of China* (Sisters, OR: Multnomah, 1996), p. 64.

1990s

1 "Uyghur Minority—Still Unreached," *China Prayer Letter and Ministry Report* (April-May 1991), p. 5.

2 Patrick Klein, *By Faith Alone: Confessions of a Bible Smuggler* (Dallas, TX; Creative Press, 2014), pp. 80–82.

3 Caleb Project, *Uyghurs of Central Asia*, p. 13.

4 Caleb Project, *Uyghurs of Central Asia*, p. 14.

5 "Where Christianity and Islam Meet," *China Prayer Letter and Ministry Report* (April 1990).

6 Personal interview with Feng Jianguo (May 2001).

7 News snippet in *Pray for China* (January-February 1997).

8 News snippet in *Pray for China* (September-October 1997).

9 News snippet in *Pray for China* (September-October 1997).

10 News snippet in *Pray for China* (September-October 1997).

11 News snippet in *The Challenge of China* (January 2003).

12 News snippet in *The Challenge of China* (January 2003).

13 Nina Shea, *In the Lion's Den: A Shocking Account of Persecution and Martyrdom of Christians Today and How We Should Respond* (Nashville, TN: Broadman & Holman, 1997), p. 62.

14 Paul Hattaway, *China's Book of Martyrs* (Carlisle, UK: Piquant, 2007), p. 588.

15 Paul Hattaway, *China's Unreached Cities*, Vol. 1 (Chiang Mai, Thailand: Asia Harvest, 1999), p. 95.

16 *UCA Dispatch* (November 23, 1994).

17 In 13 churches spread across 11 towns. Charbonnier, *Guide to the Catholic Church in China*, p. 211.

18 Feedback letter to Far East Broadcasting (February 1993).

19 News snippet in missionary magazine *Tianfeng* (March 1993).

20 Letter to Far East Broadcasting (August 1995).

21 Letter to Far East Broadcasting (February 1996).

22 *Global Chinese Ministries* (August 13, 1999).

23 *Pray for China* (November-December 1999).

2000s

1 News snippet from Chinese City Gospel Mission, a missionary newsletter, c. 2007.

2 See the Asia Harvest website (www.asiaharvest.org) for more details of this project.

3 "The Glorious Light," *The Challenge of China* (March 2004).

4 Lambert, *China's Christian Millions*, p. 274.

5 Lambert, *China's Christian Millions*, pp. 174–75.

6 Eugene Bach, *Crimson Cross: Uncovering the Mysteries of the Chinese House Church* (Blountsville, AL: The Fifth Estate, 2012), p. 83.

7   Bach, *Crimson Cross*, pp. 182–83.
8   Personal communication, January 2001.
9   Report from AVC Mission in *DAWN Friday Fax* (June 22, 2001).
10 "Female House Church Evangelists Tortured and Abused in Xinjiang," *China Aid* (August 18, 2005).
11 "Xinjiang Urumqi House Church Bible Training Attacked, 35 Christians Arrested Including an American-Korean Pastor," *China Aid* (October 26, 2006).
12 "Prominent House Church Leader Detained in Xinjiang on Separatism Charges," *China Aid* (May 19, 2008).
13 Other sources said Zhou was caught with only 5,184 illegally published Bibles, which would weigh far less than three tons.
14 Zhou Heng quoted in "Christian leader writes a Letter of Gratitude following his release from Prison," *China Aid* (April 9, 2008).
15 "A Son Among the Uyghurs," *The Voice of the Martyrs* (August 2007).
16 "Uyghur Christian Alimujiang Persecuted for Religious Conversion," *China Aid* (December 23, 2009).
17 Bob Fu quoted in "Trial Date for Imprisoned Christian Alimujiang Yimiti set for July 28," *China Aid* (June 26, 2009).
18 Personal communication.
19 Guli Nuer quoted in Brett Tarbell, "The Source of My Joy," *Open Doors* (August 2, 2016).
20 Chang Le quoted in "Christian Minor Expelled from Xinjiang High School for His Faith," *China Aid* (October 25, 2009).
21 Letter to Trans World Radio (April 2000).
22 *Global Chinese Ministries* (March 2001).
23 Letter to Trans World Radio (May 2001).
24 *Lift Up Our Holy Hands* (February 2002).
25 *Lift Up Our Holy Hands* (June 2002).
26 *Global Chinese Ministries* (February 2002).
27 Letter to Trans World Radio (July 2002).
28 Letter to Asia Harvest (September 2003).
29 *Lift Up Our Holy Hands* (August 2004).
30 *China Testimonies* (September 2005).
31 Letter to Far East Broadcasting (February 2006).
32 *Global Chinese Ministries* (February 2007).
33 Letter to Asia Harvest (July 2007).
34 *Challenge of China* (April 2007).
35 *Lift Up Our Holy Hands* (October 2008).

The Modern Back to Jerusalem Movement

1 Moses Zhang, quoted in Ruth Wang, "Moses Zhang, the Last Warrior of Chinese Back to Jerusalem Evangelistic Band, Dies at 93," *China Christian Daily* (March 19, 2018).

2 See Hattaway, *Back to Jerusalem*.

3 Chan, "Back to Jerusalem Movement," p. 75. This page number, and those below, refers to the draft article I received. The article was subsequently included as a chapter in *Mission Spirituality and Authentic Discipleship* by Ma and Ross.

4 "Who 'Owns' Back to Jerusalem?" *Back to Jerusalem* (no. 1, June 2004), p. 3.

5 Chan, "Back to Jerusalem Movement," p. 74.

6 Ai Hua, "The Rise of the Middle Kingdom: Reflections on the Indigenous Mission Movement," *World Christianity* (December 9, 2018).

7 Hattaway, *Back to Jerusalem*, p. 97.

8 Chan, "Back to Jerusalem Movement," p. 78.

9 Golf with Lee, *Coming Chinese Church*, p. 127.

10 Ai Hua, "The Rise of the Middle Kingdom," np.

11 Keep in mind that even back in the 1940s, the term "Back to Jerusalem" was first coined by a foreign missionary and had never been used by Chinese Christians themselves.

12 Gao Quanfu quoted in Golf with Lee, *Coming Chinese Church*, p. 146.

13 David Wang with Georgina Sam, *Christian China and the Light of the World: Miraculous Stories from China's Great Awakening* (Ventura, CA: Regal, 2013), p. 43.

14 Wang with Sam, *Christian China and the Light of the World*, p. 46.

15 "Overseas Missions: The Chinese Church in Action," *China Source* (November 26, 2012).

16 "Overseas Missions: The Chinese Church in Action," *China Source* (November 26, 2012).

17 Eugene Bach, *China and End-Time Prophecy: How God is Using the Red Dragon to Fulfill His Ultimate Purposes* (New Kensington, PA: Whitaker Books, 2021), pp. 189–90.

18 Bach, *China and End-Time Prophecy*, pp. 189–90.

2010s

1 Golf with Lee, *Coming Chinese Church*, p. 136. Photographs and video footage of this phenomenon were distributed after the event but do not appear to be online now. In 2015, Chinese scientists discovered that a

huge salt water "ocean" is located beneath the sands of Xinjiang that contains approximately ten times the water as all the five Great Lakes of North America combined. See Stephen Chen, "Huge Hidden Ocean under Xinjiang's Tarim Basin Larger than all Great Lakes Combined," *South China Morning Post* (July 30, 2015).

2 The Asian Workers' Fund remains active today and has grown to support more than 1,500 Asian evangelists in over 1,100 different people groups. See https://www.asiaharvest.org/asian-workers-fund for details.

3 "Xinjiang Christian Petitioner Beaten and Detained," *China Aid* (May 25, 2010).

4 "More than 30 Christians in Far West China's Xinjiang Detained, Fined," *China Aid* (February 27, 2012).

5 "Police Raid House Church in Xinjiang, Detain 70 Christians," *China Aid* (March 20, 2012).

6 See Gao Zhisheng, *Unwavering Convictions: Gao Zhisheng's Ten-Year Torture and Faith in China's Future* (Durham, NC: Carolina Academic Press, 2017).

7 "Christians Detained for Attending Bible Training," *China Aid* (April 27, 2016).

8 "China Targets House Churches, Detains Members and Pastor's Family in Xinjiang," *The Christian Times* (July 29, 2016).

9 "Police Detain Christian Camp Organizers for 'Indoctrinating Minors,'" *Christian Today* (September 14, 2016).

10 "Christian Woman Receives Three-Year Sentence for Holding Bible Study," *The Christian Times* (January 5, 2017).

11 "Three Arrested for Displaying Crosses in Home," *Christian Today* (October 28, 2016).

12 "Christian Woman Beaten by Family for Refusal to Divorce Imprisoned Husband," *China Aid* (October 16, 2017).

2017—The Year Everything Changed in Xinjiang

1 Andrew Gih, *The Church Behind the Bamboo Curtain* (London: Marshall, Morgan & Scott, 1961), pp. 14–15.

2 Jun Mai, "China Says Tough Measures in Xinjiang are to Beat Terrorism—Why Isn't the West Convinced?" *South China Morning Post* (April 4, 2021).

3 Thomas D. Williams, "China Tells Citizens to Report Parents who 'Lure' Kids into Religion," *Beitbart News* (October 18, 2016).

4 "China Bans List of Islamic Names in Xinjiang," *Fox News* (April 28, 2017).

5 "Xinjiang Locals Cite 48 Bans as Reasons for Some Arrests," *China Aid* (October 16, 2018).

6 Glyn Moody, "China is Building the Ultimate Surveillance Tool," *TechDirt* (December 18, 2017), www.techdirt.com.
7 "US Accuses China of Using Concentration Camps Against Muslim Minority," *The Guardian* (May 4, 2018); and "UN Says It Has Credible Reports that China holds Million Uyghurs in Secret Camps," *Reuters* (August 10, 2018).
8 Hasiyet Abdulla quoted in Andrea Morris, "Chinese Govt Orders Hospitals to Perform Late-term Abortions, Kill Newborn Babies of Religious Minorities," *CBN News* (August 24, 2020).
9 Joanna Smith Finley quoted in Morris, "Chinese Govt Orders Hospitals . . ."
10 "Xinjiang Increases Crackdown on Minorities, Forbids Qur'an, Arabic Language Study," *China Aid* (March 6, 2018).
11 "40 Arrested for Refusing to Celebrate Dragon Boat Festival," *China Aid* (June 24, 2018).
12 "Authorities Arrest Man Who Sought Heart Surgery Abroad," *China Aid* (September 20, 2018).

Genocide

1 "Chinese 'Surveillance Pigeon' discovered near Kazakhstan as Detentions, Blockades Continue," *China Aid* (May 5, 2018).
2 "Horrors Continue in Xinjiang Detention Camps, Further Arrests without Cause," *China Aid* (May 11, 2018).
3 "China's Treatment of Uighurs is 'Embarrassment for Humanity' Says Turkey," *The Guardian* (February 10, 2019).
4 Omir Belaki quoted in Gerry Shih, "Muslims Forced to Drink Alcohol and Eat Pork in China's 'Re-education' Camps, Former Inmate Claims," *The Independent* (May 18, 2018).
5 Omer Kanat quoted in Steven Jiang, "Thousands of Uyghur Muslims Detained in Chinese Political Education Camps," *CNN* (February 3, 2018).
6 Emily Feng, "China Targets Muslim Uighurs Studying Abroad," *Financial Times* (August 1, 2017).
7 Mihrigul Tursun quoted in "Uighur Woman Pled for Death as Authorities Tortured Her," *China Aid* (November 29, 2018).
8 Adrian Zenz quoted in "Expert Estimates China Has More Than 1,000 Internment Camps for Xinjiang Uyghurs," *Radio Free Asia* (November 12, 2019).
9 Chris Smith quoted in "US House Approves Uighur Act Calling for Sanctions on China's Senior Officials," *The Guardian* (December 4, 2019).
10 Quoted in Mimi Lau, "Wanted: Chinese Cadres to hold Beijing's Line in

Xinjiang as Han Chinese Head for the Exits," *South China Morning Post* (December 4, 2019).

11 Sayragul Sauytbay quoted in Jane Clark Scharl, "For China's Uighurs, the Red Terror Isn't Over," *Crisis Magazine* (August 5, 2020).

12 "Cotton Condemns Chinese Concentration Camps in Xinjiang Province," press release on the website of Arkansas Senator Tom Cotton (December 3, 2019).

13 Mimi Lau and Linda Lew, "China Claims 1.3 Million Xinjiang Residents Given 'Vocational Training' each Year," *South China Morning Post* (September 17, 2020).

14 Mike Pompeo cited in "US: China Committed Genocide against Uighurs," *BBC News* (January 20, 2021).

A Christian Lament for the Uyghurs

1 Quoted in "100 Christians Sent to 'Re-Education' Camps in Xinjiang," *World Watch Monitor* (February 2, 2018).

2 Samuel Smith, "Over 80 Chinese Christians Arrested for Worshipping in House Churches," *The Christian Post* (March 7, 2017).

3 "Xinjiang Court Gives 5 Christians Harsh Sentences," *China Aid* (April 25, 2017).

4 "Six Uyghur Christians Arrested," *China Aid* (September 3, 2019).

5 "A Letter to the Uyghurs in Xinjiang," *China Source* (February 26, 2019).

The Future of the Church in Xinjiang

1 Crisler, *China's Borderlands and Beyond*, p. 319.

2 "Chinese Websites Claim Kyrgyzstan, Kazakhstan part of China," *Zee News* (May 11, 2020).

3 Shan, *History of Christianity in Xinjiang*, p. 5.

A Survey of Christians in China

1 Ye's figure was quoted in numerous publications at the time, including *The 2007 Annual Report of the Congressional-Executive Commission on China: One Hundred Tenth Congress*, First Session (October 10, 2007).

2 Ku Ma, "Rule of Law best help to Freedom of Faith," *China Daily* (December 3, 2009).

Selected Bibliography

———

Ahlbert, Gustaf, *Bakhta Han, or Lucky Child: A Story of a Girl from Xinjiang* (Malmo, Sweden: Pathways, 2013).

——, *Habil: A Christian Martyr in Xinjiang* (Kindle edition, 2008).

Anonymous, *The Chinese Back-To-Jerusalem Evangelistic Band: A Prayer Call to Christian Friends of the Chinese Church* (1947).

Avetaranian, John, *A Muslim who Became a Christian: The Story of John Avetaranian, 1861–1919* (Hertford, UK: Authors Online, 2002).

Baumer, Christoph, *The Church of the East: An Illustrated History of Assyrian Christianity* (London: I. B. Tauris, 2006).

Benge, Janet, and Geoff, *Mildred Cable: Through the Jade Gate* (Seattle: YWAM Publishing, 2015).

Benson, Linda K., *Across China's Gobi: The Lives of Evangeline French, Mildred Cable, and Francesca French of the China Inland Mission* (Manchester: Eastbridge Books, 2008).

Broomhall, Marshall, *Islam in China: A Neglected Problem* (London: Morgan & Scott, 1910).

Cable, Mildred, and Francesca French, *George Hunter: Apostle of Turkestan* (London: China Inland Mission, 1948).

——, *The Making of a Pioneer: Percy Mather of Central Asia* (London: Hodder & Stoughton, 1935).

——, *Through Jade Gate and Central Asia: An Account of a Journey in Kansu, Turkestan, and the Gobi Desert* (London: Constable, 1927).

Caleb Project, *The Uyghurs of Central Asia* (Littleton, CO: Caleb Project, 2003).

Couling, Charlotte Eliza, *The Luminous Religion: A Study of Nestorian Christianity in China* (London: Carey, 1925).

Covell, Ralph, *The Liberating Gospel in China: The Christian Faith Among China's Minority Peoples* (Grand Rapids, MI: Baker Books, 1995).

Dawson, Christopher, *Mission to Asia* (Toronto: University of Toronto Press, 1987).

England, John C., *The Hidden History of Christianity in Asia: The Churches of the East before 1500* (Delhi: Indian Society for the Promotion of Christian Knowledge, 1996).

Forbes, Andrew D. W., *Warlords and Muslims in Chinese Central Asia: A*

Selected Bibliography

Political History of Republican Sinkiang 1911–1949 (London: Cambridge University Press, 1986).

Foster, John, *Church of the T'ang Dynasty* (London: SPCK, 1939).

Fritzon, Ann-Charlotte, *Passion for the Impossible: The Life of the Pioneer Nils Fredrik Höijer* (Solna, Sweden: The Swedish Slavic Mission, 1998).

Hattaway, Paul, *Back to Jerusalem: God's Call to the Chinese Church to Complete the Great Commission* (Carlisle, UK: Piquant, 2003).

——, *China's Book of Martyrs* (Carlisle, UK: Piquant, 2007).

——, *China's Unreached Cities, Vol. 1* (Chiang Mai, Thailand: Asia Harvest, 1999).

——, *Operation China: Introducing all the Peoples of China* (Carlisle, UK: Piquant, 2000).

Holzmann, John (ed.), *The Church of the East: An Edited and Condensed Version of Nestorian Missionary Enterprise* (Littleton, CO: Sonlight Curriculum, 2001).

Huc, L'Abbé, *Christianity in China, Tartary, and Thibet* (2 vols.) (London: Brown, Green, Longmans & Roberts, 1857).

Hultvall, John, *Mission and Change in Eastern Turkestan: An Authorized Translation of the Original Swedish Text* (Erskine, UK: Heart of Asia Ministries, 1987).

Kemp, Hugh P., *Steppe By Step: Mongolia's Christians: From Ancient Roots to Vibrant Young Church* (London: Monarch Books, 2000).

Lambert, Tony, *China's Christian Millions* (Oxford: Monarch, 2006).

——, *The Resurrection of the Chinese Church* (Wheaton, IL: Harold Shaw, 1994).

Mingana, Alphonse, *The Early Spread of Christianity in Central Asia and the Far East: A New Document* (Manchester: University Press, 1925).

Moffett, Samuel Hugh, *A History of Christianity in Asia, Volume 1: Beginnings to 1500* (Maryknoll, NY: Orbis, 1998).

——, *A History of Christianity in Asia, Volume II: 1500 to 1900* (Maryknoll, NY: Orbis, 2005).

Moule, A. C., *Christians in China Before the Year 1550* (London: SPCK, 1930).

——, and Paul Pelliot, *Marco Polo: The Description of the World* (2 vols.) (London: Routledge, 1938).

Platt, W. J., *Three Women: Mildred Cable, Francesca French, Evangeline French* (London: Hodder & Stoughton, 1964).

Shan, Mark Chuanhang, *The History of Christianity in Xinjiang, China: with a General History Background* (Boston: self-published, 2011).

Stewart, John, *Nestorian Missionary Enterprise: The Story of a Church on Fire* (Edinburgh: T & T Clark, 1928).

Taylor, Mrs. Howard, *The Call of China's Great North-West, or Kansu and Beyond* (London: China Inland Mission, 1923).

Wingate, R. O., *The Steep Ascent: The Story of the Christian Church in Turkestan* (London: British and Foreign Bible Society, 1950).

Young, John M. L., *By Foot to China: Mission of the Church of the East* (Tokyo: Radio Press, 1984).

Zwemer, Samuel M., *The Moslem World* (Philadelphia, PA: American Baptist Publication Society, 1908).

Contact Details

Paul Hattaway is the founder and director of Asia Harvest, a non-denominational ministry which serves the Church in Asia through various strategic initiatives including Bible printing and supporting Asian missionaries who are sharing the Gospel among unreached peoples.

The author can be reached by email at **paul@asiaharvest.org**, or by writing to him via any of the addresses listed below.

For more than 30 years, Asia Harvest has served the Church in Asia through strategic projects that equip the local churches. At the time of printing this book, Asia Harvest has successfully printed and delivered more than 249,000 Bibles to house church Christians in Xinjiang, in addition to supporting many evangelists and providing aid to hundreds of persecuted church leaders and their families.

If you would like to receive the free *Asia Harvest* newsletter or to order other volumes in The China Chronicles series or Paul's other books, or if you want to contribute to Paul's ministries to support Chinese Christian workers and their families, please visit **www.asiaharvest.org** or write to the address below nearest you:

Asia Harvest USA & Canada
353 Jonestown Rd #320
Winston-Salem, NC 27104
U.S.A.

Asia Harvest Australia
Mailbox 80, 377 Kent Street
Seabridge House
Sydney, NSW 2000
AUSTRALIA

Asia Harvest New Zealand
PO Box 1757
Queenstown, 9348
NEW ZEALAND

Asia Harvest UK & Ireland
c/o AsiaLink
31A Main Street
Ballyclare
Co. Antrim BT39 9AA
UNITED KINGDOM

Asia Harvest Europe
c/o Stiftung SALZ
Moehringer Landstr. 98
70563 Stuttgart
GERMANY